China and the People's Liberation Army

Great Power or Struggling Developing State?

China and the People's Liberation Army

Great Power or Struggling Developing State?

Solomon M. Karmel

St. Martin's Press
New York

ISBN 0-312-22389-7

Library of Congress Cataloging-in-Publication Data
Karmel, Solomon M. (Solomon Mark), 1965-
  China and the People's Liberation Army : great power or struggling
  developing state? / Solomon M. Karmel.
  Includes bibliographical references and index.
  ISBN 0-312-22389-7
  1. China—Armed Forces.   2. China—Military policy.   3. China.
Chung-kuo jen min chieh fang chün.   I. Title.

UA835.K37 2000
355'.00951—DC21
                                                              99-40510
                                                                  CIP

Design by Westchester Book Composition
First edition: April 2000

10 9 8 7 6 5 4 3 2 1

Contents

List of Tables and Figures

Acknowledgments

S pecial thanks to the following scholars who provided intellectual advice or teaching on China and questions of international security, or who in other ways helped to make this study possible: Lynn White III, John Arquilla, Mary Callahan, Michael Leifer, Michael Yahuda, David Bachman, Wen-hsin Yeh, Lowell Dittmer, David Yost, David Callahan, and David Shambaugh.

Thanks also to the following schools for providing me with support while researching and writing on the Chinese military: The London School of Economics, the Naval Postgraduate School, and the University of California at Berkeley.

My ideas on the Chinese military were previously developed in *Foreign Affairs, Orbis,* and *Defense Analysis* articles. I am thankful to those journals for allowing me to develop and publish some early research for this book.

Thanks also to my editor, Karen Wolny, for having faith in this project and promoting it; to Margaret Dornfeld, for her careful line editing; and to Rick Delaney and Brook Partner at St. Martin's Press.

Finally, thanks go to Martine Smets and Juliette Karmel, for their love and support on three continents.

INTRODUCTION

Developing World Security Priorities and the Chinese People's Liberation Army (PLA)

Many claim China is a "great power," or even a "superpower."[1] Others note with alarm that China has matched its dramatically increasing economic and political clout with rapidly expanding military capabilities. In the words of Nicholas Kristoff, *The New York Times'* respected China correspondent during many years of Deng Xiaoping's stewardship, China "has nuclear weapons, border disputes with most of its neighbors, and a rapidly improving army that may—within a decade or so—be able to resolve old quarrels in its own favor. . . . China has been using its economic boom to finance a far-reaching buildup" and "seeks the influence of a great power."[2]

Indeed, China's dramatically expanded economic and military capabilities are said to threaten states in Asia and beyond. Gerald Segal has argued that with respect to Southeast Asia, "Part of China's nationalist agenda is to demonstrate its dominance in the region. The problem is that China often defines 'normal' relations with certain neighbors—Vietnam, for example—as ones where China is dominant."[3] Similarly, Ross H. Munro, in an article appropriately entitled "China's Waxing Spheres of Influence," argues that "Vietnam's strategic position is so weak that China can move slowly and, if it wishes, rather gently, in its inexorable drive to establish hegemony over Vietnam." Meanwhile, "India's weakness vis-à-vis China affects all of South Asia."[4]

Scholars have argued that renewed national vigor under Deng Xiaoping even prepared China for a future confrontation with Japan. Nowadays, in such a confrontation, "China will expect Japan to accept a subordinate role. . . . Beijing feels morally justified in putting Japan in an inferior position."[5] Soon enough, great-power China's "expected emergence" will give China "the capacity to challenge Japan for dominance of East Asia. . . . [A] future Chinese hegemony in East Asia is a strong possibility." In 1994, Denny Roy even foresaw the possibility of "a Sino-Japanese cold war . . . more dangerous than the previous cold war" and, with China's power surge in East Asia, "the greatest threat to the region's stability since the Pacific War."[6]

A more confident but still authoritarian China—a state that suppresses pluralism, brazenly markets its weapons to pariah states, and aggressively pursues export-led growth strategies—is even looked upon by some as a threat to the United States. Presidents Bush and Clinton, and political figures on both their right and left flanks, occasionally struggled to get tough with China as the confidence of China's post-Tiananmen leadership increased, and as China's propaganda machine presented the United States in often acrimonious terms. According to Francis A. Lee, "The superpower status attained by China will pose many vexing problems for the United States and Europe. America's former hegemonic influence will be undermined in international trade and investment, as well as in the realm of international political relations."[7] Richard D. Fisher also feels a resurgent China could undermine U.S. military superiority in Asia. With more Su-27 fighter purchases from Russia, and better integration of the fighters into the air force, "China eventually could challenge American air superiority in Asia."[8]

Hence, the alleged rise of China to great power status is believed to be of worldwide significance. Harvard professor Alastair Iain Johnston reassures us that the frequency of China's involvement in military disputes has decreased as Chinese power has increased. Yet he accepts that China has become a great power, and concedes: "Thus far there is little consensus about what . . . China's rise as a great power means for regional and global peace and development."[9]

Whether China really should be considered a great power is more than an academic question, because particular answers can lead to shifts in policy. In the 1980s, Ambassador Richard Solomon secretly advised U.S. negotiators with Beijing to acknowledge, in their negotiating strategies and tactics, Chinese leaders' own self-perception of their importance. Chinese officials negotiating with the United States "consider themselves the representatives of a once and future great power,"[10] and, he suggested, face and respect are issues that therefore assume more importance in negotiations. Solomon's phrasing sidestepped the issue of whether or not China is *currently* a great power, or whether it is currently perceived as such by its contemporary leaders. But the logic appears to be that China is a contender of some kind, which demands and should receive respect. Steven I. Levine, in the leading textbook on Chinese foreign policy in the English language, echoes Solomon when he claims that a primary element of China's informal ideology is the timeless, rarely shaken belief that "The Chinese are a great people, and China is a great nation." This belief allegedly influences current views among the Chinese and their leaders on "how they believe they should be treated."[11]

The idea that the Chinese leaders view themselves as commanding a great power might convince a "dove" to provide China with some room to maneuver in its waxing sphere of influence, or it might convince a "hawk" that significant resources must be employed to contain China's new expansionist capabilities.

By contrast, if the underlying assumption is incorrect—if China is *not* a great power, in reality or even in the opinions of its own leaders—neither of these policy solutions to a nonexistent problem makes any sense.

So is China a great power, on a path that may soon challenge East, Southeast, South Asian, Japanese, and perhaps even U.S. national security interests? Or does China more resemble a struggling developing state, consumed by security problems on the home front and enervated even by half-hearted power-projection efforts beyond its poorly defined borders?

I. On Great Powers, Struggling Developing Countries, and their Respective Militaries

Analysis of a few key variables will help us to understand the difference between a great power and a struggling developing country, and it will also shed light on the purpose of military force in both cases. Further, these variables provide us with a comparative perspective on China and the People's Liberation Army (PLA).

Stability in the Capital and Key Power Centers

The first political priority of any developing state—one, which the current Chinese government, for example, has not guaranteed—is political stability in the capital and the centers of government power.

Since World War II, wars within states are far more likely than wars between them, and the phenomena of anti-colonial revolutionary wars, civil wars, internal revolts, coups d'état, or bloody, military suppressions of organized internal dissent have been primarily (although not exclusively) localized within the states of the developing world.[12] In China in 1989, brittle state organs could not cope with protest movements in Beijing, Tibet, and dozens of large cities along the coast, and the resulting crackdown was the military's largest and longest-sustained military engagement in the post-Mao period. Government organs apparently were insufficiently developed to manage peaceful dissent, and leaders responded to a primarily "loyal opposition" (Tibet excepted) with the only solution they could fathom. Not surprisingly, then, the 1997 National Defense Law lists "preventing armed rebellion and preserving national unity" as primary responsibilities of the People's Liberation Army.[13]

Admittedly, during most years in the reform period, tanks and soldiers in China's major cities are a rare sight. Yet even in more stable years, the Chinese government provides the plurality of its military funding to the Beijing and Nanjing military regions—China's traditional, land-locked, northern and southern capitals. These are particularly defensive places to station forces, and locations from which the goals of more confident states (alliance-building, force projection, securing ocean routes for trade) would be difficult or impossible to achieve.

Defining State Borders

After securing the capital and other centers of state power, the developing state's military must next define state borders. These borders are more likely to be stable in the current era if they encompass a nation, rather than some fraction of a divided people, a loose tribal collection, or an overextended mini-empire.

The goal of border delineation might be achieved de jure through historic claims and conquests, but the borders will probably not be secure in the age of modern nationalism until the nation and its state rest on solid institutional, demographic, and cultural foundations.

Many peoples in the developing world have poorly defined or undefined borders even when their nations appear to be relatively well defined. For example, North and South Korea remain entirely separated politically, economically, and increasingly, culturally, despite relative ethnic uniformity across borders. One can locate the nation of Kurdistan on the map between Turkey, Iraq, and Iran, but not its internationally recognized state. Jordan, Egypt, and especially Israel have all succeeded in creating a Palestinian nation largely by struggling to destroy it. Still, while it is unlikely that any of these countries will be particularly stable before the Palestinians have a defined state, as of yet, they don't. China's borders are more well defined, logical, and defensible than the borders in these examples, but are they *very* well defined?

China is unable to control Taiwan (its "renegade" province), has only recently managed to regain control of Hong Kong, and suffers regular (small-scale) revolts in its far Western territories. In the South China Sea, it has far less important, but nonetheless active territorial disputes with four states and Taiwan. Similarly, in the 1960s, it fought a war with India and several armed forays with the Soviet Union over territorial disputes in the Himalayas and on China's northeastern borders. These disputes (especially on the Indian border) are not yet fully resolved. China also has claims over the Senkaku Islands now controlled by Japan. For reasons of history, ethnic nationalism, and institutional weaknesses, China can by no means take its borders for granted.

The definition of borders hoped for in a developing society is usually the maximum area that reasonably could be justified when ambiguous, incomplete, or archaic historical records confront exacting modern cartography and rigid international laws. The breakup of the Malay Federation provides the best contemporary exception to the rule: The Malays willfully jettisoned their undisputed, richest city when they concluded, in the mid-1960s, that Chinese Singaporeans could not be digested into their nation-state. Their decision to break up the Malay Federation proceeded before Lee Kuan Yew and most leaders of Singapore regarded such changes as necessary or inevitable. But few states in the developing world are as ready to release territorial control as the Malays or, say, the Czechs, who cared more about joining Europe than about joining Bratislava after the fall of the Berlin Wall. Instead, the developing state will research ambiguous historical claims or conquests and assess whether the maintenance or enforcement of any claims—including ambiguous ones—are worth the very extensive risks and costs of a confrontation.

China's historical claims on Tibet through the centuries, for example, are ambiguous and difficult to define in terms understood by modern nation-states. And in any case, should the modern, legal status of the occasional protectorate of a defunct empire be determined by historical claims or the will of the indigenous people? Either way, in 1951, Mao Zedong decided that ambiguous historical claims could be solidified perpetually through an armed invasion at minimal cost. His decision, and the effort to define China's far southwestern border in a way that encompasses a relatively cohesive, very different ethnic group, has long-term consequences for the definition of China's military mission. Low-intensity conflicts are likely to exist in Tibet for some time to come, and Tibet does not yet provide China with a particularly stable southwestern border.

Those who would argue that China is winding up to project itself outward fail to acknowledge that, due to the successes of the Qing, the Nationalists, and the Communists, China is already massive—perhaps even swollen and overextended—by its own historic standards.

Admittedly, briefly under the Mongolians, China was far larger (although also subjugated under barbarian, Mongol rule in the eyes of many Han Chinese). Under the strongest Manchurian emperors (also considered foreign by many modern nationalists, such as Sun Yatsen), China encompassed all of what is now Mongolia and was also larger. Yet today, China cannot hope to swallow the generally well-defined borders and states of Mongolia, Korea, Vietnam, or Burma, where Chinese people, on and off during several glorious moments of their 4,000-year history, have staked claims. Chinese leaders are having enough trouble, on the one hand, employing Maoist political institutions to further absorb Tibet and Muslim peoples in far western border regions, and, on the other, maintaining historically legitimate claims on Taiwan and several East and South China Sea islands. From the perspective of Chinese history, current claims may already be stretching the capacity of China's leadership.

Partly because the cartographic definition of the Chinese state is incomplete, fervent nationalists bent on domination of Japan, India, or even Vietnam, Korea, or Burma are almost nowhere to be found on the Mainland. Those who argue otherwise appear to have misread the ruling ideology in the Chinese politburo, the military doctrine of its leadership, the apparent mood of its people, and the long-term projection capabilities of its armed force.

Alliances

While great powers have colonial possessions or allies that do their bidding, less powerful developing world states are unlikely to have strategic alliances in which they wield significant influence over other states. The only prominent exceptions are states that form alliances with much larger powers to guard against primarily domestic, ethnic nationalist or radical, revolutionary threats to their survival.

During the Cold War, great powers occasionally deluded themselves into thinking that greatly imbalanced alliances were of primary importance to their long-term interests (e.g., the United States in South Vietnam in the 1960s), but usually an alliance of unequals is of secondary importance to great powers or to the balance of power. In any case, today the NATO states, Japan, and South Korea are among the only states with very significant, binding alliances of any kind. Lesser powers have a difficult time creating, shaping, and maintaining alliances of significance.

An "alliance" is defined carefully by Jonathan D. Pollack and Young Koo Cha as

> . . . a host of interrelated policy understandings and agreements that, when fully developed, include
> - a strategic concept defining the shared obligations of alliance partners
> - a defense strategy through which the roles and responsibilities of each partner are specified
> - an agreement on types and levels of forces to implement a common defense strategy
> - a range of more-specialized agreements on command relations, base arrangements, and burden-sharing.[14]

The example of the United States's binding alliance with South Korea is the focus of Pollack and Young Koo Cha's study.

Whatever its strengths, in contrast to the United States and many of its allies, China is a state without close allies of any kind. Readings that discuss the alleged ambitions of China or its leadership frequently ignore this awkward stumbling block to aggressive international action.

In the Cold War, bipolarity emerged when the Soviet Union formed long-term, binding alliances with several states in Eastern Europe, Asia, and the Caribbean, often with the coercive support of an occupation force. Again, China does not have even one very close military ally of even minor significance. Its navy has made official port calls with dozens of other states, and its soldiers have worked on projects abroad (e.g., in Burma). But it has no overseas military bases or binding military agreements that would allow it to legally station troops abroad for outward power projection.

In terms of economic alliances, China has none, and few significant bilateral or multilateral agreements with any other state. Several sources suggest China has arrived, at least, as an economic superpower, or is heading in that direction. But in terms of economic alliances, China is not even a member of G-8 talks, nor, at the time of this writing, of the World Trade Organization (although this may soon change). Even within what could be considered its sphere of limited influence, China is unable to control and has no diplomatic relations or established trade agreements with, de facto, one of its most important trading partners (Taiwan). China's weak economic diplomacy results in part from a weaker economic presence in world trade than is often presumed. China is not the most important trading partner of any other relatively strong state in Asia. Its most important trading partner is Japan, but Japan's most important trading partner is the United States. Some assert that China is poised, at least, to dominate Vietnam, and ties between the two countries are certainly improving. But ironically, Vietnam's most important trading partner is China's nemesis, Taiwan. One finds unimpressive evidence of hegemony even if the focus is on the two states whose leaders get along better with Chinese leaders than with any others (North Korea and Burma). China is not definitively the most important trading partner or economic ally of either. North Korea receives more of its foreign exchange from Koreans in Japan, and more economic support, at this stage, from South Korea. China's influence, particularly in northern Burma, is clear, but Burma's most important trading partner is Thailand. And on the world stage, these two "pseudo-allies" are insignificant economic players. Finally, China has rapidly expanded its trade, and its trade surplus, with the United States and Europe. But economic superpower currently implies more than the successful marketing of a wide range of inexpensive, low-tech consumer products.

Military Professionalism

A great power will probably possess a professionally run military with a well-defined mission. By contrast, because political systems and military organizations in the developing world are frequently unstable, corrupt, poorly administered, or legally troubled, strategic missions for the developing-world military may be clouded by apparently non-military, potentially unprofessional goals.

Here, concerning the meanings of "professional" and "unprofessional" in a military context, one should quickly "round up the usual caveats." The military's proper role in domestic politics is a multi-layered topic.[15] One must acknowledge that all militaries play a role in the domestic politics of their state. Even coups d'état are not necessarily unprofessional. While one study, using data from 74 countries, concluded that military rulers are fundamentally unconcerned about most types of social change and oppose reformists,[16] scholars of developing-world militaries have recognized that many military interventions are justified by the genuine need to remove corrupt predecessors. A coup that restores order can be a professional act, as the control of violence on behalf of the state is a primary objective of all militaries. When opposing civilian authorities with competing legitimacy claims actively seek support from a military during power transitions, it is difficult to define military professionalism. Similarly, corresponding military coups—not even clearly definable as such—can be labeled reformist when regime change promotes reform or installs reformers.[17] Indeed, a historically common means to change a corrupt or incompetent regime is regicide, and, in short, an attack on the highest (incompetent or self-destructive) leaders of the country may be professional in some cases.

Like political interventions in domestic politics, economic interventions by the military also can be considered professional, and they are not confined to the developing world. The "guns and butter" dichotomy is not complete, as militaries can create a stable environment for business, contribute to development projects, spark industrial growth through defense conversion, and train or educate sectors of a work force. Further, the military frequently plays a similar role in advanced and developing states. In a stable, long-standing, liberal democracy, the military, de facto, may maintain a somewhat strong hand in domestic economic policy formulation or enforcement. It is frequently asked to carry out apparently civilian goals, ranging from the completion of engineering projects to the organization or financing of educational programs with large civilian components. In both the developed and the developing world, the military is usually one of the most technically advanced organizations in society, and its influence on the domestic political economy, as an instrument of state force or economic development and technology transfer, may be willingly accepted by a well-informed electorate. This may be particularly true if the developed state has pretensions to be a great power, and funds its military accordingly. Further, it should be noted that Western writings on military economics suggest no clear causal relationship between military spending and higher or lower growth rates,[18] so from an economic perspective there is no known proper or particularly professional level of military spending at any level of economic development.

However, the usual caveats notwithstanding, there are many elements to frequently listed conceptions of poorly trained, poorly organized, poorly directed, and financially mismanaged militaries worthy of mention: Some militaries lack technically trained or even literate staff, and this makes the use of complex ordnance difficult or impossible. Others lack logical bureaucratic organizational methods, or coherent, legally delineated relationships with civilian authority. Military unprofessionalism, if it has any meaning, must also refer to a lack of clearly defined military objectives: The military should be considered "unprofessional" when it *emphasizes* tasks that are only tangentially related, or unrelated, to the definition and defense of the state and the state's organized management of violence and force. Unprofessional activities could include everything from sectarian party formation for the personal gain of generals to rentier and profit-making activities.[19]

In a state with an advanced legal system, it is likely that the military will play a legally proscribed role that is more exclusively international, or that at least focuses on security questions, both foreign and domestic. One definition of a developed polity would include the principle that leaders—military and civilian—are not above the law, and the security mission of a developed state is likely to be at least legally proscribed. In the United States, for example, laws clearly delineate, for defense organizations and bureaucracies, their defined roles (broad, enduring purposes for which organizations are established in law), missions (broad tasks, combined with a description of purpose, indicating action to be taken), and functions (powers, duties, and responsibilities that organizations are intended to hold).[20] Of course, some defense organizations (e.g. the CIA) carry out operations that break domestic laws and violate international treaties, but powerful legal documents (e.g., the National Security Act of 1947 and subsequent amendments and the U.S. Constitution) help to proscribe the activities of even the most secretive defense organizations.

By contrast, to a much greater extent, rule by law in many developing societies is the goal rather than the practice. (In China during the Cultural Revolution, it wasn't even the goal.) Further, the military's mission and methodology may intentionally be particularly vague and difficult to pin down. The military of a developing state is likely to emphasize as key elements of its mission a host of tasks unrelated to security questions that are nonetheless central to the activities of government: Beyond economic developmental goals, this could include everything from the pursuit of social revolution to the eradication of an opposition (loyal or disloyal, armed or peaceful). Robin Luckham makes a broad distinction between military establishments that arose out of colonial state formation and those that sprang from struggles of national emancipation. In Asia and elsewhere, "those which originated from anti-colonial armies and took part in struggles for national independence were overtly political from their inception."[21] China's People's Liberation Army essentially fits into this category. It is no surprise that the absolutist, revolutionary goals of a liberation organization have only very recently begun to be limited and codified, as the revolution's leaders die off and many of their revolutionary goals are similarly extinguished.

Specifically with respect to financial mismanagement, another caveat is in order: To varying degrees, every state suffers from some level of financial corruption in every bureau of the government. In Asia, this is true even in the states that are far more developed and advanced in the democratization and legalization process than China.[22]

Yet the developing world is especially plagued by militaries that involve themselves in all manner of monopolistic economic practices that may increase corruption, siphon money out of a country, and, in general, weaken respect for all government institutions. Prominent examples of militaries with missions that, de facto, involve unprofessional profit-seeking that compromises state institutions include those of Indonesia under Soeharto, Burma under Ne Win, and Zaire (the Congo) under Mobutu.

China's military professionalism, organization, clarity of mission, and levels of corruption are not as compromised as in some regional cases (e.g., Burma, Indonesia), and not as much as in the past, under Mao. In China in the late 1960s, financial corruption may have been a smaller problem; it is at least less well documented. But the People's Liberation Army under Lin Biao became preoccupied with the spiritual and cultural liberation of both soldiers and civilians, and it contributed to anarchic acts of destruction (particularly in urban areas and minority regions), acts that compromised Chinese domestic stability and from which the Chinese state has yet to fully recover. To the extent that its mission was defined at all, one of the military's Maoist goals, especially from 1966 to 1968, literally included its own self-destruction as a functioning bureaucracy with clearly delineated hierarchies of power. Partly due to the influence of Lin Biao, any laws marking the proper role of the army would have been particularly dangerous to push through and impossible to enforce from 1966 to 1969. Similarly, a clear military hierarchy, with unequal ranks for officers and privates, was completely abolished.

The reform period in China has led to a more technically competent military and also has sparked important efforts toward legal reform. China's National Defense Law, adopted in the spring of 1997 after approval by the National People's Congress Standing Committee, stipulated in law, for the first time, the Maoist principle that the Communist Party should control the gun. Jurisdiction and authority of the State Council and the Central Military Commission (CMC) also are to some extent delineated.[23]

Yet despite legal improvements under reform—with dozens of less prominent laws, regulations, and stipulations delineating the proper role of the military—the reform period has actually provoked some *regression* in the military's ability to focus on international security concerns and the pursuit of any defense strategy. Reforms include the codification of bizarre, counterproductive, or archaic practices that may be detrimental to China's political modernization in the long term. For example, should the Party "control the gun," as stipulated in the National Defense Law, instead of government officials and bodies, such as the President or State Council? Will the Party still control the gun if it loses control of the government? Legal codification of an undemocratic and legally compromising institution (one-party control) may not, in the long term, represent true reform.

Since the Cultural Revolution, one surprisingly prominent military preoccupation is for-profit business. Some of the thousands of military-controlled businesses in Mainland China do earn money, and some are becoming more logically organized and more efficient. Yet these businesses have little to do with conventional notions of international power or security, and they return almost nothing to any civilian or military bureau of the state. Meanwhile, they compromise strategy, spark corruption, and probably represent a long-term drag on China's economic growth. And while the guns and butter dichotomy is not complete, neither is it the case that guns and butter are necessarily complimentary, as all politicians in China suggested, with respect to military businesses, until 1998. The effort to force the Chinese military to pay its own way, advance economic construction as a central goal, and, generally, participate very actively in the civilian economy was previously associated with the most radical periods in Mao's rule, such as the Great Leap Forward. Deng's decision to run the military as a profit center adds a new twist, but it is not necessarily a reform that will help China to become an emerging great power. When, for example, the military sells missile or nuclear trigger technology for profit to pariah states in China's neighborhood, China's strategic interests—and ultimately its power vis-à-vis other states—may be compromised rather than promoted.

In many developing countries, there is a belief that the state will be stronger if the military becomes weaker, because the military's domestic political ministrations are viewed as destructive. Some Western analysts fail to realize that some of China's civilian leaders would feel threatened if the Chinese military became significantly more empowered, especially in terms of autonomous budgetary and decision-making capabilities.

Jiang Zemin apparently realized potential problems in 1998, when he urged the military to cease its business activities. Still, the military is likely to have unprofessional dealings in the domestic economy for some time to come.

Military Strategy and Tactics

The military strategy and tactics of a great power are likely to set the pace for most other states of the world. Technological superiority, advances in logistic management, superior intelligence systems, greater industrial capacity, superior access to resources, and more advanced educational attainments should allow a great power to make its military combat units strategically and tactically advanced by the standards of the day.

The same is unlikely to be true in a twentieth century developing state. In China, for example, Maoist "People's War" strategies of guerrilla warfare represented a genuine advance on tactics to fight a liberation struggle, but their application has been far more limited than many are willing to admit. Once the liberation (from both international and domestic opponents) was essentially achieved, People's War became a far less relevant concept. These days, few inside or outside of China have acknowledged that *China is quietly working to jettison entirely the legacy of People's War as an archaic holdover of the Maoist past.* In its place, military planners have promoted what is labeled here a strategy of technocratic command, although the strategy probably will never receive such an elitist appellation officially. This strategy emphasizes skills and tactics that parallel those already present in many states with more technically advanced militaries.

For the Chinese military under reform, strategy and tactics designed by combat and missile units to fight wars are admittedly developing rapidly. Nuclear forces are behind those of the United States and Russia, but otherwise quite impressive. China is also studying and copying (often in violation of international copyright regulations) Western books on ordnance, logistics, and tactics. The increased emphasis on secondary and tertiary educational attainments as an internationally recognizable, technocratic mark of status for officers will also help China to improve its strategy. Further, efforts to purchase and copy foreign hardware that China cannot produce at home have created modern pockets of tactically advanced combat power.

However, generally, China is not a technical leader in many industrial fields of military significance, and its logistic systems are mired in Maoist organizational bureaucracies. Its military leadership admits that with respect to both strategy and tactics, China is woefully behind world leaders. With respect to some technologies (e.g., electronic systems), China is falling even further behind.

Definitions of Great Powers and Developing States

By summarizing the discussion above, one can come to workable definitions of modern "great powers" and "developing states." A great power is one whose capital, strategic centers, and outlying regions are all comparatively secure and well defined; one that is able to link the interests of other states to its own, and significantly influence the actions and security policies of other states through alliances (or, in a previous era, through colonial proxy relationships); one with a military that is professional in the sense outlined here (technically competent, possessing a clear mission that emphasizes defense of the state, logically managed, and legally and financially proscribed); and one whose military is advanced strategically and tactically by contemporary standards.

By contrast, a developing state is not only a state that is still striving to achieve comparatively high economic wealth. It is also one that has not yet achieved the characteristics of a leading great power outlined here.

Mohammed Ayoob, in a well-formulated book on what he terms "the Third World security predicament," lists basic characteristics of Third World states:

> The most important of these are lack of internal cohesion, in terms of both great economic and social disparities and major ethnic and regional fissures; lack of unconditional legitimacy of state boundaries, state institutions, and governing elites; easy susceptibility to internal and inter-state conflicts; distorted and dependent development, both economically and socially; marginalization, especially in relation to the dominant international security and economic concerns; and easy permeability by external actors, be they more developed states, international institutions, or transnational corporations.[24]

In fact, in the modern world most developing nation-states are not easily permeable from a military perspective. Advances in military technology and the powerful organizing force of modern nationalism enable states in the developing world to build genuinely potent deterrents against foreign military intervention and subjugation. These deterrents vastly raise the cost of international wars of conquest, to the point where conquest and subjugation are all but impossible against a viable, resourceful, but still developing nation-state. However, Ayoob's book generally provides a description of politics in the developing world, which is supported here.

More Caveats

Admittedly, like realist views of the world, the discussion above presents a static image, which fails to show how and when a state or state system can change, in this case from one point on the scale (developing world state or power) to another (advanced power, or great power). There is clearly not one formula for every great power in every epoch. Needless to say, when Mongolian generals galloped thousands of miles from Ulan Bator to build the greatest empire of the Middle Ages, they did not require or employ, as elements of their success, urbanization, industrialization, extensive international trade, control of shipping lanes and sea power, enlightened management of divisive ethnic nationalist urges on their borders, developed legal and bureaucratic norms, or aerospace capability. Today, each of these factors can be critical.

China's current leadership is convinced that in the contemporary world, the comparatively rapid, long-term expansion of the national Gross Domestic Product (GDP) provides the simple precondition and essential catalyst of transformation from developing to developed power. The consequent, overwhelming emphasis on economic construction by both military and civilian forces is not misguided, and the economic results have been impressive. Yet the above discussion suggests that the foundations of development and especially the foundations for great power frequently require more than one building block. Perhaps most importantly, the single sine qua non that can move one state from developing and inward-looking in its security concerns toward powerful and outward-looking is domestic political stability. This is a multifaceted variable that is both a cause and effect of the power of a state. And political stability might not be secured even after a series of successful, sagacious leaders implement intelligent political reforms.

Also, "great power" and "developing state" are labels that to some extent compare apples and oranges. One cannot discount the possibility that a state—China, for example—could be both a developing state and a great power. The dichotomy above does not compare developing states with developed ones or great powers with weak powers. Even a comparison of these more polar opposites would have to allow for equatorial states somewhere in between, and the discussion above clearly leaves even more room for states that straddle the line.

The Soviet Union may present an example of a state that, for decades, exhibited many features of both developing states and great powers. Yet such exceptions are rare, and it is argued that China is not in this position, for several reasons. Further, even the Soviet case is not much of an exception: Until it was overwhelmed by nationalist separatism, the Soviet Union exhibited the characteristics of a great power far more than it exhibited developing state characteristics.

The preceding discussion is summarized in the table below.

Table I.1   Illustrative Great Power and Developing State Security Dichotomies

	Great Power	*Developing State*
1. Capitals and strategic centers Secure	Yes; to the point where power is defined externally	No; the most primary security objective of all states is not entirely resolved, and a military cannot ignore this.
2. Outlying regions well-defined	Yes; to the point where it may be hard to define an "outlying region" meaningfully	No; another primary security objective of all states is not resolved, and a military cannot ignore this.
3. Alliances	Potentially quite significant force on international goals and security policy.	A developing state has no alliances, or is a junior partner that probably joined an alliance to quell instability at home
4. "Strategic mission" and military "professionalism"	Primarily involves national defense and external power projection	Can emphasize economic and political goals only tangentially related, or even counter-productive, to national defense and power projection
5. Tactics	Invented and refined by the Great Power in response to its own technological innovations and hands-on experiences	A response to techno-logical and international developments over which the developing state has very little control

II. On Chinese Power and The Role of the Military in Chinese Politics

We return to a central question of this introduction: Is China an emerging great power or a struggling developing state?

Despite sources of strength, China most resembles a developing state—not a great power or even a very stable and fully established, modern nation-state.

It should be noted that while Chinese leaders frequently extol their own sagacity in the Chinese press, they rarely openly claim to their people, or to foreigners, that they consider China to be a great power. Deng Xiaoping once suggested that China's nuclear capacity did make it a great power under Mao, but that its power was threatened by the greatly advancing technological capacity of others.[25] Yet generally, Chinese leaders more frequently describe China as a state in need of strong, authoritarian leadership—specifically because it is backward and needs to be driven from its backwardness by revolutions or reforms from above.

Like the leadership's words, their actions also suggest hesitancy with the idea of hegemonic influence regionally or internationally. Chinese leaders abstain from many important United Nations resolutions; do not actively lead most international treaty negotiations; do not participate in most peacekeeping operations; have rarely sent forces beyond their borders or coastal waters for any reason (except friendly port calls) since 1980; and generally assume a low profile in international diplomacy. While some Chinese soldiers are working outside of China selling weapons or building roads (e.g., in Burma), at the time of this writing, a few dozen observers in conflict resolution efforts in Iraq/Kuwait, Liberia, and the Western Sahara represent the only Chinese military presence in any international operation.[26] Indeed, unless one counts the brief border war with Vietnam, in which Chinese forces were barely able to enter Vietnamese territory and couldn't hold it, China has almost no international military experience under reform. This lack of international military experience over the past two decades stands in stark contrast to the forces of many other contenders for great power status (the United States, Russia, India, Great Britain, France). In each one of these five cases over the past two decades, significant military contingencies have been sent to foreign countries to wage war, separate combatants, or occupy territory to conduct relief efforts in low-intensity conflicts.

The strategies, force structure, and economic policies of China's military industrial complex reflect the fundamental fact that it is not a great power. Sources that describe China as an emerging great power may be correct, but for this to have any meaning one needs some sense of when China might emerge. Will China emerge in ten years or fifty? The question is important, not only because different answers imply very different levels of urgency about the issue, but also because in fifty years time, China's regime, many other regimes, and the international system all will have changed dramatically. Indeed, in an age of information and communications revolutions and service economies, the attainment of great power status might require dramatic transformations toward greater economic and political liberalization. If these transformations occur, the nature of the threat fundamentally changes.

Meanwhile, sources that suggest China is already a great power or superpower demonstrate unrealistic impressions of China's power or provide incomplete or unrealistic definitions of power. For example, one source saluting China's status as a superpower defines a superpower as exhibiting four attributes:

1. Large diversified national economy
2. Major conventional military force
3. Nuclear weapon capability
4. Strategic geographic location[27]

It would seem that many countries fit this bill, and superpower in today's world is not all that super. "Nuclear weapon capability" could include a state like Japan, which has the technical capacity and materials to build nuclear weapons quite quickly (in several months or even weeks) should it choose to do so. Indeed, it is probably the case that any state in the contemporary world with a nuclear capability could fit this definition of a superpower, but Israel, for example, is not generally viewed as a superpower. The definition suggests that several states besides China (the United States, Russia, India, perhaps Great Britain, France, perhaps Japan, Germany, Pakistan, and Israel) all deserve consideration as superpowers. Within the East and South Asian regions alone, one would have to consider China, India, Pakistan, Japan, North Korea, Taiwan, and South Korea all as potential superpowers (although some of these countries and territories do not have *very* large or *very* diversified economies in comparison to current leaders).[28]

In China's case, the dilemmas of development are simply too great for the state to exert the type of great power influence over East Asia that the Soviet

Union exerted over Eastern Europe and many satellite states throughout the world. China is too poor to appear as a role model; its politics and political ideology are too insular and unstable; and it is not technically advanced enough to achieve Soviet-style hegemony over any competently led state in East Asia. One strains to imagine the world war that would provide it with a large occupation force within its still-inhabitable buffer states.

The discussion above should not lead to false exaggerations of China's weaknesses. It would be foolish to suggest that China's political handicaps render it internationally insignificant or particularly vulnerable to external pressure. Almost all developing world states are smaller in terms of geography; all are smaller in terms of manpower; and many are far younger and less cohesive than China. One should not forget simple facts: China possesses nuclear weapons and a gigantic army that would not be overwhelmed easily in any conflict on Chinese territory, initiated by any power.

But saying that China would be a prickly rose bush—or a wild and wholly unmanageable white elephant—for even the most heavily armed occupation force is not the same as saying that China is a great power. France, the United States, and China all essentially worked to occupy Vietnam in the postwar period. Does their failure imply that Vietnam is a great power?

Also, new advances in security paradoxically do not necessarily lead to power-projection. China has no real external security dilemma, but neither can it concentrate on filling external power vacuums—vacuums that are themselves rarely defined, poorly documented, but frequently sighted—in the South China Sea or elsewhere. China's military is too busy challenging a viable civil society at home, and faithfully working to secure the short-term stability of a communistic, autocratic leadership with ambiguous claims of political legitimacy.

Ironically, new advances in security vis-à-vis other states are caused in part by the same factors that breed new *insecurities* at home in less developed states: These include technological factors (such as cheap but very destructive weaponry) that make occupation of a hostile population costly, and political factors (especially ethnic nationalism). So China's security and freedom from occupation threats in the postwar period has done little to enhance its power over other states. Instead, external security, in this and other developing states, frequently has led the military toward unfettered introspection and domestic interventionism in internal conflicts that are far from resolved.

III. The Goals and Themes of This Study

This book is a study of the Chinese military-industrial complex. It was inspired by a series of writings suggesting an emerging, or very likely to emerge great power and potential military threat. These writings appeared to fundamentally misrepresent the goals, the force structure, the economic foundations, and the budget of the Chinese People's Liberation Army and the state leadership that it is designed to defend.

The threat to Taiwan's independence and contemporary way of life is real, and China's interest in uninhabited islands in the South China Sea could be portrayed as aggressive or irredentist. But I suspect that, like the Loch Ness Monster, the threat to other great powers, regional powers, or even small but well-defined nation-states is unlikely to emerge anytime soon.

For China to achieve its reform objectives, it will inevitably be forced to adopt international standards and practices, economically, politically, and militarily. From a security perspective, it is led by status quo figures, who are very open to a reformist agenda but nonetheless, on issues of state rights, the sanctity of domestic politics, and the current status of China's borders, are extremely conservative and justifiably so. China's leaders realize that they are playing a game like "Go" (*weiqi,* or Chinese chess) but even more complex, in which they have already captured more areas of the board than they usually would hope to influence. Their current, almost unparalleled successes are challenged by dramatic and constant economic, political, and cultural threats in the very heartland of their power. Simply securing the base areas that they already have claimed will be the work of decades.

As stated in one open report published by two prestigious Chinese military academies:

> As the world's largest developing country, China is facing challenges and pressures in many areas. The international anti-China forces will not easily give up their plots to "divide," "Westernize," and "contain" China. Certain national separatist forces will act in what they hold to be a suitable international setting and political climate, to add fuel to the fire. And, meanwhile, China still remains subject to certain problems left over from history with certain surrounding countries, with disputes in areas such as island jurisdiction, sea space delimitation, territorial division, and maritime rights and interests, all of which involve national sentiments and interests; thus are very sensitive and complex. So we will need to always stress and deal conscientiously with the realities and potential threats to our national security and development in the new century.[29]

This openly published report could of course be interpreted as propaganda. But one would expect the propaganda of an expanding, confident great power to include phrases like "Manifest Destiny," or discussions of hegemonic leadership in a "co-prosperity sphere". Instead, this military security report emphasizes the threat of divisions, separatism, historical quagmires, and border disputes. This report and many, many others suggest a fundamental lack of confidence in the future, which, following China's turbulent modern history, comes as no surprise.

The first chapter of this book discusses China's emerging strategic doctrine. Contrary to the beliefs of some, China's leadership is working quietly to bury the now outdated concept of People's War. The replacement is a far more technocratic, elitist strategy that is a step in the right direction—but hardly a dangerous or threatening one. Also, the "new" goals of the Chinese leadership are neither fully implemented, nor new in the West. In the United States and elsewhere, these strategic and tactical goals have been established, proven achievements for years.

The second chapter discusses China's force structure. Where are its troops stationed, and to what extent are they geared up to fight wars of the twenty-first century? China is working hard to modernize its bloated force—the largest army in the world—yet I argue that despite noted successes, the PLA's apparent source of strength, sheer size, is the army's most crippling weakness. China is struggling to develop crack troops and build its naval and air power, but its efforts are hindered by an oversized, outdated, decentralized force structure.

The third chapter of this book focuses on the changing priorities of the Chinese military-industrial complex with respect to the management of ordnance production, military and civilian economic development, and profits. The economic goals and priorities of the entire defense establishment are multidimensional, but generally I argue that China still requires significant changes in the organization of its military-industrial complex if its fighting force is to be significantly modernized and coherently led.

The fourth chapter attempts to provide the most detailed, unclassified analysis of the Chinese defense budget available. Chinese sources that are unclassified, and even some that are intended only for internal use, provide only the sketchiest details about the budgeting and management of defense appropriations. Nevertheless, revealing discussions of shortcomings in the budget and budgetary process are analyzed in some detail.

The conclusion of this book presents China's force modernization in comparative perspective. The goal is to assess whether the Chinese leadership or neighboring leaders foresee much of a future—glorious or horrifying—for Chinese political, economic, and especially military hegemony.

Modern wars may be more difficult to win than a game of Chinese chess. It is rarely clear in a real game of domination and influence if the last stone has been played. Still, for China to be a great power by the standards of the day, it must excel in comparison to other states that have also rapidly improved their forces. Is China's great power just around the corner, or can its neighbors comfort themselves with the knowledge that China will be, at best, emerging for some time to come?

CHAPTER 1

The Goal: Overhauling China's Military Strategy

P eople's War" is dead, and "People's War under Modern Conditions" is an essentially misleading and meaningless appellation for China's struggle toward very new strategic directions. Yet the emphasis is on the word "struggle." China's leadership is burning a Maoist bridge behind it without a secure replacement.

Some Western sources published early in the reform period (especially in its first decade) were unwilling to sound the death knell of People's War: People's War was said to have survived in the Central Military Commission of the Chinese Communist Party, perhaps with face lifts of one kind or another. Harlan Jencks, for example, recognized many changes in Chinese strategy during the early 1980s, but still saw People's War under Modern Conditions as China's most important, albeit constantly changing, strategic doctrine: " 'People's War under modern conditions' is China's defensive strategy during its long transition from 'underdeveloped' to 'world-power' status—a transition that still has decades to go."[1] Publishing five years later, Rosita Dellios similarly regarded People's War under Modern Conditions as China's guiding strategic doctrine, and she set out to analyze this doctrine, counter-intuitively, as it might be applied to China's nuclear force modernization.[2]

More recently, Kenneth W. Allen, Glenn Krumel, and Jonathan D. Pollack, in their impressive 1995 RAND study on the problems China faces in its struggle for air force modernization, highlight many dramatic changes in China's strategic conception. But they claim weakly, "Although necessarily a somewhat amorphous concept, People's War retains a measure of influence in Chinese thinking, at least in broad conceptual terms."[3] To be fair, they are focused on what China's military planners are struggling to shake off, rather than on what China has endorsed as its road to the future.

Other scholars publishing in the 1980s and especially more recently have concluded that the concept of People's War—"under modern conditions" or otherwise—is now of limited importance to Chinese strategy. Paul Godwin may have been the first to write a tentative eulogy to the illusive concept of People's War, as far back as 1984: "There is now sufficient evidence that the current military elite seeks to reject People's War, however modified, as an approach to strategy and force structure requirements. While the label of 'People's War' may well be retained, the content of Chinese strategy is likely to be very different from what has gone before."[4] Similarly, by 1986, June Teufel Dreyer suggested that newly emphasized strategic and tactical goals point to more disruption than continuity in China's post-1978 strategic priorities.[5] A recent book on Chinese security policy by Mel Gurtov and Byong-Moo Hwang also suggests that while People's War under Modern Conditions is still relevant to Chinese strategic planning, new goals to promote active defense in limited wars continue a process, begun in the 1950s, to throw off many key, outdated elements of Maoist People's War doctrines.[6]

Evidence of corrosive cracks in People's War even when Mao Zedong was alive include conventionally fought battles against Chiang Kai-shek from 1947 to 1949; conventionally fought battles in Korea; and the increasing reliance on nuclear weapons and technical modernization as deterrents against superpower attack. Then the death of Mao, the definitive completion of Maoist social revolution, the disappearance of a direct threat of attack from any superpower, increased interest in sea power and offshore resources, and revolutionary technological developments in warfare all helped to chart the end of People's War.

So why do opaque sightings of People's War or People's War under Modern Conditions still appear in many Mainland and Western sources on contemporary Chinese strategy? Why has this strategy never been rejected outright?

The phrase "People's War under Modern Conditions"—a title for the current strategy endorsed by central planners—allows for dramatic force-restructuring in an atmosphere of absolute political stability. It is a contradictory and archaic but politically palatable label that allows China to overhaul its army to adapt to modern conditions, but still highlights the army's unchanging political status, subordinate to a party whose nominal task is to defend and mobilize the people. It should not be looked upon as an extant military strategy, at least not among strategists in the high command. Rather, it is a doctrinal phrase that, like the Four Cardinal Principles of Deng Xiaoping, preserves the Communist Party's absolute leadership (in this case, over the military) in a strategic and political atmosphere that is otherwise highly fluid. The preservation of the Communist Party's dictatorship is the only real principle of the Four Cardinal Principles, and the desire to preserve the political power of "the People's mass Party" is the primary political legacy of People's War.

China is struggling to shake off every other remnant of People's War. This is because the strategy and tactics of modern war little resemble those of the Red Army's war of resistance against Chiang Kai-shek and the Japanese, or the strategies and tactics subsequently pursued by Mao that were tied to the lessons of that resistance period. China's military modernization effort has forced a retreat from the idea that the military should be preparing for a war of resistance, in which the masses would arraign themselves against overwhelming technical force. The size of China's army and human support base, the zeal of its soldiers and citizenry, and any effort to promote political ideology over technical capacity or "mind over machines" are all rejected by Chinese strategists as a means of creating an effective defense force.

Instead, much of the modernization program is an effort to catch up with leading military and technological powers, by studying and copying them, sometimes through technology transfers or foreign purchases, and sometimes through detailed analyses of their strategic doctrine and the duplication of many tenets. Where remnants of the former strategy linger, in the form of unnecessary political personnel or secretive, autonomous offices with duplicative and overlapping functions, Chinese strategists have rightly concluded that they are simply wasting resources.

A new strategy is emerging, and it is labeled here a strategy of "technocratic command." This unrevolutionary label will never be endorsed by the high command, but the high command has already quietly (even secretly) endorsed the central precepts outlined here. They include (1) a more powerful, more centralized, better educated, highly trained, leaner officer corps as the central component of military strength; and (2) the development and acquisition of affordable, manageable, select, high-tech ordnance that will advance and diversify Chinese capabilities.

This chapter reviews how China's strategic doctrine has changed from an emphasis on the concepts of People's War to an emphasis on elite command and control systems and more diversified forces, technologically armed to fight regional, international conflicts.

I. People's War Under Modern Conditions

Any summation of People's War concepts must admit that this doctrine was always elastic, and changed through various periods of Maoist revolution and rule. Yet June Teufel Dreyer summarizes key strategic precepts of People's War as follows:

> The army, supported by paramilitary forces and a sympathetic populace, would lure the enemy deep into its territory until the invading force was overextended and dispersed. Communist troops would avoid the defense of fixed points, preferring highly mobile guerrilla-type tactics to isolate enemy units from one another. The element of surprise was considered crucial. When superior force could be concentrated against the dispersed units, communist troops were to surround and destroy them. When this could not be done, they withdrew and practiced harassment. After a protracted period, the exhausted, demoralized enemy would surrender.[7]

Other elements of People's War and China's military doctrine under Mao are outlined by Georges Tan Eng Bok: First, politics is primary; war serves political aims and relies upon politically correct decisions. Second, there is a primacy of men over weapons; zealous fighters imbued with the proper revolutionary spirit can win against superior technology. Third, Maoist war fighting is designed to counter imperialism and hegemonism—and is hence defensive in nature and focused on all-out conflicts.[8]

Bok would emphasize that these Maoist, revolutionary strategic conceptions actually borrowed a great deal from Sun Zi, Lao Zi, and Zhuang Zi, who all argue that "mind is superior to matter," "thought more powerful than weapons," and "doctrine overcomes (bare) strength."[9] Yet People's War struggled to apply these ancient principles to a new kind of conflict that would promote socialist revolution, and therefore would emphasize the "masses" (not sagacious generals); guerrilla tactics against foreign and foreign-funded armies (not binary struggles between Chinese forces); and wars of attrition in which a side with socialist, superior political ideals triumphed against a side wizened by its archaic, immoral, and alien viewpoints.

One recent Mainland source argues that under reform, despite changes, People's War has not been abandoned, and indeed it should not be. The reasons provided (contradicting the analysis presented here) are as follows:

First, People's War emphasizes strategies to fight superior weaponry with inferior weaponry, and China would still be in an inferior technical position in a war with a superpower. With the help of People's War, China might "triumph from a position of weakness." Second, People's War accepts the fact that war is an all-out struggle of one society or nation against another. This is in accord with war in the contemporary world: "Modern war is a war of military sciences, politics, economics, foreign relations, science and technology, and culture altogether." The third reason is tied to the second: Any future war of resistance would be fought on land, at sea, in the air, and in the stratosphere. People's war is a valid strategy, it is suggested, because such a war would inevitably involve more than the army. The militia, the people, and every layer of society would need to play its part in the defense of the Party and state. Fourth, People's War emphasizes the primacy of people and political will over economics and technical capacity. And it is still the case that modern ordnance and weaponry can only be employed effectively if people remain central to strategy. The fifth and final argument is similar to the fourth: If war is a competition of national power and economic power, increasing the quality, wealth, and production of the people is critical.[10]

So how has the allegedly extant doctrine of People's War been slowly transformed into a doctrine of People's War under Modern Conditions during the reform period? The Mainland editors of a textbook on the Chinese military discuss very briefly, but do not define, what might be meant by the term People's War under Modern Conditions. Highlighted phrases allude to how and why People's War under Modern Conditions appears to be different from People's War:

> From the end of the 1970s, especially after the 1980s, the Central Military Commission fundamentally revised its strategy to resist invasion and train soldiers in light of international developments: Taking Marxist-Leninist-Maoist thought as a guide, and according to a strategy of active defense, we studied how to resolve the problems of strategy and tactics when fighting a "People's War under Modern Conditions."
>
> *Based on now-available equipment,* we studied how to prepare for *conventional war and nuclear war;* how to win a war with inferior equipment against superior equipment; how to engage in *joint-force fighting;* how to train to fight based on the enemy's position, the special characteristics of the terrain, and the exigencies of battle when war breaks out.[11]

The passage suggests that people are still regarded as a key to victory, yet they are trained by modern forces that work more closely together, employing joint-force tactics. China is still training to triumph over better-armed opponents, as the Red Army needed to do during its war of resistance and civil war. Yet it is preparing to fight with the highest technology, including the ordnance of nuclear wars. Finally, it is recognized that tactics cannot be static, and must adapt to the exigencies of battle. The passage suggests that Marxism-Leninism is still a strategic guide, although there is no information as to how or why.

Western sources provide further clarification on the meaning of People's War under Modern Conditions: " 'People's War under Modern Conditions' [is] a strategy combining guerrilla warfare, positional defense, and mobile operations principally conducted by the militia, regional forces, and main forces, respectively. Guerrilla and light infantry operations are not to be abandoned by any means. The Chinese recognize, however, that positional and mobile defense conducted by modern combined arms forces would play the decisive role."[12] The shift, then, is away from the least organized militias of the people and toward the most organized and well-trained units, and, in particular, the best-trained and equipped divisions of the People's Liberation Army (PLA).

Rosita Dellios never defines People's War under Modern Conditions in her work focused in large part on that subject, but she suggests that the most important addition to People's War provided by modern conditions is the emphasis on the nuclear deterrent:

> [P]eople's war under modern conditions is no mere "human wave" response to armed aggression, but rather the strategy for psychological pre-emption for such aggression. However, if the opponent cannot be forced to "resign" on the cerebral battlefield then its *will to fight* must be undermined on the physical one. With GNW [guerrilla nuclear warfare] as the culmination of *people's war under modern conditions,* China cannot only defend itself against a better equipped aggressor, but may also reverse the adversarial relationship so that it becomes the more powerful party.[13]

People's War under Modern Conditions further employs traditional Chinese thinking on psychological warfare and trickery (sapping an enemy of the will to fight, hopefully before the battle). Also emphasized are Maoist guerrilla strategies applied to unconventional warfare, and efforts at force modernization and regularization dating back to the Korean War.[14]

The most recent Chinese sources in the second half of the 1990s still suggest that People's War is alive and well, yet the concept is modified further and further as memories of Maoism fade in China. Defense Minister Chi Haotian worked move China's rhetoric beyond support for People's War and "People's War under High-Tech Conditions": As of 1997, China supposedly would promote "Modern, High-Tech People's War." What does this mean?

> The first and foremost task of creatively developing a high-tech people's war is, in accordance with the principles for building crack, combined, and efficient troops, to build revolutionized, modernized, and standardized standing armed forces oriented to the needs of the 21st century, and also to build strong reserve forces which are "ample in quantity, well-trained, highly mobile, and well-equipped." In other words, the country will have a combination of elite standing troops and powerful reserve forces.[15]

The emphasis on reserves in Chi's discussion creates a kind of compromise that bridges old concepts (relying on the masses) and new ones (relying on crack troops), but the rest of the discussion—with its focus on efficient crack troops and joint warfare waged by a professional standing army—strays far from Maoism.

While continuity theses suggest a few worthwhile points, the reality is that publicized efforts to promote an appearance of strategic continuity are evidence of conservative politics rather than conservative strategies. Most Chinese strategists are recommending and struggling to implement radical shifts. For example, Chi Haotian, quoted above, is in fact struggling to cut China's unspecialized regular forces and undifferentiated reserve forces, and this is no secret to the officers who are asked to follow the rapidly changing nature of modern, high-tech People's War.

II. Jettisoning a Doctrine

Chinese views on the importance of People's War overemphasized the degree to which this strategy was relevant, even during Mao's lifetime. The overemphasis on People's War as an overarching strategy made Mao appear as a brilliant military figure whose theoretical strategic conceptions, first glorified from the period of the Long March (1934-35), were universally applicable. But we should remember that in the "anti-Japanese war," Mao did not triumph over foreign forces through a guerrilla war of resistance. Rather, the United States bombed Hiroshima and Nagasaki with nuclear weapons in a much wider conflict, and within China the Japanese surrendered, on U.S. terms, to the government of Chiang Kaishek. Mao himself must have realized that he was more than a nuisance to the Japanese, but less than a liberator. Ultimately, it was the state with the superior technology that liberated China from a Japanese imperial threat.

From 1947 to 1949, and from 1950 to 1953, the war against Chiang Kai-shek and the Korean War were also fought largely through conventional battles, in which the much-trumpeted strategies and tactics of People's War only applied marginally. From 1947, to dislodge Chiang Kai-shek from major industrial bases near and along the coast, Mao and his generals employed the PLA to fight conventional battles. Later, as commander of China's armed forces in Korea, Peng Dehuai did employ overwhelming numbers against a technically superior opponent, because he had no choice. But his own assessment of China's military after that battle was that it needed a major overhaul. China's forces suffered terrible casualties despite mixed successes, and many of the policies of Deng Xiaoping under reform drew lessons from the slaughter of the country's poorly-equipped forces (and the death of Mao's own son) during that conflict.

John Lewis and Xue Litai's excellent studies of China's nuclear and naval modernization rightly emphasize a slow break with People's War concepts starting from as far back as the Korean War:

> The Korean War challenged [Maoist] dogma. It brought Chinese troops face-to-face with the devastating lethality of modern air and naval power. The threats by the United States to use nuclear weapons in Korea and against China itself during the war and subsequent crises activated Mao's ambition to make China forever immune to such intimidation. Despite the apparent perpetuation of People's War as scripture, Beijing secretly started Projects 02 (nuclear weapons), 05 (ballistic missiles), and 09 [focused on nuclear-powered submarines and their missiles]. It strengthened its conventional forces and updated its views on military intelligence, mobility, and troop concentration. Revolution's theories and modern practice began to diverge, though the term "People's War" could never be questioned.[16]

Significant modifications of People's War concepts in the 1950s also included the establishment of a defined hierarchy of Soviet-influenced ranks, the weakening of political commissars, less attention to economic development projects for men in uniform, and an attempt to stress professionalism and the army over more amateurish militia forces.

Mainland and foreign arguments suggesting strategic continuity correctly identify the ways in which already vague strategic concepts have proved to be even more fungible, and the politically undesirable task of spitting on Mao and his legacy has admittedly been avoided.

Yet Chinese leaders are convinced that China cannot triumph from a position of overwhelming technical weakness. China has moved away from the idea that most wars it is likely to fight would be all-out wars of resistance against a superior occupation force. Chinese leaders are preparing instead for limited, high-tech wars and regional struggles. These wars would probably be waged conventionally, and could involve disputes over uninhabited islands and other strategic locations that are far from most of the people. These include the Spratly Islands, the Himalayan border with India, and the deserts of China's northwest.

Since reform, specific elements of People's War rejected by Deng Xiaoping and his successors can be listed as follows:

Politics over Economics

A central element of People's War was the belief that the country with the most political resolve, the most unified and unswervingly loyal command, and the correct political doctrine was bound to triumph over a country governed by capitalist, imperialist, or archaic ideologies. This was a lesson derived from guerrilla warfare against hated Western and Japanese imperialists and especially against corrupt Nationalists. In an environment of revolutionary discontent, more airplanes and more factories did not necessarily yield victory against Mao. Mao transformed the ancient idea that mind could triumph over matter into the socialistic idea that political will and the correct line could triumph over capitalistic business leaders and their industrial output.

Yet the most important contribution of Deng Xiaoping to China's strategic thought was the idea that power in the modern world is defined by economics. Under the section "Taking Action to Promote the Overall Public Interest of National Construction," a textbook on the Chinese army published in Beijing outlines the theoretical underpinning of the deemphasis of politics and military readiness under Deng and the shift, even within the military, toward the goal of economic construction. Power is defined in economic terms from the beginning of the reform period, and in order to correct the economic deterioration that took place under the Cultural Revolution and reverse the consequent backwardness of China's production power, the military would work single-mindedly to promote China's overriding concern under reform: economic development.[17]

Deng argued that significant military power could no longer be secured without modern industry, tremendous technological capacity, and an understanding of modern economic management. At the very beginning of the reform period, at the Third Plenum of the Eleventh Central Committee meeting in late 1978, China already began to emphasize military "construction in peacetime" (*heping shiqi jian she*) and technological modernization rather than the militarization of society to counter total war.[18] Military modernization was regarded as the fourth modernization, behind agriculture, industry, and science and technology, because military modernization was regarded as simply impossible from a backward construction base. The emphasis on economic development, technically competent personnel, and modern management was antithetical to Maoist People's War, especially as People's War was presented during the civil war, the Great Leap Forward, and the first years of the Cultural Revolution.

Masses over Matter

A point related to the one above is the new focus on ordnance modernization. The goal of ordnance modernization dates back through every period of Chinese PLA history but was not a prominent element of the People's War doctrines. In 1977, Deng Xiaoping's call for "fresh air within the Party . . . respecting knowledge, respecting skills," immediately led to an increased emphasis on technocrats and technology. The military lists 12,000 weaponry and ordnance innovations between 1978 and 1983; these were said to have increased firepower, attack strength, mobility, and defensive capability. Institutional reforms were promoted in 1982 to rectify command structures in the development of weaponry, and in 1983 a particularly large meeting was held in the military to promote new weaponry and military technological improvements.[19] Since then, outside analysts estimate that at least 10 of China's 24 land-based, group armies have been re-equipped with many types of advanced conventional weapons.[20]

Rather than focusing on weaponry, People's War relied obsessively on huge masses of poorly equipped soldiers, reserves, border police, and militia units struggling to overwhelm any enemies through their zealous, collective willpower and overwhelming numbers.

A strategy implying strength in numbers made sense for a resistance movement against a technically superior Japanese occupation force, and also for a movement designed to counter the Chinese armies of Chiang Kai-shek. In both cases, low-tech guerrilla operations were more effective and more destructive if more numerous and widespread. This is largely because guerrilla warfare is designed to counter the effectiveness of a military or government already occupying the country. Yet in more likely international struggles that China might face in the future, masses of poorly equipped personnel are unlikely to be decisive or even useful.

Red Masses over Expert Elites

The goal of professionalism was tainted under Mao by its association, especially in the 1950s, with Peng Dehuai, a former defense minister purged by Mao during the Great Leap Forward. Peng's program as Minister of Defense from 1954 included modernization of weaponry, training and discipline, a rank system, and conscription.[21] By contrast, Lin Biao, the commander of the armed forces through the most violent period of the Cultural Revolution, promoted a program that de-emphasized professionalism and focused instead on good class backgrounds and apparent fervor for a communist cause as defined by factional leaders.

During the reform period, politics still matters, but political qualifications have been watered down considerably. Nowadays, according to one Chinese source, "The essence of being 'politically qualified' is to ensure that the gun always obeys the Party's command."[22] Beyond this basic political requirement, the emphasis is on education and expertise.

Generally, the emphasis by Deng Xiaoping and Jiang Zemin on professionalization of the officer corps marks a return to the goals of Peng Dehuai. Through all of the reform period, Deng and Jiang have promoted a younger and more educated officer corps in order to overturn the "soft, lazy, and loose" (*ruan, lan, san*) style of leadership that, Chinese sources admit, developed prior to the reform period.[23]

According to Chinese sources, China's military modernization would "raise education and training to the stature of 'strategy'" (*ba jiaoyu xunlian tigao dao zhanlue diwei*). The military now "takes cadre education and training as the focal point" (*ba ganbu de jiaoyu xunlian zuowei zhongdian*): "Each level of cadres form the powerful backbone of military construction, the organizational leaders and commanders of any future war. Hence, cadre education and training are the mainstay of military education and training in the new period." Cadre education and training here includes both the study of "military theory and war command under modern conditions," and the study of science and technology.[24]

The new policy continues to result in a far more educated officer corps through the 1990s. Before 1980, less than 10 percent of military cadres held university or some junior college qualifications; by 1997, 56 percent held at least junior college qualification, and among leading cadres ranking at and above the regiment commander level, over 90 percent were college-educated. By 1997, the army also had established 173 doctoral tutoring units and 644 master's degree tutoring units. "A batch of military specialists who are experts and scholars straddling the turn of the century have gradually emerged." The army boasts 20,000 holders of doctoral or master's degrees.[25]

Much of the military modernization effort also has focused on the struggle to cut staff. Official accounts claim that in 1975, Deng Xiaoping already recommended staff cuts, and by 1977, with Deng Xiaoping's encouragement, the Central Military Commission outlined an "Army Organizational Structure Rectification Plan" based upon Deng's recommendations. Supposedly, by 1980 Deng Xiaoping had promoted a now frequently quoted goal of "reducing army size, increasing fighting power" (*jingjian jundui, tigao zhanzhengli*). The plan would demand reforms, emphasizing increased quality and staff cuts in every military region and command.

The giant staff cuts decided upon in 1985—of perhaps a million soldiers—would be achieved, first, by cutting offices and work units across the board, from the general staff to the regional commands and the service branches. Cuts may have been scaled back in the wake of student protests (1987, 1989), workers' protests (1989), ethnic nationalist protests in Tibet (1987-1989), and the Tiananmen Massacre. Still, within a decade the General Staff was said to have cut 60 percent of its officers, the Political Commissars 30 percent, and the Logistics Department over 50 percent.[26] With the goal of achieving an officer to private ratio of 1:3.3, from 1985 to 1988, 600,000 were cut from the rolls, and the ranking system was simplified. In all, the "staff cutting and rectification" effort, especially the cuts from 1985, were regarded as unprecedented.[27] They created a leaner army and a much leaner officer corps (see also next chapter).

From Guerrillas and Standing Army Forces to Crack Troops, Sea, Air, and Space Forces

The heavy emphasis on land-based forces under Mao was a side effect of People's War and Mao's emphasis on the masses: How could one fight a people's war of resistance without a support base comprised of the people? Under Deng Xiaoping, militias and an overwhelmingly land-based force have lost their luster. Instead, the emphasis is increasingly on the defense of coastlines, offshore islands and reserves, and strategic installations and ordnance (e.g. submarines, missile silos), with specialized forces. This necessarily has implied less militia training and more joint force exercises that encompass amphibious operations, in-flight refueling, and other elements of contemporary war fighting.

Specifically, military theory and war command under modern conditions is said to include as a central element far better coordination of the services and joint warfare training between air, naval, army, and missile forces.[28] In the words of Shu-shin Wang, an analyst publishing in Taiwan:

> China has strengthened its military mobility and has changed its military tactics and strategy from a unilateral combat of various armed forces to the combined combat of ground forces, air force and navy, from negative defense to positive defense, from short-range attack to long-range attack and from total war to local war. The reasons for these changes chiefly resulted from China's new modernization programs for its air force and navy and from its new domestic and external environments."[29]

This transition is still far from complete, as I show in the next chapter. Many Chinese sources argue that China must push further toward the "building up of crack armed forces" and "organizing combined forces."[30] Still, the effort to move away from another central principle of People's War is clear.

The Move Away from Total Wars and Total Victories

Another element of People's War was the belief that a total war of resistance against an invading superpower was highly likely and "winnable". The Soviet Union had discussed war with other nations as inevitable and certain to advance socialism, and Mao similarly suggested that a likely People's War against the Soviet Union or the United States could culminate in an important victory for revolutionary movements worldwide. The likelihood of war and its importance to the revolution reinforced the need for the militarization of Chinese society in preparation for the impending struggle.

In the age of "Mutually Assured Destruction" (MAD), with legitimacy defined largely through an economic development program, the reformist leadership quickly conceded that a total war against a superpower would be unlikely and, in any case, could not be won on terms that would in any way benefit China's long-term interests.

Unlike under Mao, when the masses were asked to prepare for a People's War against a superpower, any form of war preparedness, even of organized forces, is low on the list of priorities for reform. In the fall of 1984, Deng gave a speech to the Central Military Commission, in which he suggested that the threat of total war—or of any international conflict between China and a superpower's occupation force—had been obsessively overemphasized under Mao: "We've already spoken of the threat of war many times." Deng preferred to focus on his new paradigm under which "the army would unswervingly serve national construction, the overriding public interest."[31]

In a meeting of the Central Military Commission in Beijing in the late spring of 1985, Deng outlined similar themes, stating that while the threat of world war existed still, the forces that supported world peace were growing. It was at this meeting that the strategy of countering "early, massive, nuclear war" (*zaoda, dada, dahe zhanzheng*) was passed over completely for the new strategy of "construction in peacetime" (*heping shiqi jianshe*).[32]

Preparing for total war has therefore sunk low on China's list of priorities. A recent discussion of Chinese strategy under reform spanning 26 pages and covering everything from the role of the military to warning systems, civilian defenses, construction corps, public safety, the militia, and the masses, focuses for only a page on the subject of war preparedness.[33]

To the extent that victory against a great power is discussed in military circles, it is discussed in defensive terms: Winning a war of resistance against an invading force no longer implies advancing world revolution; it simply means the successful effort to repel an attack.[34]

Alastair Iain Johnston argues that as with conventional war, China's poorly-defined strategy to prevent nuclear war is similarly unrevolutionary. Chinese strategists are promoting the concept of a limited deterrent, according to Johnston. Through this strategy China would not struggle for a first-strike capability or even parity against a superpower, but would settle instead for flexible defenses, specifically to ensure against conventional or nuclear escalation.

From the late 1980s on, Chinese strategists have developed a concept of 'limited deterrence' (*you xian wei she*) to describe the kind of deterrent China ought to have. While the concept is still evolving, limited deterrence, according to Chinese strategists, requires sufficient counterforce and countervalue tactical, theater, and strategic nuclear forces to deter the escalation of conventional or nuclear war. If deterrence fails, this capability should be sufficient to control escalation and to compel the enemy to back down.[35]

Whether China has struggled to develop any nuclear firepower other than a minimal deterrent (which is much less than the flexible, limited deterrent described by Johnston) is still an open question.[36] Yet the important point is that Johnston's argument suggests accurately that "total" victory in nuclear war against a nuclear power is far from the minds of Chinese defense planners. Further, while some would argue that People's War under Modern Conditions is relevant to China's official thinking on nuclear deterrence,[37] in Johnston's discussion of China's emerging strategic thought, People's War is a concept that is justifiably ignored.

Generally, by 1984, Deng Xiaoping made it clear that no war (conventional or nuclear) against a superpower could lead to the victory of Deng's reform program or the achievement of China's long-term goals. Deng argued that China would badly need to modernize its army—because it was technically backward compared to others, because China by no means possessed a leading army—simply to resist invasion or repel attack in the unlikely event of a superpower war under modern conditions.[38]

Meanwhile, victory of the reform effort, during which political legitimacy is defined in economic development terms, can only be achieved during a time of peace. In Deng Xiaoping's words: "China's promotion of an independent foreign policy has restrained war and safeguarded world peace. . . . China needs peace, and would last wish to see war break out. China needs a long period of a stable, peaceful international environment, and needs the friendship of every nation's peoples to jointly carry out economic construction and to transform [China's] poverty and backwardness."[39]

In accord with a new desire to work with superpowers toward peace is the recognition that military-to-military exchanges might help to avoid disastrous, unplanned, and pointless encounters that provoke accidents and bloodshed. One new element of strategy discussed in many Chinese sources is the desire to build military-to-military relations between China and foreign nations. This has resulted in many military exchanges, for example, between U.S. and Chinese defense personnel.[40]

Space and Time: Key Advantages or Crippling Handicaps?

Many Western sources cite a recent emphasis on regional wars or local wars, but the most contemporary Chinese sources have moved beyond this already "un-Maoist" terminology to focus on intelligence wars and information wars that might be vastly destructive to all regions and localities at lightning speed and simultaneously. A central idea of People's War was that vast space and time horizons could only favor a force staffed by millions, because any army lulled into China would eventually be enervated by its giant army, its militarized society, and its slow, crippling guerrilla attacks. Yet electronic wars and information wars can bypass ground forces and occur in seconds. Partly as a result, the false sense of security suggested in older Chinese doctrinal texts has disappeared in more recent ones. Now, according to an article in *The PLA Daily*,

> Modern warfare is characterized by its short duration, fast rhythm, great intensity, limited operational objectives, extensive battlefield, precision strike, controllable damage, complicated troop structure and precise and fragile systems. Due to these changes, the outcome of future hi-tech local wars will be determined mainly by the destruction of the enemy's combat system rather than by the annihilation of enemy personnel. . . . The main factor for victory will be shifted to control of time from control of space. When a battle unfolds, strategies, campaigns and tactical actions interact and proceed in great harmony. The initial battle will quickly and directly develop into the decisive battle in which the winner and the loser is decided. . . . The core of these ideas . . . is that the initial battle is the decisive battle.[41]

Mao struggled to develop China's Third Line to ensure that hundreds of hinterland cities and towns would have the resources to serve like guerrilla hamlets, repelling foreign invasion. But China's vast geographical size is no longer described as strategically advantageous. In an age of information warfare, size merely implies a potential command and control problem for those forced instantly to defend themselves:

> Our country is a large country with frontiers and coastline extending for tens of thousands of kilometers. Rapid economic development along the coast and in the depth of the hinterland means that there are many vulnerable targets. Without the guarantee of modern early warning systems, we will sustain heavy losses in the initial battles and be reduced to a passive position. Thus, we should build a full-air-space, omnidirectional, total-depth, all-weather, large-capacity, over-the-horizon, time-efficient, stable, reliable, flexible, encrypted, and integrated early warning system which has great adaptability and survival ability in electromagnetic environments. We should develop a modern information network to increase our ability to analyze, process, transmit and use early warning information data.[42]

This goal is a logical one based on new assumptions about war; the next chapter discusses the extent to which it has been achieved in practice.

The Threat of Unconventional War

Beyond the discussion of new forms of electronic war and information war, public sources are more revealing than in the past about fears concerning the increasingly dispersed and complex threats of chemical, biological, and nuclear weapons. Chinese commanders look with increasing concern at the threats posed by unconventional technologies to China's standing army and vast population. Despite a famous Maoist quotation, the blustering idea that a nuclear-armed superpower force was a mere paper tiger against China's massive population was never really endorsed even by Mao, who worked successfully to build China's nuclear deterrent. These days, one struggles to find any relevant references endorsing the famous paper tiger quotation in China's increasingly diversified media. Further, there is more evidence than ever that Chinese leaders question the effectiveness of their nuclear deterrent and fear new unconventional threats, including those posed by terrorist organizations.

China's nuclear fighting capability has developed steadily since the 1960s, but its second-strike capability against Russia and especially the United States is not guaranteed. More importantly, Chinese leaders share the renewed, post–Cold War worries of many other secular, establishment powers about the security threat posed by unconventional terrorism and fundamentalist or millenarian religious organizations. China is often accused of activities that encourage nuclear proliferation, in Pakistan and elsewhere, and it is working to improve its nuclear capabilities (discussed in the next chapter) through external intelligence and internal technical discoveries. But, perhaps more than the United States (which is working toward new-generation missile defenses and Star Wars systems that would shatter the Anti-Ballistic Missile Defense Treaty), China might be looked upon as a wary and conservative, status quo nuclear power.

One Mainland article on unconventional weapons, in the monthly journal of the PLA General Logistics Health Department, acknowledges the positive impact of treaties such as the Nuclear Nonproliferation Treaty, Comprehensive Nuclear Test Ban Treaty, and treaties banning the use of chemical and biological weapons—all of which China has signed and publicly endorsed. However, the article also highlights the limited effect of these treaties with arguments that parallel (and probably borrow from) those of Western realists:

[O]f the 3000 tons of highly enriched uranium flowing in the world, only one percent is under the actual monitoring of the international atomic energy organization. Of the 1000 tons of plutonium known to exist, less than one third are theoretically under international supervision. Inspection plans on missile, chemical and biological weapons are even more difficult to be carried out. At least [until] now, there is not one effective system to stop proliferation of large-scale destructive weapons. Information necessary for developing nuclear, chemical and biological weapons is unavoidably proliferated, and material needed to develop the weapons can be acquired by [more ways] than one.[43]

China further fears new nuclear weapons being developed by powers more advanced than China:

To destroy enemy communications equipment in the future information war, some major military countries are vigorously developing nuclear weapons of the third generation like weapons of laser beam, electromagnetic radiation, x-ray radiation, microwave radiation and blast wave; along with neutron weapons, nuclear bombs that penetrate through ground, laser beam gun tips, and nuclear scatter bombs, etc. Nuclear weapons of the third generation are even considered as a key part of the new military revolution. It is predicted that these weapons will possibly appear in about ten years from now, and the possibility of strategic use of nuclear weapons will be increased.[44]

Authorities also fear new chemical weapons being developed by both governments and nongovernmental organizations:

In the area of chemical weapons, in addition to nerve poisonous agents which are the most possible to be used, there have been some new chemical agents like the deadly poisonous agents and disabling agents, which cannot only be inhaled through air passage to be poisoned, but also be absorbed through skin to pose a dual threat. Biological and chemical agents of small molecule peptide type like battlefield toxin agents, whose toxicity is one hundred times higher than that of chemical agents currently available, a minute amount of which can be poisonous to humans, are also new agents. Other examples are . . . agents which can penetrate through gas masks and protective clothing. Direction of development of new chemical battlefield agents are towards high toxicity, multiple paths, penetration, obvious effects of disability and hard to protect and treat. In recent years, spread of chemical weapons have heightened the threat of chemical terror and chemical terror activities occurred often. The serin poison gas incident at a subway station in Tokyo, Japan in 1995 is one example.[45]

Finally, authorities fear the threat of new biological weapons being developed by both governments and nongovernmental organizations. The same source implies a fear that these weapons could be more debilitating, or more easily directed against, a somewhat ethnically uniform country like China:

> The rapid development of biological technology may bring a more important revolution in the history of mankind, which is called "biological revolution" by some people. The greatest hazard to mankind posed by biological technology is that it may be used to develop biological weapons. When humans can differentiate the gene sequences of different races, there is a possibility that terrible "race gene weapons" can be developed. If this technology is seized and utilized by ethnic cleansers, unprecedented catastrophe will be brought to mankind. At present time, utilization of gene engineering and cell engineering will not only make the large-scale, industrialized production of biological battlefield agents a reality; it will also enhance the ability of biological battlefield agents to cause disease and their resistance to environment and drugs, change the antigen structure of biological battlefield agents to render the originally effective vaccines useless; it is also possible to develop and produce new toxins or gene weapons, making detection, diagnosis, prevention and treatment of damages by biological battlefield agents more difficult. It can be said that technological developments of nuclear, chemical and biological weapons have not really been truly stopped. They have just become more surreptitious.[46]

This source presents an ambiguous but unnerving conclusion on the results of newly possible unconventional weaponry, suggesting that technologically inferior powers may increasingly rely upon unconventional weapons to repel more advanced adversaries. The conclusion is ambiguous, because it does not state whether China should be considered one of those technologically inferior countries:

> Even though the possibility of actual battlefield use of nuclear, chemical and biological weapons in future wars is relatively slight, these weapons [continue] to be important deterrent weapons. The huge battlefield military effects of these weapons was amply demonstrated in the Gulf War. Since Iraq threatened to use chemical and biological weapons, multinational troops had to make adjustments in their operational plans, troops deployments, and operational protections, and amount of war preparation work was doubled. Time of air raid operations was extended in order to destroy eleven Iraqi chemical weapon storage points. Large amounts of manpower and capital were spent to produce and acquire protective

machines and material. . . . Troops carried out emergency anti-chemical exercises and went into high alert and preparation status. All of the above caused serious psychological burden to officers and men. . . . Even after the Gulf War, suspicion about "Gulf War Syndrome" remained.

In future wars, possibly due to the relatively large difference among military power of various countries, there may be warfare situations where nuclear, chemical and biological weapons are lined up against high-tech conventional weapons. Eventually, nuclear, chemical and biological weapons may be considered the best means against high-tech conventional weapons.[47]

The implication of this and other discussions on new forms of warfare is clear. If war is increasingly high-tech, and less contained in conventional battlefields than ever before, then China's massive, low-tech land force may be of little import to truly international security concerns.

No Mainland source would yet admit that China has abandoned People's War. But many list, as Deng Xiaoping's primary strategic contribution to China's defense modernization, goals antithetical to People's War. So China is driving on a road that leads away from People's War—but in what direction is it heading?

III. Toward a New Military Doctrine of "Technocratic Command"

China is clearly in a transition period in which its military leaders are struggling to build a new doctrine. Central tenets of the new doctrine that have already emerged focus first on elite leadership and the modernization of command and control; and second on technological modernization as the keystone to success.

The degree to which elite leadership must be concentrated and centralized is a controversial point. Decentralization is encouraged not only by the Maoist People's War legacy but also by Deng Xiaoping's emphasis on autonomous military-economic units managing their own budgets, paying their own way, and hopefully (at least until recently) earning profits. Yet the high command appears to feel that decentralization in China has gone too far, and it is lobbying for a "neo-traditional" recentralization effort, emphasizing elite technocrats with significantly more concentrated decision-making power. As Jiang Zemin gains further confidence in his control of the armed forces, a subtle, nascent re-centralization effort may be one of his few significant military legacies in the 1990s.

The focus on elite leadership and unified command and control is traditional because sagacious, well-organized command, strong leadership, and effective intelligence have been strategic concerns in China since the days of Sun Tsu. However, the focus is new in its emphasis on command and control systems completely unknown before the twentieth century, including those involving high-speed computers, anti-missile defenses, and electronic warfare.

In terms of training, the new focus is on perpetual upgrading of technical skills, rather than a solid grounding in supposedly timeless doctrines. In the words of Deng Xiaoping (spoken in 1980, long before the Gulf War shocked many Chinese strategists into drawing similar conclusions): "On wars nowadays: If our military officers don't have the knowledge to fight modernized war it is unacceptable. . . . Because equipment is not the same, commanding modernized war will require many new facets of knowledge."[48]

China has struggled to promote military technical modernization since the Qing dynasty. These days, the new technologies sought include the revolutionary technologies of unconventional warfare, electronic warfare, information warfare, and intercontinental missiles. "Information and knowledge have changed the previous practice of estimating military strength by merely calculating the number of armored divisions, airborne combined troops, and aircraft carrier fighting groups. At present, it is also necessary to calculate invisible strengths, like computational ability, communication capacity, reliability, real-time reconnaissance ability, and so on."[49]

These elements of China's emerging doctrine are designed to be effective in regional wars under high-tech conditions, which Chinese strategists have focused on as a type of war China is likely to face in any near-term conflict, and also against information-based wars unconstrained by geographic regions or territories.

One relevant military text published by the National Defense University, discussing "high-tech war and army quality building," contains a theme that is increasingly popular in military circles. "[H]igh-tech war has already changed the traditional concept of 'certain victory in numbers' (*duobing zhilu bisheng*). . . . Instead, one must rely upon superior quality to attain victory."[50]

What is quality? Quality first implies limiting army numbers, and second improving weaponry. The authors are fascinated by the capabilities of American F-117 fighters, missiles, M1A1 tanks, and defense-related electronics.[51] It is argued that to boost weaponry, one needs (1) to understand what is required to prepare strategies for high-tech war; (2) to work from a scientific base to develop the weaponry; and (3) to devote a larger percentage of the defense budget to weapons construction. This is the first example in the book of a prominent lobbying request.[52]

Quality further implies improving the technical capacity and skills of one's personnel, and improving the "war-fighting capacity of the entire force"—through greater coordination between the branches and different military regions.

Improving intelligence and placing greater demands on army logistics are also critical. This source suggests that each day of the Gulf War cost the allied forces some one billion U.S. dollars, merely to pay for expended fuel, bombs, and miscellaneous replacement fittings and costs. The unstated question is whether China has the economic base to sustain this kind of regional war, but the focus here is also on intelligently organized, logistic organizational structures. Organization must be able to manage similarly limited (yet still vast and expensive) conflicts without excessive waste.[53]

Next, quality means more training and preparation in peacetime, and, finally, advancing theory and doctrine on military affairs. To improve its theory and doctrine, China must study both Maoist thought ("seeking truth through facts") and the experiences of foreign armies.[54] Apparently, doctrine would be studied, ironed out, and espoused by the high command and its elite military academies, with the help of intelligence personnel studying abroad.

Generally, the most prominent illustration of quality, for these officially sponsored authors, was the allied campaign in the Persian Gulf war. Iraqi forces relied on quantity rather than quality, and the American-led side was victorious. Unlike the American-led, allied forces, "the Iraqis were incapable of carrying out high-tech war."[55] Iraq also is faulted for having invested in an almost exclusively land-based force before the Persian Gulf War. Chinese analysts suggest that 96.5 percent of Iraq's army was in its land forces, only 0.4 percent in its navy and 3.1 percent in its air force. This is seen as a primary reason for Iraq's crippling inability to fight high-tech war, despite over 10,000 tanks at its disposal.[56] The lesson is obviously relevant to China, a nation with an overwhelmingly land-based army (although it is not as imbalanced as Iraq's), in which the majority of more than two million infantry soldiers behave like a dispersed standing army, stationed away from any national border.

The conclusion of this text reiterates that to improve quality in the army, China's scientific and technological capacity must improve. China must "decrease quantity and increase quality," pay more attention to army construction, upgrade its weaponry to the highest technological levels, and improve the knowledge and effectiveness of its soldiers.[57]

An even more important, very up-to-date "internal circulation only" (*neibu*) source—intended for circulation among China's military and defense-planning elite, published by the scientific research branch of the National Defense University and the Army Command Study and Research Office—discusses parallel themes of "war command under high-tech conditions." There has been some censorship of passages and articles, which implies that the copy summarized here was disseminated to lower levels of the military command structure with some information deleted. I nevertheless analyze the book in detail because it clearly has been promoted and endorsed at the highest levels, primarily for internal consumption. Authors of individual chapters are listed throughout, and include several lieutenant generals (*zhongjiang*), major generals (*shaojiang*), and senior colonels (*daxiao*).

Generally, the book, *Research on War Command under High-Tech Conditions* (*gao jishu tiaojian xia zuo zhan zhihui yanjiu*), argues forcefully that military modernization must begin with proper leadership and organization at the top.[58] A lieutenant general who wrote the book's introduction admittedly begins with a quick kowtow to Marxism. Command under high-tech conditions must first grapple with basic theory, including Marxist theory: Not People's War as such (which is not mentioned) but rather Marxist historical materialism, the overriding basic theory that allegedly unites the Chinese high command. Yet what is the relevance of historical materialism in practice? The essay states only that the central element of Marxist doctrine as applied to command is the understanding that war-fighting under modern conditions changes with changing socio-economic structures.[59] One can conclude from this, then, that Marxism—or the weak trace of it here—justifies a strategic overhaul under new socio-economic circumstances.

Beyond the curt, courteous reference to Marxism, other points are directly in accord with themes more relevant to "technocratic command" and the discussion here. The second point outlined in the introduction to this internal circulation text is that China's military needs to create a more unified command. It is incorrect to suggest that commands for the land force, air force, and the navy could ultimately be separate or autonomous. Military regions also should not host truly independent commands, and different command bureaus or functional divisions (e.g., logistics, intelligence) cannot work in a fully autonomous fashion. Hence, while the model of guerrilla warriors in autonomous hamlets is not explicitly rejected, the call for a stronger, more centralized command structure (permitting coordination of branches, sectors, and functions) implies a rejection of guerrilla-style organization.[60]

Third, there is a need for China to grapple with new command methods and technologies. This implies in particular more use of computer simulation and automation. This source refers to the need to build "C4I" (command, control, communication, computers, and intelligence), employing up-to-date Western terminology for command structures. (Later in the work and in many other Chinese military sources, the less contemporary term, C3I—leaving out computers—is used.) The focus on C4I also means paying more attention to ensuring that technology and doctrine are complementary.[61]

Fourth, there is a need to improve and update strategy. This refers in particular to the creation of a strategy that considers the far-reaching implications of electronic warfare and its threats to command and control. China needs to build strategies to defend itself against electronic wars under high-tech conditions, and to develop the capacity to fight such wars.[62] Poorly equipped, poorly trained, and poorly educated masses of soldiers are the least appropriate means of countering truly advanced attacks on electronic systems.

Finally, there is a need to improve China's theoretical understanding of and research on command under modern conditions. This book is an effort to meet that need, and future research, training, and war-games must also be directed toward similar ends.[63]

Other articles in this source flesh out important details on China's current defense goals that reinforce the introductory themes. A lieutenant general from the Jinan Military Region, writing specifically on new techniques for fighting land offensives, states that command under conditions of modern warfare must be more concentrated than is currently the case in China. It is no longer possible that people from different branches of the armed forces or different military regions can work separately to fight a land war.[64]

In "Recognizing Some Problems of United Command and Control Across War Zones," a major general from the Beijing Military Region argues that there has been a clear "revolution in military affairs" in recent years, and the revolution's impact on command and control is enormous. In the post-1970s "age of microchips" (*xinpian shidai*), of electronic warfare, and of rapid, multi-tiered, jointly fought battles, China's military command and control must become more centralized; must have better coordination between the center and the branches; must have more automation and computerization, and generally must be more agile. These goals should be achieved partly through reorganization and continued managerial work to improve command and control structures. The improvement of "automation" technologies like computers and advances in the technical capacity of China's command receive even more attention. The major general describes China's command, from a technical perspective, as weak and unreliable.[65]

Another major general lobbies similarly for the creation of a more unified command structure, with more centralized control not only of field divisions, but also of intelligence, communication, electronics, and automated systems.[66] The repeated references to China's overly dispersed intelligence structures throughout the book never discusses more specific proposals, but suggests that a restructuring of intelligence is indeed long overdue.

Major General Wang Liangjun, in "Securing Command Stability under Unified War Fighting," again discusses the threat of electronic war, and of warfare that attacks command and control systems conventionally or through a nuclear assault. The major general suggests that the stability of China's command would be severely strained by technologically advanced attacks directly on command systems, and that China must counter this threat through "secrecy" (*zai yinbizhong qiu wending*), "motorization" (*zai jidongzhong qiu wending*), resistance, and agility. Not surprisingly, the implications of an emphasis on secrecy are discussed only briefly, but the author implies that China needs a simplified command structure, without too many layers, that could hammer out solutions to attacks on command behind closed doors, perhaps behind one closed door. Resistance implies better electronic backup systems to counter the threat of electronic warfare. There is no discussion of what agility might imply in practice, except some coordination between each branch of the armed forces.[67]

Two senior colonels, Chen Yong and Liang Yongsheng, writing on "the stability of a unified wartime command" suggest similarly that for major decisions, China's chain of command may be too long, arcane, and complex. It is argued that for China, the ideal chain of command would involve only three to five levels, and certainly should not exceed ten. The authors suggest that for major decisions, this apparently moderate recommendation frequently does not represent current practice.[68]

Two senior colonels suggest that the first key to raising the quality of decision making in battle is better intelligence, and more unified intelligence across branches. These authors specifically compare China's intelligence gathering personnel, technology, and organizational structures to those of the United States and Russia, and they find China's severely wanting.[69] Command personnel and military strategists are also said to require more training for more years at the highest levels of military decision-making. In terms of training, the senior colonels again compare China unfavorably to the U.S.[70]

Indeed, the most striking, specific weaknesses of command is China's backward intelligence systems and controls, and the parallel weakness of Chinese communications. A senior colonel from the Intelligence Bureau of Shenyang Military Headquarters argues most forcefully, in "Securing Intelligence under a Unified, War Fighting Command," that China simply has no means to organize and sift through the intelligence provided by various branches and regional divisions of the armed forces.[71] Zhang Liangfu, a senior colonel from the Communications Bureau of the headquarters of the Nanjing Military Region, similarly hones in on the problems of communications under high-tech war, and describes them as numerous. There will be problems of communication between different branches of the armed forces and different defense organizations (army, People's Armed Police, militia); between forces fighting in different media of the war zone (land, sea, air, stratosphere, and electronics); and between command headquarters, intelligence organizations, and divisions in the field. Exact numbers are censored, but Colonel Zhang estimates that in an attack on China, the nation must be prepared to remove obstacles to hundreds of aerial communication lines, and to repair thousands of them.[72] There is no information provided on which communication systems, in addition to old-fashioned telephone lines, China would need to build to counter information and communication warfare. Satellite communications, short-wave, microwave, "relay communication" (*jieli tongxin*), underground and underwater field lines, and fiber optic systems are each employed to varying degrees by various branches of the armed forces. Yet this source admits that the systems of the different branches are not always compatible, and not always mutually accessible. The result is an undue reliance on backward communication channels (e.g., it is implied, the telephone). The article argues that the lack of coordination of communications within the armed forces is detrimental to the pursuit of modern defenses, and that this weakness must be rectified.[73]

Some parts of this textbook on command are more subtle than others. For example, Senior Colonel Wang Jianghuai, of the Command School and Research Branch of the National Defense University, concedes that there are advantages to each branch of the armed forces and each military region having somewhat autonomous command structures. The advantage of this system is that the independent commands have genuine power and resources to identify and carry out important goals at middle levels of military organization. But the disadvantage is again emphasized over the advantage: Overlapping and unclear divisions of authority between the General Staff, the branches, and military regions weaken China's defenses.[74] The solution is to establish a clear chain of command, in which intelligence is shared, and decision making, planning, and control are carried out in a coordinated fashion. Again, this essay is one among many suggesting that intelligence is *not* sufficiently shared between branches, and that China can still only carry out joint-force exercises with difficulty.[75]

Another comparatively subtle essay, written by a major general from the Xinjiang Military Region and two lieutenant colonels from the Command School and Research Branch of the National Defense University, further suggests that command must accept differences in function across branches of the armed forces. For example, due to the tremendous destructive power of China's missile force, or "Second Artillery," and its overwhelming reliance on technology, it seems logical that the command structure of the missile force would be more concentrated than that of other branches of the armed forces. Due to the tremendous distances covered by the navy, by contrast, its command should be concentrated and united, but its control comparatively dispersed.[76] Generally, the emphasis of this important book is on a more unified, more centralized, more technically capable, more educated, more powerful central command.

Chinese sources focusing on the modernization of specific branches of the armed forces often touch on similar, technocratic strategic viewpoints, which suggests that these viewpoints are being circulated at every level of command. For example, an open military source focused exclusively on air force modernization (published in a prominent series on high-tech war), hones in on developments in air force technology, and what these might imply for the tactical potential of modern fighter planes. If technology does not drive the modernization goals of the Chinese air force completely, it can be said at least that it drives the entire discussion in this source.[77] Chapters survey new shielding technology, air-control technology, guidance systems, reconnaissance systems, photo-electronics and general electronics, power and propellants, in-flight refueling, anti-missile technology, and other scientific developments. The book was probably targeted for military personnel or civilian defense planners, and it was considered either sufficiently important or commercially viable to be printed in at least two editions.[78]

Another military-funded study on the use of missiles in modern warfare stresses the increasing importance of C3I systems. The authors again borrow the obviously English-derived "C3I" term, and emphasize the centrality of missiles—the technology about which they have the most expertise—in the defense and attack of C3I.[79] The book also emphasizes the centrality of highly skilled, technical personnel (*rencai*) in the development, deployment, and use of missiles in "missile wars."[80]

Commanders of various military regions provide a similar emphasis in their most recent speeches and writings. For example, a recent article attributed to the commander of the Nanjing Military Region focuses almost exclusively on shortcomings in China's command and the importance of rectifying them:

> To engage in local warfare under the conditions of high technology, the command system must be highly capable of processing information, conducting reconnaissance, making prompt decisions, and launching concealed movements. In modern local wars such as the Gulf War, the command posts are invariably the initial major targets of assault by the belligerent parties. Our army's command system is still far from meeting the requirements to organize and direct local warfare under the conditions of high technology. For example, the procedure in directing a military operation is quite detailed and complicated. Our methods in conducting military operations are relatively backward, and our command system remains inefficient. Our reconnaissance, early warning command and control, and electronics countermeasures capabilities are still relatively weak.[81]

Finally, Mainland analysts of military financial management and logistics support similar themes. In a section of an article by leading Chinese defense analysts outlining shifting budgetary goals for the future, the first goal listed is the development of high technology. The *way* it is listed suggests that People's War has been discarded:

> Take the development of high technology products as the key; raise national defense capacity to create new technological and industrial products: Modern war is high-tech war. Science and technology are the first sources of productive force and constitute the most worthwhile and basic element in an army's battle power. The regional wars of the current era, especially the Gulf War, entirely prove this point.[82]

No mention is made of people being the key to production, war-fighting, or anything related to defense.

IV. Conclusion

A legacy of People's War is the fact that the political branch of the armed forces is still surprisingly prominent. "The separation of Party and army functions" is still more of a slogan than a genuine goal. "Political work in the armed forces" includes ideological education, Party building and Party organization, cadre development, and mass work to build proper relations between the army and the people. This political work is valued, most obviously, in the Political Commissar branch of the PLA, which is considered the second of four primary administrative branches of the army (behind the General Staff, ahead of Logistics and General Armaments). In effect, political work, bureaucratically, is listed as more important than the logistic management of millions of soldiers and civilians and an unknown percentage of China's GDP, and ahead of weapons development.

Yet in terms of China's contemporary, applied military strategy and doctrine, this bureaucratic atavism from the Maoist era is not particularly important. It primarily reflects the goal of political continuity and the continued drag of communistic management.

From a strategic perspective, China is moving steadily toward a more technocratic command. In the words of one Chinese defense analyst not previously cited: "To unceasingly improve the components that make up our army is the essential goal of our national defense development strategy. In fact, quality has increasingly become the trend for our nation's battle force—moving from extensive to intensive models, moving to quality construction, moving on the road toward a scientifically and technologically strong army."[83]

Giant obstacles may block the Chinese high command from achieving success in its strategic modernization effort. These include fears of internal turmoil that distract the army away from international objectives, a communist organizational legacy, still-bloated staff, limited defense budgets, and frequently distracting economic goals (e.g., self-sufficiency and the management of profit centers). However, the goal—a move away from People's War toward an emphasis on elite leadership and lean, specialized, technically equipped forces—is now clear.

CHAPTER 2

The Reality: Implementation and Force Structure

While emerging strategic viewpoints outlined in the previous chapter appear to be universally endorsed by the high command as long-term objectives, in practice China's army is an amalgamation of old and new. This means an activist, socialistic state still maintains a bloated armed force, which is called in to resolve sundry problems and conflicts. These range from infrastructural weaknesses to ethnic nationalist turmoil. The state is also committed to the public employment of citizens, and overstaffing in the military parallels overstaffing in most public offices and state enterprises.

Consequently, the implementation of any international, strategic goals, and especially the implementation of a strategy that would dramatically cut staff to promote a very "un-Maoist" elite, centralized, technocratic command, remains problematic.

Lingering reminiscence for People's War strategies may drag the reform process to an extent, but more important problems are the fact that the army is and has always been a bloated organization for the execution and enforcement of domestic policy. The size of the armed forces and the location of army bases reflect this fundamental fact.

This chapter measures the extent to which China has implemented its newly emerging strategic goals in practice, with an emphasis on China's overall force structure and its effort to cut military staff. Despite some improvements, including force reductions, China remains technologically behind the times. The most important source of the problem is not low budgets, as some Chinese sources claim. It is rather the budgetary drain of surplus labor.

I. The High Command

In a Marxist-Leninist state, military commanders answer to the leaders, not of the state, but rather of the Communist Party. Admittedly, the Party's chairman or secretary is likely to also hold executive posts in the government. For example, Jiang Zemin at the time of this writing is both the Party secretary of the Chinese Communist Party (CCP) and president of the PRC. Yet his authority over the military derives from his Party, rather than state, credentials. Indeed, all military and defense bodies are supposed to answer to the Party, as in Mao's famous dictum, "Power flows from the barrel of a gun; the Party must control the gun."

The Central Military Commission, or CMC, is China's highest ranking military body. Before 1982, the CMC was listed simply as the military organizational wing of the Communist Party. As part of his reform effort to separate and further define Party, government, and industrial organizational structures, Deng Xiaoping promoted a subtle change, more in theory than in substance, in the 1982 Constitution of the PRC: The Constitution listed a CMC that would form the military organizational wing of the state. In theory, this meant that from 1982, the chairman of the CMC could be elected, or recalled, by the People's Congress and its standing committee. The People's Congress would then play a more significant role in the management of military affairs.[1]

In practice, the CMC of the Communist Party and that of the Chinese government consist of the same people, and the Party decides who these people will be. Further, in recent years China has retreated from this reform on paper. A national defense bill has formally re-subordinated the military under the CCP.[2]

The CMC develops China's military strategy. It oversees military equipment modernization. It determines the structure and responsibilities of subordinate organizational branches, services, and regions. It promotes combat readiness and training. Finally, the CMC is supposed to work jointly with the State Council (the executive branch) in the overall management of the defense budget and defense capital expenditures.[3]

The most powerful figure in the Communist Party usually also serves as Chairman of the CMC, and the most powerful figures in the politburo (the standing committee of the Communist Party Central Committee) frequently serve in the CMC. For example, soon after Jiang Zemin became Deng Xiaoping's hand-picked successor as Communist Party General Secretary, Jiang also became Chairman of the CMC.

Below the CMC, through most of the reform period, there have been three general headquarters, or central administrative branches of the high command: The General Staff Department, General Political Department or Political Commissars, and General Logistics, almost always listed in that order. In July of 1998, the State Council announced the creation of a fourth central administrative branch of the high command, the General Armaments Department (GAD). Because its functions relate to the management of weapons development and China's military-industrial complex, GAD's organization and significance is outlined more thoroughly in Chapter Three.

The goals and interests of these central administrative branches sometimes overlap. For example, at the time of this writing the General Staff and General Logistics Department run competing businesses and industrial factories that are only loosely connected with their central administrative tasks. Yet the General Staff Department is primarily responsible for the formulation of strategy and for war command. The General Political Department is primarily responsible for the enforcement of Party control and the Party line, and for the Communist Party's "thought work" and "organizational work."[4] The General Logistics Department is primarily responsible for all questions of logistic supply and distribution. Finally, the General Armaments Department manages weapons modernization and procurement.

The four general headquarters directly control the seven military regions of the Chinese army, the three military regions of the Chinese navy, the military regions of the air force, and China's strategic missile force, or "Second Artillery." Meanwhile, some sources suggest that the National Defense University, the Academy of Military Science, and many other military colleges are directly subordinate to the Central Military Commission. Others suggest that these organizations are jointly supervised by the General Staff Department, the Political Commissars, and General Logistics.[5]

To what extent has this basic command and control organizational structure been reformed in practice? Again, in terms of technological improvements, China is struggling to bolster command and control through long-term investments in "high performance computers, optics, and electronics, air-to-surface and surface-to-air observation, and modern telecommunications."[6] Military planners are working to ensure that the electronics industry will become the defense establishment's lead industry (see also next chapter), and this would pave the way for improved command and control.[7] Specific technologies under development include new airborne early-warning systems, which may, with Russian or Israeli help, be operational by 2005.[8] Plans also are underway to build a constellation of 10 lightweight satellites with impressive image precision and infrared sensors.[9]

Generally, the blurring of civilian and military research has advanced with respect to command and control systems. For example, the State Science and Technology Commission (a civilian body) is studying materials used in both military and civilian electronics and information gathering.[10] The National Defense Science and Technology University (a military research center) has developed a high-speed fiber-optic computer network and other products of importance to both military and civilian telecommunications.[11]

Still, Chinese experts have argued that China's technological capacity in command, control, and related electronics and communications development is sorely in need of improvement. The PLA "is currently saddled with an obsolete and vulnerable command and control network," primarily composed of short-wave radio and telephones.[12] Economic reforms have greatly advanced China's electronics industries, but ironically, some economic reforms cut into military development due to a brain drain from military bureaus to civilian, profit-making industries.[13]

Beyond technological advances, a more significant reorganization and recentralization effort would demand a thorough overhaul of some of the central headquarters listed above. For example, China's military logistics, organized by the General Logistics Department, have long been highly decentralized.[14] Reforms of logistics began around 1982, with significant cuts in redundant staff and market-oriented reforms in organization and procurement. Yet Chinese strategists are convinced that China's logistic systems are still woefully inadequate considering the threats posed by the speed, depth, and diversity of modern warfare.[15]

Meanwhile, the military's ability to lobby for the changes it seeks may be decreasing. Deng Xiaoping was a Long March veteran and boasted impressive military credentials, but he apparently used these credentials to check military power and limit the financial impact of the military on the defense budget. While military personnel comprised 31 percent of the politburo in 1977, he had limited the military to only 9 percent of politburo positions by 1992.[16] And throughout his term, the military remained only the fourth of four primary modernization priorities.

Jiang Zemin, by contrast, has an entirely civilian background. When he first became Party secretary in 1989, in the wake of the Tiananmen Massacre, he appeared to pander to military interests. This was either as a payback for the suppression of protests or because of his lack of confidence in his control over the military. Yet as Jiang gains confidence, his primarily civilian connections may further distance the military from positions of power in the politburo and elsewhere in the Communist Party hierarchy. By 1997, apart from Generals Liu Huaqing, Zhang Zhen, and Chi Haotian, all of the 20-odd army and air force generals and admirals owed their promotion to Jiang Zemin in his capacity as chair of the CCP CMC. Liu Huaqing had the highest Party rank of all of the military figures and was probably the most powerful among them, but by 1997, he was the only military leader left on the politburo.[17]

Tied in with the effort to reform the high command is the effort to retire hundreds of thousands of soldiers in the officer corps. This may be even more problematic.

II. Force Structure

Definitive numbers on the actual size of the Chinese armed forces do not exist, and even historical information is vague and inaccurate. Many sources claim that China cut one million soldiers from the ranks between 1985 and 1987, for example, while others suggest that only around 700,000 were cut.[18] More recently, China claims exactly 1.039 million were cut—but the cuts were not complete until 1990.[19] While this revised figure appears precise, its credibility is weakened by the 1990 date. Were cuts really pursued the year after the Tiananmen Massacre? Why were they then halted as the situation became *less* tumultuous?

While precise numbers may never be obtained, many cuts clearly came from retiring or transferring vast percentages of the high command. Fifty percent of the General Staff, Political, and Logistics Departments were supposedly cut in the second half of the 1980s.[20] But it is difficult to know how many officers were actually cut, and how many were transferred to units like the People's Armed Police (PAP), the militias, or the reserves. If such groups expanded in size or bureaucratic organization (and the PAP, at least, almost certainly did), then this does not necessarily represent a step forward toward China's new strategic goals.

The International Institute for Strategic Studies (IISS) lists the size of the Chinese armed forces in table 2.1.

Shu-Shin Wang, publishing in *The China Quarterly,* offers competing statistics, published a few years before those from IISS (see table 2.2):

The evidence suggests that, in line with current strategic thinking, first, the PLA is indeed shrinking, although at a varying pace from year to year (cuts between 1990 and 1995 do not appear to have been signifi-

Table 2.1 **Chinese Defense Forces**[21]

Force	Troop Size
1. PLA	2,840,000 total
army	2,090,000
air force	470,000
navy	280,000
strategic missile force	125,000
2. Reserves	1,200,000
3. People's Armed Police	800,000
TOTAL	4,840,000

Table 2.2 **Chinese Defense Forces**[22]

Force	Troop Size
1. PLA forces	3.4 million in total
land force (army)	2.3-2.4 million personnel, in seven military regions and 24 group armies
navy:	360,000 personnel in three military regions
air force:	470,000 personnel, including air defense forces and paratroops; incorporated into more than 50 combat divisions
missile force:	100,000 personnel, manning more than 100 strategic missiles
2. People's Armed Police	1.5 million personnel
3. Reserve force	700,000
TOTAL	~5.6 Million

cant if they occurred at all). Second, the size of the land force is shrinking faster than that of the air force and navy (see also below). Third, while the armed forces' major divisions (army, navy, air, missile) are shrinking, and may indeed approach 2.5 million troops by the millennium, the size of the People's Armed Police (PAP) is almost certainly increasing.

In the second half of the 1990s, the most recent reductions are supposedly slated to shave 19 percent, 11.6 percent, and 11 percent respectively from land, naval, and air forces.[23] These differing percentages, with land forces receiving somewhat more significant cuts, are in line with China's new strategic outlook: "To develop a force to fight a war under high-tech conditions, our army must promote the naval and air forces and cut land force troop numbers. Only in this way can we fight a modern, regional war under high-tech conditions."[24] Yet in Chinese sources, the army is still usually described as comprising some three million soldiers, and two-thirds of the PLA is still said to be land-based (Wang's figures suggest just under 70 percent).[25]

What is the People's Armed Police, and why has it become a "drop-out" destination for so many surplus soldiers? Briefly, in June 1982, the CMC decided to transfer the internal security duty task of the PLA to the public security force. On 5 April 1983, the PAP force was founded, head-quartered in Beijing. It may have begun with a force of 500,000. This gradually increased in size through the mid- to late-1980s as economic units (managing hydropower, communications, and gold mining) and then the armed forest police were subsumed under the PAP. Major reforms under Jiang Zemin include bringing the PAP under the joint command of the CMC and the State Council, and subsuming other military units into the armed police, further increasing its size.

In 1997, Jiang Zemin announced that China would reduce its army further by 500,000 in three years, which would leave the force at "precisely" 2.5 million, according to official sources.[26] Many accounts suggest that most of these 500,000 soldiers to be cut are likely to become armed policemen.[27]

In the recent administrative shifts, reserve units also may be gaining some prestige and resources. The NPC adopted the "Reserve Service Officer Law" in May 1995. A year later, the CMC decided to confer military ranks on reserve service officers, and in March 1997, the NPC approved and promulgated the National Defense Law. These legislative and administrative measures laid the foundation for the further development of reserve service units.[28]

Like the PAP, the reserve units are supposed to support the major armed force divisions in wartime, but their primary strategic responsibility in times of peace is assistance toward the maintenance of public order.[29] Currently, the reserves are not well equipped for modern war. They train for only half-a-month a year. If any weapons are used during the training exercises, they tend to be light and low-tech.[30]

Each of the four major branches of the armed forces are advancing strategically and technically, but even these regular forces are crippled by important weaknesses:

Army

The PLA land forces are divided into seven military regions, which in turn support group armies, provincial military districts and subdistricts, municipal garrison commands and many special forces. The group armies are the largest combat units and the main forces of the regular troops.

Different sources cite different numbers of group armies and infantry divisions. According to Shu-Shin Wang, there are 24 group armies, 80 infantry divisions, 20 tank divisions, 30 artillery divisions and many other combat and logistic support troops.[31] A more recent official U.S. source lists the number of infantry divisions (army maneuver divisions) at 75, not 80.[32] And exact administrative divisions of the seven military regions listed by the PLA suggest 30 group armies, not 24, as follows:

Regional Army Commands[33]

1. Beijing Military Region:
   - Beijing Garrison Command (*beijing weishu qu*)
   - Tianjin Garrison Command (*tianjin jingbei qu*)
   - Hebei Province Military Regional Command
   - Shanxi Province Military Regional Command
   - Inner Mongolia Military Regional Command

2. Shenyang Military Region:
   - Liaoning Province Regional Command
   - Guilin Province Regional Command
   - Heilongjiang Province Regional Command

3. Lanzhou Military Region
   - Gansu Province Regional Command
   - Shenxi Province Regional Command
   - Ningxia Regional Command
   - Qinghai Regional Command
   - Xinjiang Regional Command

4. Jinan Military Region
   - Shandong Province Regional Command
   - Henan Province Regional Command

5. Nanjing Military Region
   - Jiangsu Province Regional Command
   - Anhui Province Regional Command

- Zhejiang Province Regional Command
- Jiangxi Province Regional Command
- Fujian Province Regional Command
- Shanghai Garrison Command (*shanghai jingbei qu*)

6. Guangzhou Military Region
   - Guangdong Province Regional Command
   - Hunan Province Regional Command
   - Hubei Province Regional Command
   - Hainan Province Regional Command
   - Guangxi Regional Command

7. Chengdu Military Region
   - Sichuan Province Regional Command
   - Yunnan Province Regional Command
   - Guizhou Province Regional Command
   - Tibet Regional Command

The staffing of these military regions has never been measured with any degree of precision in open sources. For example, the Economist Intelligence Unit quotes unnamed military analysts who claim that as many as one million soldiers may be stationed in Xinjiang.[34] This seems highly unlikely and strategically unnecessary, but this statistic and others are simply unverifiable at an unclassified level.

However, in broad terms, the complaints of the high command about these forces appear to stem from real problems. Military leaders complain that their land forces engage in largely duplicative functions, work poorly together, and are unprepared for many possible combat situations. A glance at the names of the regions and group divisions listed above, and at the apparent locations of major bases as listed by U.S. intelligence, helps us to understand how and why. China's ground forces are not at all concentrated toward any national border or potential battlefront. Instead, they are scattered, and for the most part located far inland. They therefore have the appearance of a standing army designed to promote internal order, engage in construction activities, and carry out other largely domestic functions. In the words of Chinese military analysts: "Presently our force [numbers] are extensive, [yet] the troops truly organized to promote fighting power are minimal, while it is the unorganized, auxiliary forces that are extensive."[35]

To provide one important example, Taiwan's sources suggest that around 80,000 soldiers are currently deployed by the 31st Group Army in Fujian Province, and these forces would be the most likely ones to actively engage in a cross-strait military conflict.[36] While Taiwan regards this group army as threatening, it is strange that China's most prominent territorial dispute—its claims on Taiwan—would not lead China to send a larger force to Fujian. As China has some 30 (or 24) group divisions for its land force of 2.3 to 2.4 million soldiers, this implies a land force in Fujian that is roughly average in size.

The military regions with the largest number of listed group armies have as their capital base the traditional northern and southern capitals of China, Beijing and Nanjing, and both of these cities are located inland. Indeed, in accord with Mao's Third Line strategies, designed to provoke enemy losses deep inland, *most* important military bases are at least 200 kilometers from any border.

The forces are frequently stationed in large, regional capital cities. This is only partly because these cities and their facilities are strategically significant. Other reasons include comfort, convenience, and the occasional perceived need to employ the PLA to maintain domestic stability in urban areas.

In truly remote border regions where frontier disputes have caused conflict in the past, some sources complain that China is understaffed. "Some commands don't have a camp hospital for several hundred kilometers, while the cities have many."[37] At the same time, regional commands remain powerful due to the historical legacy of Mao's People's War doctrine, and this can compromise the military's efforts to modernize its mission.[38]

To the extent that the army focuses on international security questions and international strategies, each of its military regions defends vastly different frontiers to address vastly different external threats, some of which in contemporary times are highly improbable or impossible (e.g., "Soviet" attack).

Each military region, at least, defends a border, and this is a reform from before 1987, when some military regions were entirely landlocked. Yet the borders of military regions have not changed since 1987, before the Soviet collapse, and even then a reorganization from eleven to seven military regions was largely attributed to cuts in staff, not to any changes in China's international security environment or strategy. After major reductions in troop size (although again, it is not clear if these proceeded quite as quickly as claimed), the commands were billed as too thin and overextended to be meaningful.[39]

China's elite army corps supposedly include the 27th, 28th, 38th, 39th, and 54th group armies, comprising some 275,000 personnel. China also has worked hard to create "fist units" or crack troops. Meanwhile, perhaps 20 percent of the army's units can be considered rapid reaction forces.[40]

Yet again, the responsibilities of the crack troops, or of any elite, land-based forces may be as muddled as those of ordinary forces. The five elite corps listed above are poised to counter both "domestic insurrection and foreign invasion."[41]

Navy

The pursuit of naval modernization reflects not only a move away from People's War but also a retreat from Mao's Third Line strategy, which emphasized the bolstering of hamlets in the hinterland. With China's Open Door mostly open for coastal areas, these have grown rich far more quickly than China's inland areas, and China's new emphasis on the navy is therefore logical. "By 1988 an open economic coastal belt with almost 300 cities stretched from Liaoning Province in the northeast to Guang-dong Province in the south," with these areas housing more than 80 per-cent of the country's foreign joint-venture enterprises.[42] Once the return of Hong Kong was essentially guaranteed (by 1984), China also con-cerned itself more with the defense of Hong Kong. Further, it set its sights more seriously than before on defending claims over Taiwan and the Spratly Islands.

The new emphasis on the navy reflected changes not only in China's domestic political economy, but also in perceptions of the importance of the sea as a strategic resource and battleground. "Navies in the present era create great power, strong mobility, and the capacity for worldwide inter-vention. In modern warfare, more than before navies are of substantial significance; their technological foundation, their position and use are increasingly prominent and important."[43] China now views the seas as "the new high ground of strategic competition,"[44] and the military is likely to emphasize naval modernization as one of its highest priorities for many years to come.

In all, naval personnel are said to number around 260,000 (U.S. Department of Defense),[45] 280,000 (IISS, quoted above), 340,000 (Insti-tute of Southeast Asian Studies),[46] or 360,000 (Shu-Shin Wang, also quoted above)—roughly 10 percent of China's armed force.

The PLA navy is divided into the East, South, and North China Sea Fleets. IISS provided useful information on major naval bases and fleet deployments in China at the end of the 1980s. The South China Sea Fleet bases are concentrated in and near Hainan and near Hong Kong. In 1997,

Hong Kong became its capital base. The East China Sea Fleet bases are concentrated in Shanghai and northern Zhejiang. Finally, the North China Sea Fleet is concentrated in and near Qingdao and Dalian.[47]

The three regional divisions of the navy originated in part from concerns that no longer appear valid. The North China Sea Fleet, for example, traditionally focused on defending China against a Soviet sea attack and invasion. The regional organization also suggests a relatively dispersed force, divided somewhat evenly for bureaucratic rather than strategic reasons. Presumably, it would be easier to reposition naval forces than to reposition regional land-based forces. Still, the most up-to-date sources suggest that at least in the short term, the Chinese navy is by no means poised to attack or defend anything in particular. Service resources and staff appear evenly spread between north, east, and south. China is very interested in the maintenance of territorial claims defended by the East and South China Sea Fleets (Taiwan and the Spratlys respectively), but predictably, the North China Sea Fleet, assigned to defend the capital region, appears to be the regional naval force that (by a very slight margin) receives the most resources years after the Soviet Union's demise.[48]

The navy's forces can also be broken down by function into five categories: warship, submarine, marine, naval aviation, and coastal defense force.[49] Coastal defense forces are said to comprise 29,000 soldiers, a marine corps of around 5,000, and a naval air force of around 25,000.[50] One source maintains: "The new marine corps is perhaps one of the clearest indications of the PLA's efforts to develop its power-projection capabilities to secure China's interests in its periphery."[51] To the military's credit, if China were ever to seek to capture its offshore claims (Taiwan, the Spratlys, the Paracels, the Senkakus) through force, the marine corps presumably would provide a necessary contribution in amphibious landings. On the other hand, for such a large navy, the marine corps appears to be surprisingly small. 5,000 soldiers cannot be considered evidence of the implementation of dramatically new priorities in an army of a few million.

The navy suffered from decades of technological stagnation before the 1970s, but some efforts at technological modernization have been carried out since then. Through the 1970s, naval forces received perhaps 20 percent of the overall military budget, an increase from previous decades. The result was a tripling of the size of the submarine force and the development of new nuclear-powered submarines. Manpower increased, and training was upgraded, according to a CIA research report of 1980.[52]

Tai Ming Cheung concludes that the naval portion of the defense budget remained higher post-Mao than during most of Mao's reign, at between 10 and 15 percent of overall military spending.[53] Deng Xiaoping suggested early in his stewardship that the development of China's naval force was one of the most critical tasks facing the PLA,[54] yet, in contrast to previous years, the focus was on "upgrading technological levels rather than increasing warship numbers."[55] By 1982, the navy's annual congress was already focusing on technological advances of the navy and "scientific fortresses, moving on the sea."

An article reviewing the military thoughts of Deng Xiaoping states that he chastised some naval officers for emphasizing quantity over quality, and promoted the idea that instead, quality should be emphasized, in a quotation that is not dated.[56]

At the end of 1985, the Naval Military Academic Research Institute was established to coordinate and provide research and analysis for the formulation of naval strategy, operations, and tactics.[57] Naval forces were necessarily stationed and directed away from the Chinese hinterland. Hence, according to Bruce Swanson, with respect to naval strategy, already in the early 1980s, "The Maoist doctrine of 'man over weapons' was not in evidence."[58]

China completed the testing and development of a nuclear-powered submarine, supposedly designed entirely at home, in 1986. By the late 1980s, the commander of the navy (Zhang Lianzhong) supported the further development of three systems that would permit continuous offshore deployments: underway replenishment ships, a long-distance communication system, and a global navigation system.[59] And in more recent years, naval planners have called for changing from a coastal defense (*jinhai fangyu*) strategy to an offshore defense (*jinyang fangyu*) strategy. According to Lewis and Xue, they hope to extend China's defense perimeter to between 200 and 400 nautical miles from the coast, and even farther in the case of the South China Sea islands. The navy hopes to have a so-called offshore navy on patrol by the year 2000, and, in the far-off future, a blue-water navy (*yuanyang haijun*) with one or more aircraft carriers.

Again according to Lewis and Xue, by the early 1990s, the navy's four principle missions included (1) safeguarding China's territorial integrity—increasingly including the active defense of islands in the South China Sea; (2) having the capacity to conduct a blockade of Taiwan; (3) blocking the threat of a sea-based invasion; and (4) creating a survivable nuclear retaliatory force.[60]

Whether or not China can achieve these missions in the short term, Chinese leaders have backed their somewhat more ambitious goals for the navy with a few important improvements in ordnance. According to Renato Cruz de Castro, "the best indication of the PLAN's changing status is the modernization of its surface and submarine units," with the construction of new ships and submarines; the development of improved heavy caliber naval guns; and the attempt to develop the PLAN's fleet air arm.[61]

Sources describe the modernization of major surface combatants as particularly important, with the Luhu-class destroyer and Jiangwei-class frigate both representing a marked improvement over previous vessels developed in the 1970s.[62] China has also bought Russian Kilo-class submarines.[63] Other high-tech imports to China that should improve the capabilities of its submarine forces include side-scan sonar, deep sea cameras, remotely activated undersea manipulators, and special deep diving lights, all capable of operating at depths of 12,000 feet.[64] China has also sought to lift the European Union's arms embargo to buy European submarine technology, such as German underwater diesel engines.[65]

Home-grown improvements besides the nuclear submarines are further boosting Chinese naval power. China's 863 project (a government-funded initiative to promote the development of civilian and military high-tech products) has helped China to model a submarine that, China claims, should be able to operate at a depth of 6,000 meters.[66] Other naval improvements include new missiles, radars, and electronics devices. A radio navigation guidance system developed for the navy supposedly extends China's naval intelligence-gathering 2,000 nautical miles.[67] There is evidence that China is working to develop a tactical nuclear weapons capability at sea, and generally, advances in missile capabilities should improve China's naval warfighting capability.[68]

Naval improvements also increase the credibility of China's nuclear deterrent. China's decision to develop a submarine launched ballistic missile (SLBM) reflects its justifiable fear that its entire land-based nuclear force would not survive a first strike by a superpower.[69]

The Chinese Navy has a new Naval General Equipment and Technology Department. One source suggests that its goals, from the end of this century through the first five years of the next, include: "To develop a new strategic missile nuclear submarine, develop a third-generation new missile destroyer and missile frigate, further improve the technical performance of [the navy's] tactical missiles, and develop new navy aircraft such as an anti-submarine bomber, missile attack plane, medium- and long-range bomber, and an early warning plane." These are said to be goals that would reinforce China's coastal defense capabilities rather than further promote its blue water capabilities.[70]

Despite these improvements, in the short term the navy still faces crippling weaknesses. It has focused to some extent on long-term goals, but it is most concerned with retiring old ships and equipping new ones with technology that might survive a technically and strategically advanced attack. And while money for the navy did increase in the 1980s, the evidence suggests that much of the money spent in that decade was wasted on outdated ships and poorly run projects.[71] By the early 1990s, the navy staffed some 2,300 ships of every type except carriers,[72] but many of these ships may not have been operational. Indeed some sources suggest that the bulk of the navy's aging ships are being retired.

Even in the mid-1990s, Chinese sources on the navy regularly implied (contradicting current strategic directions) that more is better, and due to this archaic outlook, old materials were held onto far longer than they could be usefully employed. Even the more modern ships equipped for naval combat are, at the time of this writing, mostly out of date. For example, China maintains around 50 to 55 fully-equipped warships. This is a large force for East Asia, but the vast majority of these warships are said to employ archaic technology.[73] One might also expect more warships with such a large navy; Japan's much smaller navy employs more destroyers, nearly as many frigates, and, generally, far more advanced technology.[74] Taiwan also employs more destroyers than China overall, and far more in the Taiwan Strait or nearby waters.[75]

Similarly, despite significant improvements in the submarine force and despite its size, the majority of the force consists of 52 aging diesels.[76] China has very little money for full-scale exercises and training involving submarines, and the exercises off Taiwan in 1996 represented the expensive exception rather than the rule. In the early 1990s, Taiwanese analysts claimed that less than 20 percent of the Chinese submarine fleet were at sea at any one time.[77]

Key equipment and ordnance for naval modernization also appear to be beyond China's reach either technologically or financially. For example, many sources highlight China's efforts to purchase an operational aircraft carrier (apparently from at least four countries: Russia, the Ukraine, France, and Spain). But other expenses have drained the budget to the extent that even a used, aging carrier is currently too expensive to purchase, refit, and defend in any adequate way.[78]

To summarize naval developments, the strategy is clearly changing. In the words of Tai Ming Cheung, in the 1980s " 'People's War at Sea' was quietly replaced with more sophisticated concepts."[79] The Naval Air Force is only behind those of the U.S. and Russia in terms of size, and it is working to build a strong joint operations capability. Its submarine force is the largest and one of the most technically advanced in Asia. However, Chinese naval analysts frequently claim that China is decades away from developing a blue water navy, and Western analysts concur that China remains well behind the United States, Russia, and some regional powers (e.g., Japan) in the quality of its naval ordnance.[80]

Air Force

The People's War legacy is awkward enough for naval defense planners. For the People's Liberation Army Air Force (PLAAF), it is even more inhibiting. The air force is a capital-intensive branch of the armed forces which, to be effective, relies almost entirely on modern logistics, high technology, advanced and consistent training, and developed command and control systems. Chinese defense planners in the reform period realize that outdated, Maoist strategic views must be jettisoned for China's air force modernization to proceed smoothly. Yet jettisoning the legacy of the past has proved to be an overwhelming task, due to bureaucratic and strategic inertia; the financial, technical, and logistic difficulties involved in air power modernization; and the substantial time lags between research and full-scale production of new airplanes.

During the 1950s, the air superiority of U.S.-led UN forces in the Korean War taught China an invaluable lesson in the strategic importance of a modern air force. The alliance with the Soviet Union through the 1950s further provided China with the means to create relatively advanced air power. The PLAAF consequently progressed from almost non-existent to advanced by the standards of the developing world.

Yet even in the 1950s, People's War concepts inhibited the development of air power. The air force remained quite subordinate to the land forces, and limited coordination between branches on all questions concerning air defenses meant that from a strategic and logistic perspective, the air force was poorly managed and led.

The break with the Soviet Union was catastrophic for China's air force modernization effort, crippling China's technical capacity for aeronautic advances. During the Cultural Revolution, the close association between the air force and Lin Biao further poisoned air force modernization efforts until Mao's death.

At the outset of the reform period, Deng Xiaoping argued forcefully for a jettisoning of outdated views on air power and a reversal in the fortunes of the air force:

In the future, it will be unsatisfactory to fight a war without an air force, indeed, entirely unsatisfactory without control of the air. . . . [A] navy without air support is also no good. We need to enter the seas to fight. Without any control of the air, our enemies can 'walk all over us' (*keyi changtong wuzu*). No matter how—from now on, in any war—between land, sea, and air forces, above all one needs a powerful air force, to promote control of the air. No war can be fought without it.[81]

In this quotation, Deng Xiaoping identified the pressing need for air force modernization and even boldly claimed that the air force might be the most important branch in a modernized army. Many in the military have followed his example and emphasize air force modernization as China's highest priority.[82]

Yet identifying a goal is not the same as achieving it. In the early 1980s, after some efforts to overhaul the air force, assessments of China's air power, especially compared to the air power of either superpower, remained cutting.[83] The inherent difficulties of using air power to defend a giant geographic territory and the tremendous aeronautic advances by major adversaries through the 1960s and 1970s posed part of the problem. But for China, the central issue was "the lamentably poor quality of China's own equipment."[84]

As with the navy, China's air force is now the third-largest in the world in terms of the size of its inventory. Two sources provide similar figures on the impressive number of airplanes China's air force allegedly shelters: 5,900 and "over 6,000."[85] Yet these planes are of greatly varying quality and purpose, and it is not clear how many of them are operational. Another source suggests China maintains 4,970 combat planes of re-engineered Soviet designs produced from the 1960s through the 1970s;[86] the U.S. government estimates the PLAAF maintains 4,500 combat planes, in some 30 air divisions. Meanwhile, 2,000 PLAAF aircraft (including MiG-19s, MiG-21s, and TU-16s) are said to be *1950s*-era Soviet designs comparable to outdated U.S. fighters like the F-100, F-8, and B-47.[87] While the exact numbers vary from source to source, even analysts who are apprehensive about China's growing military potential admit that the vast majority of Chinese planes are no match for up-to-date U.S. fighters like the 150 F-16s sold to Taiwan.[88]

The apparently gigantic size of China's outdated air force suggests that the emphasis is still on quantity rather than quality, but China is also working to improve quality. This is reflected in new purchases and development programs and the development of elite air force units.

In the 1990s, Russia sold China a few dozen Su-27s, Russia's most effective warplane, and many reports have suggested that, despite China's cost constraints, Russia is likely to sell more of these fighters or has already done so.[89] The licensed production of the Su-27 or MiG-31 fighter on Chinese soil is also highly possible, although it might take years for factories to have the capacity to produce entire planes, and significant numbers of them.[90]

China has had difficulty integrating the Su-27 into its overall force structure. Many air force runways apparently cannot handle its weight and power, and the army may be afraid to test its full powers or to provide pilots with adequate flying time in practice flights due to the cost burden of the aircraft. Yet the PLAAF apparently has begun employing the Su-27 in some exercises. In August 1995, Chinese Su-27s approached the Senkaku Islands (claimed by China, Japan, and Taiwan). In March 1996, the Su-27 flew in major military exercises intended to intimidate Taiwan on the eve of its presidential election.[91]

Responsible sources also have claimed that China is working to develop a new fighter jet, the J-10, which is based on the Israeli Lavi (a plane in turn based on the American F-16).[92] These could be fitted with engines built by several technologically advanced military powers, including Russia.

Like the army, the air force is struggling to develop elite units that would be trained to employ China's newest hardware. The 15th airborne army is said to be the most advanced group within the air force.[93] While training, even for elite forces, does not match that in the West, it is improving not only in the air but also on land. At an exhibition set up in the summer of 1997 to mark the 70th anniversary of the founding of the PLA, China showed off a virtual-reality simulator with a three-dimensional headset, allowing trainee aviators to practice in-flight refueling.[94]

Overall, China provides no figures on the extent to which spending for the air force has increased, but leaders admit that overall defense spending is increasing. Further, at least one internal source suggests that the air force comprises an increasing percentage of China's overall defense spending.[95] Many foreign procurements are probably not even listed in official defense budget calculations, so official figures admitting a new emphasis on the PLAAF may still understate the shift in resources from civilian to military budgets, and from land-based forces to air (and naval) forces. One Western source claims the 24 Su-27s purchased in 1991 cost around U.S. $1 billion. Former Russian Defense Minister Pavel Grachev claims a second batch of 22 Su-27s was delivered to China in 1996.[96] Also in 1996,

Moscow and Beijing may have reached agreement on a $2.2 billion deal for China to begin co-producing the Su-27.[97] These large purchases and domestic production contracts should have created noticeable "camel humps" on an official chart of China's annual defense spending. Yet there is no evidence in Chinese or Western sources that the cost of these aircraft was included in official defense budget calculations. If further money is spent on the domestic research, development, or production of Russian- or Israeli-designed planes, a portion of this money also will almost certainly be excluded from official budgets.

However, despite new acquisitions and apparent new budgetary expenditures, both admitted and veiled, China's air force is still said to be in bad shape, especially compared to those of leading military powers. One of the best open publications on East Asian militaries to come out of RAND in recent years is a study funded by the U.S. Air Force entitled *China's Air Force Enters the 21st Century*. The authors, Kenneth W. Allen, Glenn Krumel, and Jonathan D. Pollack, are well informed by historical data, primary research, and classified information, and they conclude that efforts at modernization through the mid-1990s have not allowed China even to advance at the same pace as its competitors, let alone to catch up:

> The PLAAF's overall capabilities relative to most of its potential rivals will diminish over the next ten years. These circumstances are a product of constrained strategic thinking in China about the role of airpower, the lack of funds needed for a comprehensive modernization program, logistics and maintenance problems, the limited training available to its pilots, and the absence of a capability to develop and manufacture advanced airpower systems.[98]

Part of the problem is organizational: Because the air force has always been subordinate to the army, its principle fighter airfields and the locations of its surface-to-air missiles are concentrated around China's large cities, at least 200 kilometers from the nearest potential hostile border. The dispersion of these forces, the short ranges of the fighters, and the current lack of an aerial refueling capability all weaken the air force's ability to wage an effective air defense against a very powerful opponent.[99]

Other related weaknesses are the result of poor logistic systems:

> [The PLAAF] has yet to create an integrated air defense system that melds fighter aircraft; surface-based defenses; and command, control, communi-

cations, and intelligence elements into an efficient defensive network. For example, although the PLAAF merged with the separate surface-based air defense forces in 1957, the resulting administrative and operational structure continues to reflect two separate organizations. In an internal air force analysis prepared in 1990, the PLAAF identified the lack of a unified air defense system as among its most serious problems. Each service has its own air defense structure, and it has proven extremely difficult to coordinate the various components, even within a single service, under a single air defense plan.[100]

It was not until 1985 that the air force's military region boundaries completely coincided with the army's military region boundaries. According to RAND's analysts, it took another four years for the military region air force commanders to be fully integrated into the military region command staff as the air component commanders.

Deng Xiaoping argued that the air force would have to work closely with the navy for China's naval defenses to be credible, and the large, 1996 exercises off the Taiwan Strait represent the best example of new efforts by these forces to stage coordinated war games. Still, there is no evidence that the air force and navy train together with any frequency, "nor do they have a coordinated command and control system in case of any future conflict."[101]

The air force remains weak in its ability to provide direct fire support to ground forces and in its ability to deliver air-to-surface ordnance. It also lacks precision-guided weapons, which were employed to great effect by allied forces in the Gulf War.[102] Although some problems are currently being addressed, other up-to-date sources list many other technological weaknesses of the Chinese air force, including a lack of AWACS aircraft; no advanced, long-range air-to-air missile systems; no anti-radar missiles to attack enemy air defenses; no precision-guided munitions (PGMs) like laser-guided bombs; no airborne radar and warning capability; and again, a limited or nonexistent ability to refuel combat aircraft during flight.[103]

Other PLAAF problems highlighted by RAND are a rapidly aging and obsolescent aircraft inventory and an inability to design and produce a modern aircraft in meaningful numbers.[104] Specifically, the RAND study highlights the tremendous lag times in the development of new air force systems that involve technology transfers, from the planning stage to actual production and integration. Technology transfers begin when ordnance is already becoming obsolescent, and by the time the technology is developed, China manages to perfect wholly obsolescent systems.

Other problems listed in the RAND study focus on the logistics of training (Chinese fighters are unable to generate more than one sortie every four to five days); a rudimentary command and control system; a lack of airborne reconnaissance, airborne early-warning systems, or ordnance to attack enemy air defenses; inadequate combat training; and, generally, a tightly structured system that stifles initiative and fails to make full use of available resources.[105]

Chinese sources are equally grim in their assessment of their ability to develop advanced air force weaponry. Even when China is developing more contemporary, or more home-grown systems, the logistic problems are severe. A buzzword in the navy and air force modernizations of the 1980s and 1990s is combat effectiveness or "combat power" (*zhandouli*) which is valued over sheer numbers of soldiers and machines. Yet one Mainland article highlights the tremendous budgetary and logistic problems of increased combat effectiveness as it translates into new and expensive airplane designs: When planning the production of a new plane, one must consider new airports that correspond to the requirements of the plane; new technologies and logistic support networks to ensure proper construction; the proper quantity of production to ensure that increased combat effectiveness has really been achieved; and some degree of long-term policy stability to ensure that projects are actually completed. It is admitted that so far, China has been ineffective in managing this type of broad logistical planning.[106]

These and other problems at least in large part stem from the strategic legacy of Mao and China's inertia in its move toward new strategic directions that leaders have identified as necessary. While China is clearly working toward new strategies for air power that would emphasize a more unified command and a dramatically improved technical capacity, in practice it can be said that "the PLAAF still lacks a formal air defense strategy."[107]

Even against smaller, regional powers, the PLAAF would face difficulties. One Mainland article focusing on the Taiwan question states that China's armed force is so heavily weighed down by land-based commitments that competition with Taiwan's military modernization program is a daunting task: "Compared to the Taiwan 'region', our military equipment is more numerous, yet has lower performance, with poor quality, inappropriate speed, and backward attacking capacity." Taiwan's modern equipment and especially its 150 newly imported F-16s are regarded as a threat. "In order to resolve this threat, we need to improve the fighting capacity of our most sophisticated equipment."[108]

From 1951 to 1997, China's aeronautics industry supposedly produced an accumulated total of 14,000 military airplanes of more than 60 models.[109] Yet despite the impressive "bean counts," for all of the reasons outlined above the Chinese military admits crippling air force weaknesses: "Our air force has developed over several decades, but the plane models are old, the machinery incomplete, and the fighting power limited, to the point where we have fallen far behind world standards."[110] And acknowledged advances should be weighed against the advances of other armed forces in the region. It seems China's Su-27 purchases were largely designed to dissuade Taiwan from drifting further away from a one-China policy.

Missile Force

One might assume that China's missile force, or Second Artillery, would have suffered during the Maoist period for the same reasons that the air force did. Indeed, Maoist People's War rhetoric suggested that nuclear weapons were paper tigers, and that a sufficient portion of China's giant population would survive any nuclear attack.

The development and maintenance of a missile force requires a larger-than-average coterie of well-trained scientists and technicians, and one would expect that under Mao, especially during the Cultural Revolution, these technicians would have been in short supply. However, despite the rhetoric, Mao consistently emphasized China's nuclear deterrent, even in austere times: Secret projects numbered 02 (nuclear weapons), 05 (ballistic missiles), and 09 (focused on nuclear-powered submarines and their missiles) all received enough attention under Mao to produce successful results.[111] It would be fair to say that, with respect to the missile force, Mao's People's War precepts were pushed aside with particular haste, even when Mao was alive.

After 1964, when China exploded its first atomic bomb, and 1967, when it exploded its first hydrogen bomb, China conducted dozens of nuclear tests, including a one-megaton hydrogen bomb explosion in Xinjiang on May 21, 1992. China also developed its first generation of ballistic missiles from 1956 to 1981. These were liquid-fueled missiles designed to carry large warheads, with a range sufficient for striking some Russian cities and U.S. missile bases located in American-allied territories near China. For example, the DF-5, developed by 1981, had a range of 12,600 to 13,000 kilometers. More recent accomplishments with respect to the missile force include the launching of China's first carrier rockets over the South Pacific (1980), the development of intercontinental ballistic missiles (ICBMs, also in 1980), submarine-launched ballistic missiles (SLBMs, 1982), the development of a road-mobile, solid-fueled rocket (the DF-21, in 1985; tests on ICBMs that employ multiple independently targeted reentry vehicles (MIRVs, 1987), and a mobile ICBM (1995).[112] China has developed short, medium, and intercontinental long-range missiles, including surface-to-surface, surface-to-air, air-to-air, ship-to-ship, and submarine-to-surface missiles.[113] In all, while China is the smallest of the first five declared nuclear powers in the number of nuclear warheads it possesses (around 300), it is only third behind the U.S. and Russia in its ICBM and SLBM capacity.[114]

With improvements in Sino-Russian relations, China now employs Russian technicians for further advances, for example, in the production of cruise missiles. One American military analyst suggests that China might soon gain access to the latest generation of Russian supersonic tactical missiles, and anti-radiation missiles capable of defeating airborne warning and control systems (AWACs) aircraft or AEGIS naval radar-equipped ships. This analyst and others are concerned that Russia also has sold advanced Russian air-to-air missiles (AAMs) to China since 1991.[115]

China also has profited from commercial deals with the United States, and, possibly, the theft of secret U.S. technologies. In the late 1980s, China developed the technical capacity to build neutron bombs, possibly through espionage efforts that targeted United States scientists and labs. Further, China is allegedly close to deploying a Dong Feng-31 missile with a small nuclear warhead whose design draws on stolen American secrets, according to U.S. intelligence officials.[116] China may have further increased the pace of its long-range missile development with the help of supercomputer purchases from the United States In 1996, Silicon Graphics sold China a supercomputer that performs six billion operations per second; the U.S. government fears that the science academy that placed the order is involved in long-range missile development.[117]

In terms of personnel, according to Shu-Shin Wang, the Second Artillery staffs about 100,000 soldiers, who are stationed in six army-level bases, fourteen launching brigades, and one independent launching regiment with more than 100 strategic missiles.[118]

China's strategic doctrine on the development of nuclear weapons and missiles is more shrewd and reflective of reality than its air or naval doctrine. The development of a powerful nuclear missile force is not cheap, but it is by far the cheapest and most realistic way for China to maintain a massive deterrent against superpower attack. As a result, Chinese strategists have emphasized the importance of missiles in modern warface throughout the reform period.

A book published by the Chinese military specifically demonstrates why and how China emphasizes its missile force with respect to its force structure overall. The book sketches the contemporary world's military history, and argues that since Germany's first deployment of missiles, their use is increasing, as is their diversity. It recounts the effective employment of missiles by many countries (e.g., Israel in the 1973 war with the Arabs), and in particular during the Gulf War by the United States, where over 30 types of missiles were allegedly used to great effect. In their analysis of the Gulf War, Mainland strategists emphasize the use of missiles as an attack weapon, or weapon for battle campaigns, and the shortcomings of missiles as a defensive tool in conventional battles (e.g., the Patriots did not really work as anti-Scud weapons) are more or less ignored.[119]

This source also highlights the deterrent value of missiles. It claims that from World War II to the 1980s, the U.S. armed forces were employed some 200 times, 78 percent of the time as a deterrent, five percent to oppose a deterrent, and only 17 percent in battle. These statistics (for which no sources are provided) help to emphasize the importance of deterrent force in the use of modern militaries. Generally, missiles are accurately identified as crucial deterrents and military tools for mid-level powers in the contemporary period.[120]

One section hones in on the uses of missile war: Missiles are valuable as a strategic deterrent that restricts the enemy's strategic objectives. Missiles broaden and reinforce the effectiveness of joint war fighting methods. Missile weaponry can be economical, it is suggested, both because of possible technical spinoffs and because they are a far cheaper means than planes to bolster air power for nations weak in the air. Further, "purchases of missile weaponry will not be obstructed or condemned." This means, compared to some other advanced technology (e.g., unconventional weapons), the world recognizes the centrality of modern (conventional) missiles in every modern military force. Outside forces will be less interested in restricting their sale or purchase by "mid to small" economic powers, like China.[121] A section of the book on "special characteristics of missile ordnance technology" further emphasizes how and why missiles can help a nation like China fight a regional, high-tech war.[122]

While nuclear weapons managed by the Second Artillery serve as a powerful deterrent, they are also costly and dangerous to test and maintain. Recent diplomatic successes by China suggest that the nation is working to contain the threat that its nuclear force poses to China's own environment and security. China signed the Nuclear Non-Proliferation Treaty (NPT) in 1992. It also worked to purchase U.S. technology that would help to ensure the security of its weapons in 1994, and more recently signed the Comprehensive Test Ban Treaty (CTBT), suspending nuclear weapons testing as of July 30, 1996.[123]

To summarize, the Chinese missile force is threatening to Taiwan, and its nuclear capability threatens more unlikely antagonists such as India (which has only developed a nascent nuclear capacity) and Japan (which is technically able to develop nuclear weapons but has not tried to do so). However, China at least publicly advocates a somewhat consistent no-first-use policy,[124] and the missile force appears primarily to be a very effective and comparatively cheap deterrent against superpower attack. Overall, the missile force, while impressive, cannot compare with that of the United States or Russia. The International Institute for Strategic Studies credits China with only 14 ICBMs, and only four can reach the United States.

While the Chinese military has updated its force structure on several fronts outlined above, it still faces serious problems. Even if we assume that China has updated some 10 percent of its army groups (all those listed as crack troops for whatever reason), this still leaves well over two million soldiers in the standing army with aging weapons and an unclear mission. Because of the cost drain of the massive troop base, further modernization of other divisions of the armed forces will prove difficult. And the focus on capable leadership, new training, and more professional methods of organization can only go so far.

So despite increased spending in the 1990s and some acknowledged improvements, why is China struggling and, in some fields (e.g. the air force, command and control) even falling behind the leading military powers? The key to China's military problems is, ironically, what appears on the surface to be the military's greatest source of strength: Its gigantic labor force.

III. Army Surplus: An Intractable Problem?

In the Maoist period, People's War strategies; the reliance on the army as the ultimate arbiter of domestic turmoil; the loose administrative lines between military, civilian, and Party bureaus; and a highly militarized political atmosphere all contributed to overstaffing. Apparently, by the end of the 1970s if not sooner, Deng Xiaoping and other military leaders began to regard the vast sums spent on soldiers as "wasted" (*chidiao*).[125]

By 1985, cutting hundreds of thousands of soldiers from the ranks was justified both to save money for domestic development and to provide for "new scientific and technological improvements in military weaponry and ordnance."[126] Yet while troop cuts by 1987 must have provided at least some new funds for modernization, after 1987, the size of the army decreased much more slowly if at all. The arguments against a swollen army never changed,[127] but as inflation and the Open Door sparked workers' discontent and student protests throughout urban China, a nervous leadership sent in the tanks and then backed away from further demobilization efforts.

After several years without a significant change in policy, the Gulf War again shocked China's strategists and led them to reconsider further cuts. Iraq's own swollen army, equipped in large part with Chinese weaponry, was trampled by better-equipped, better-trained opponents. Chinese leaders saw Iraq's army as a burning metaphor for the failure of their military modernization effort.[128]

Jiang Zemin's political report at the 15th National Congress of the CCP in September 1997 was an unusual place to discuss further troop cuts of half-a-million. The location implied both the importance of the cuts for the military and resistance to the cuts by elements within the military.[129] The latest round of troop cuts is supposed to take place by the year 2000, and the officer corps is said to be a prominent focus of the cuts.[130] The goals of all of these cuts are to limit defense resources spent on surplus soldiers to save money, buy weaponry, or organize more specialized units. These goals may not be fully realized for years, according to Chinese military analysts themselves.

The evidence suggests that military planners are wisely cutting more from the land-based army than the air force or navy. Yet while U.S. forces are fairly evenly split between army, naval, and air forces, land-based army forces still comprise two-thirds of the Chinese army.[131] These poorly trained and equipped soldiers are dragging down China's modernization efforts. Further, "cuts" are frequently just transfers to even less professional (or at least less outward-looking) forces within the military-industrial complex. Again, while China is attempting to reduce the size of the PLA, the size of the People's Armed Police is slated to increase.[132] The PAP is sure to take many of the soldiers allegedly cut from the defense budget. According to one Hong Kong source:

After October, 1996, as the downsizing of the PLA [re]commenced, some second-line army divisions (altogether 14 divisions over a period of time) were reorganized into the armed police and formed a number of mobile armed police divisions directly under the armed police headquarters. They greatly enhanced the armed police's mobile combat capability.[133]

Yang Guoping, the commander of the armed police at the time of this writing, was the first PAP commander to be promoted to the rank of general, and China appears to be increasing the status of this paramilitary branch even as it struggles to modernize its power-projection capabilities and develop outward-looking security forces.

While the PAP has also become a more professional force during the reform period, this is a somewhat ambiguous development for China's force modernization effort. Briefly, the Chinese armed police interior guard units, armed police border defense units, armed police security units, armed police mobile units, and armed police special police units undertake such tasks as border defense, guard duty, protection of government facilities, fighting crime and terrorism, and preventing riots: "The main targets they have to tackle are not foreign invaders, but criminals and the mobs that may go into a riot." Much of the armed police's new technological investments include weapons for riot control, armored trucks for blocking roads, and other light weaponry.[134] These are not the weapons of a leadership focused on international power projection.

Resistance to cuts in the regular forces appears to be highest in the officer corps, which is scheduled to bear much of the pain. According to one Hong Kong report, PLA General Political Department Director Yu Yongbo acknowledged during a recent inspection of units that "officers represent the key and the point of difficulty in this demobilization."[135]

The army is hoping to speed up its decommissioning effort, again, with over 100,000 officers scheduled to be decommissioned in the latest round of cuts. However, so far there is said to be no proper system of unemployment benefits, or systemic management of work arrangements, for officers who leave the services. Some easily find arranged positions in wealthy areas, but those returning to bankrupt regions appeal to governments that cannot or will not find work for them. The officers then become a burden on the military, and the benefits provided to them may be unequal to those provided for officers who were decommissioned elsewhere.[136]

Civilian work transfers are said to be "hot with the higher-ups" but "cold at the grassroots" (*shangtoure, xiatouleng*). Specifically, the Central Committee of the CCP and governmental leaders favor civilian transfers as a means to save money and modernize the military, but work units forced to accept officers are said to regard the officers as "millstones around their necks" (*baofu*).[137]

These cadres are expensive for work units, because they wish to retain privileges gained in the army. They expect not only their salaries, but also high (civilian) ranks, free housing, and other free or subsidized goods and services.[138] Most officers also hope to be placed in comparatively comfortable Party and governmental positions rather than in enterprises struggling to compete under "market socialism." Among the officers decommissioned by the air force in 1995, 99 percent searched for positions in party and government organizations, industrial, and tax bureaus, and other "hotter" work units; only four requested jobs in private industry.[139]

While a 1986 rule dictates that commercial bureaus and enterprises should take more decommissioned officers, many cadres are still assigned to government and Party bureaucracies that are viewed as saturated or supersaturated. A 1995 directive legitimates the status quo by dictating that government departments and work units—even departments regarded as overstaffed—are not permitted to refuse transferred officers assigned to them.[140] In general, work units clearly resist the burden that these officers create; they are regarded by many as the chaff of the army.[141] As a result, officers are often relocated in less desirable, poorer regions, and benefits (especially living quarters) in these regions may be of significantly lower standard than those to which the officers have grown accustomed.[142]

Few officers have skills that they could put to use in truly "market-oriented" firms even if they landed jobs in those firms; and others who do have technical skills and specialized training complain that they are underutilized.

Finally, with changes in work employment patterns, it is harder for the military and local governments to find work for family members who accompany soldiers (probably all officers) at their stations. There were some 210,000 such family members, according to one secret source from the mid-1990s, and among them, 28,000, or 13 percent, failed to find work.[143]

The effort to decommission tens of thousands of officers is the most easy to thoroughly document and also, for China's new command priorities, the most significant element of the demobilization effort. Yet this discussion suggests that the decommissioning effort in particular is beset with difficulties.

IV. Conclusion

Mao Zedong argued that "Power flows from the barrel of a gun; the Party must control the gun." China's new leadership would update the dictum:

Now power flows from laser guns, brilliant bombs, stealth fighter planes, and nearly silent submarines. Still, China faces many technical, economic, and political obstacles in its efforts to implement a new strategy. Even if China develops the technical and economic capacity to promote military modernization more quickly, leaders are afraid that a shift away from the rank and file and toward these high-tech goods might cause the Party to lose control of the gun.

In the meantime, China's military leaders remain unsatisfied with the current force structure and capabilities. In the words of the commander of the Nanjing Military Region:

> After going through several adjustments and reforms, our army's size and structure have gradually become more scientific and rational. However, there are still some areas that fail to meet the needs of future military operations, such as the amphibious assault capability, the air defense capability in field operations, the electronics resistance capability, the air mobility capability, and the capability to provide logistic supplies on the seas. The system to provide technical support and equipment is not so efficient. The system of combined operations by various services and arms has not been truly established. Departments in charge of command, information, telecommunications, and logistics show little coordination in operations.[144]

Even with Deng Xiaoping, a Long March veteran, firmly in charge, except from 1985 to 1987, his hoped-for demobilization effort proceeded slowly. Now, with a military outsider, Jiang Zemin, at the helm, China may not have the internal political will to throw off the Maoist legacy of a bloated armed force at a pace that will enable China to keep up with the modernization efforts of more advanced powers.

By 1994, the military had again raised compensation and pensions to a level that some military advocates regarded as "proper"[145]—but at a cost to other goals and programs. Military analysts echo Deng when they warn: "Our military's ordnance modernization . . . must keep up with the improvements in salaries."[146] Yet to maintain satisfaction in the ranks, the military more often than not has chosen a divergent path: "First secure a living, second secure equipment" (*yibao shenghuo, arbao zhuangbei*).[147]

The Mainland's land forces are starting to work more closely with air and naval commands, and better coordination will increase the effectiveness of each branch of the armed forces. An amphibious exercise of November 1995 was said to comprise "all ground, naval, and air forces,"[148] and the more infamous exercise off Taiwan in the spring of 1996, designed to scare independence supporters on the eve of Taiwan's presidential election, was China's most impressive combined exercise to date.

Yet this chapter concludes with a quotation from a recent U.S. Department of Defense Report comparing the Mainland Chinese to the Taiwanese forces. U.S. military authorities note important advances in the PLA cited above. Yet, the U.S. report concludes,

> Ground force leadership, training in combined operations, and morale are poor. The PLA is still a party army with nepotism and political/family connections continuing to predominate in officer appointment and advancement. The soldiers, for the most part, are semi-literate rural peasants.[149]

In sum, to achieve "First World" military capabilities and a sharper focus on international security, China's three-million-man army needs a major overhaul; yet in the short term, much of China's defense budget continues to be wasted on army surplus.

CHAPTER 3

The Military-Industrial Complex and the Ephemeral Hunt for Profits

This chapter focuses on the changing nature of China's military-industrial complex with respect to the management of ordnance production, military and civilian economic development, and self-sufficiency. Because the defense establishment broadly defined manages perhaps one-fifth of all Chinese industry and a large proportion of its GDP, its interest in the fields of economic development, industry, and business is a huge topic. Indeed, it is a topic that appears to be more important to the central government and many military planners than any international strategic goals or assignments.

Many outside analysts feared through the mid-1990s that the self-sufficiency efforts and the hunt for profits by bureaus of the military-industrial complex provided cash cows that helped China to dramatically modernize its military. Yet now, even Chinese sources have begun to admit that the effort to retool parts of the military-industrial complex into semi-public, semi-private profit centers has not led to a stronger military. It certainly has not been part of a grand strategy for outward expansion. Instead, reform-era changes in the military-industrial complex have been part of a poorly-defined, domestically focused strategy, promoted by Deng Xiaoping, Jiang Zemin and others, to keep the factories open and running. The central leadership responded to its shrinking control and, from 1989, lack of ties to the military by permitting virtually all of the bureaucracies of the disparate military-industrial complex to go into business. The hope was that, because military and civilian personnel were freer to pursue wealth, they would remain content, loyal, and cheap.

The reforms led to some successes; key bureaucracies have begun to function more like modern businesses, and the military as a whole has grown more efficient. But many of the reforms were clearly a mistake, and some have recently been reversed.

This chapter studies trends in management, identifies the ever-shifting borders of the military-industrial complex, and then hones in on key military and civilian bureaucracies. It is argued that the military's shaky relationship with profits has been a great distraction in the 1990s, and throughout this decade fluctuating efforts to link and (most recently) detach the military from business profits have yielded very mixed results.

I. Trends in Defense Economic Management: From "Strategic" Construction to Profit-Seeking—and Back Again?

The military's involvement in the domestic economy has always been justified as important from a strategic as well as economic perspective. However, in the 1980s and 1990s the profit motive became extremely prominent, so much so that large sections of the military-industrial complex were pushed away almost entirely from military control. A brief overview of the history and organization of the military-industrial complex demonstrates the extent to which it is moving away from strategic goals of any kind.

China's military began with only 19 functioning military-industrial enterprises at the time of liberation, but it immediately took over several factories and mines formerly controlled by Nationalist soldiers.[1] From 1949 until Mao's death, military-led production expanded greatly, although erratically.

One should keep in mind that the separation between the two poles in the phrase "civil-military relations" can never be complete, and in a nation promoting a military-led liberation and a communist People's War, it was not, under Mao, even attempted. During the Maoist period, centrally controlled bureaucracies assumed the responsibility for almost all industrial production carried out by, or for, the military, and many bureaucracies with primarily economic tasks were led by active or retired army officers. In 1950, under the direction of the Ministry of Heavy Industry, China set up an Ordnance Industry Office and a China Northern Military Industrial Bureau. From then on, a steadily increasing number of central government ministries, bureaus, and commissions took on the burden of military industrial production and development.[2] By the early 1960s, the government had created a handful of ordnance ministries differentiated by the type of product produced, with separate ministries producing nuclear materials, electronics, machinery, general ordnance, ships, and missiles.

Transferred PLA reservists also became prominent in the management of economic questions through civilian bureaus,[3] further blurring the lines between civilian and military issues. And while many of China's original ministries of machine industries were directed by PLA officials for defense construction work, these ministries always included civilian development goals among their long-term objectives.

The goal under Mao for industrial development was increased production capacity, not profits, and the emphasis was often on quantity rather than quality. Military industrial production and development also involved a multitude of bureaucracies and a jungle of red tape. Nevertheless, quality control in national defense industries tended to be stronger than in national industrial bureaus generally. These industries were also more ready and able to study foreign technologies and (more irregularly) to import foreign machinery and technology from abroad.[4]

In addition to weapons development, PLA commanders have been asked to devote their forces to infrastructural improvements, irrigation and other farming projects, and Maoist industrialization goals. In the development of transportation (especially rail and roads) and China's post and telecommunications, the military has played a particularly important role.[5]

The military was also a significant player in the management of much of the energy required to fuel military industries, and in many other industries that are only remotely tied to traditional ordnance production: It processed textiles for uniforms, produced medicine for military hospitals, farmed agricultural goods for soldiers' consumption, and built transportation and telecommunication facilities for military transport and propaganda.

The military's economic involvement has been particularly significant in national minority regions. In Xinjiang, the PLA launched an ambitious five-year irrigation plan in 1950, and its cadres personally supervised land reform. According to John Gittings, "The majority of Xinjiang's state farms were started by the PLA, and by 1958 their acreage amounted to 30 percent of the total arable land in the province or 20 percent of the sown area."[6] The PLA was also prominent in projects in other frontier regions, as soldiers volunteered without pay on civilian projects on agricultural cooperatives and wasteland reclamation projects.

The involvement of the PLA in large-scale production work was interrupted by the Korean War but reinvigorated by 1954.[7] From the Anti-

Rightist Campaign and Mao's "Ten Great Relationships" speech, the military was asked to pay even more attention to the production of civilian-use goods and to aid the overall economic development program (especially in steel production). In all, during the first and second five-year plans, around 55 percent of the total value of military production went to civilian-use products.[8]

The late 1950s was a period of decreased military budgets and increased self-reliance, because of Mao's fear that military spending took funds away from civilian projects and administration.[9] So PLA soldiers were employed to promote Mao's goal of rapid, state-led industrialization, most prominently through industrial construction. In the three years of the Great Leap Forward, the PLA built the Guangzhou (Canton) railway station and worked on 25 different railway lines.[10] Great Leap Forward era statistics on the production of ordnance vs. civilian products by the Ministry of the Ordnance Industry may have greatly overstated the success of early efforts at defense conversion, but they suggest a tremendously rapid shift toward civilian priorities (see table 3.1).

The effort to make economic development projects the PLA's highest priority was reversed and criticized by December 1960. One reason for the 1959 dismissal of Peng Dehuai (the nation's most prominent general through most of the 1950s) was his complaint that mass efforts at military involvement in civilian projects were carried too far and compromised the military mission. Apparently, a secret PLA Bulletin of Activities listed as one of Peng's major mistakes, "oppos[ing] army participation in production," and favoring professionalization of the officer corps with "unreasonable military systems and formalities."[12] Yet many supported Peng Dehuai's goals, and although he was forcefully retired, his view briefly prevailed. General Xiao Hua wrote in August, 1959: "There

Table 3.1   1957-1960 Civilian Product Development by Defense Industrial Bureaus[11]

Year	Number of enterprises producing civilian goods	Percentage of enterprises producing civilian goods	Value of production of civilian goods (in millions of yuan)	Percentage of total production by ministry of ordnance
1957	39	67.2	139	19
1958	56	91.8	656	48
1959	56	91.8	1,058	60
1960	58	95.0	1,353	74.9
Total			3,206	

is a definite conflict between participation in national construction and training in their respective demands for time. . . . Needless to say, as the army is an armed combat organization, it must carry out its task as a 'work force' in such a way that its task as a 'combat force' is not affected."[13] After the Great Leap Forward, in 1961 army production work was cut to half the 1959 level. It continued to decline until the Cultural Revolution.[14]

A shift toward construction goals was evident again by 1965. The Third Line strategy was launched that year. This strategy was designed to develop inland areas and strengthen their ability to carry out a People's War against any foreign invader. Yet its most lasting influence was that Third Line development plans were instrumental to the industrialization of many inland cities and towns.

From 1966 to 1976, the Cultural Revolution created a huge setback for military-industrial development. Scientists and skilled personnel were sent to the countryside for reeducation through labor, production in factories was severely disrupted, and imports of almost any foreign machinery or military technology became impossible. Military technicians who actually managed to hold technical positions were instructed to follow broad industrialization and infrastructural goals similar to those of the Great Leap Forward, and the quality of most ordnance production deteriorated. Chinese sources credit Zhou Enlai, Ye Jianying, and Deng Xiaoping for at least preventing the destruction of already-existing technology, and research on nuclear production and nuclear weaponry was protected even during the most radical years of "politics in command." Yet Chinese historical sources race through the Cultural Revolution period, describing it abruptly as one of unmitigated disasters for the defense-industrial complex. While this is almost certainly the case, any statistics (reliable or unreliable) concerning the military-industrial complex during this period are hard to come by.

The attack on intellectuals and professional urbanites during the Cultural Revolution particularly affected military industries. Some were bereft of qualified technical personnel, and ordnance development stagnated. Still, even during the Cultural Revolution, defense industrial ministries were said to have maintained superior equipment and supplies, better quality control on products, a better-trained labor force, special access to information on technology and markets, and perhaps better access to financial resources than their civilian counterparts.[15]

During the Cultural Revolution, in addition to developmental goals reminiscent of those of the Great Leap Forward, Mao employed the military to depopulate the cities of educated youth. By 1969, it was the PLA that was primarily responsible for the organization of a massive population transfer of urbanites, in order to re-establish stability in the cities, educate students about the life of the commune-peasants, and increase the size and quality of the labor force in rural areas.

To summarize military-industrial achievements under Mao, despite shortcomings, China's military industrial bureaus were well connected, housed many of China's leading scientists and technicians, and boasted many successes. Military-industrial production proceeded almost entirely without the help of any private companies or foreign technological support after the break with the Soviet Union. Still, under Mao, largely based upon Soviet prototypes, China was able to develop or begin to develop its first nuclear weapons, attack aircraft, first amphibious vehicles, first nuclear-powered subs, first high-altitude aircraft, intermediate-range missiles, and satellites. The military's involvement in civilian infrastructural projects and civilian industries was also vast, with many improvements, especially in inland cities, that could later be capitalized on by reformers employing market measures for further advances.

It is also important to note that army production work in China's early post-revolutionary history was associated with the radical politics of the Great Leap Forward and with Mao Zedong, not with military professionals like Peng Dehuai nor with reformist factions. It was only when Deng Xiaoping introduced the profit motive and cut defense budgets that the whole army came around to regarding production and industrialization as key missions, or *the* key missions, of military-industrial bureaucracies.

In July 1975, Deng Xiaoping first struggled to advance a modernization campaign with important implications for the military. By 1978, when Deng had firmly secured power, the new goals of military defense economics for the next decade became clearer. These goals had almost universally negative consequences for military power and wealth in the short term, and it is possible that only a leader with Deng Xiaoping's stature in military circles could have achieved them. They included reductions in overall troop strength, reductions in the ratio of officers to enlisted men, improvements in discipline, reassertion of Party control, improvements in strategy and tactics, and a reduction of the PLA's entanglement in local politics. The Third Plenary Session of the 11th Central Committee meeting of 1978 in particular was a watershed event, giving priority to modernization, yet with military development as only the fourth on a list of four modernizations.

The modernization program almost immediately impacted the military budget, which by 1980–1981 began to drop sharply even as spending levels of greater powers held steady or increased dramatically. Chinese procurement levels may have been reduced to those of the early 1970s. At the same time, as the central government money earmarked for the military decreased, the government promoted limited experiments to find unconventional means to support military budgets and programs.

As Deng Xiaoping's influence was strong in military circles even before he achieved unquestioned authority in civilian politics, some economic-related reforms began very early in the military. Already in 1978, the General Logistics Department put forward a directive on the "rectification of military-run industrial factory installations" in which it was decided that the primary business of purely economic installations (cement factories, chemical fertilizer factories, medicine factories) was production, not more overtly political goals.[16]

Meanwhile, production and enterprise reforms for military-controlled agriculture began in the Shenyang Military Region, where an early effort at a personal responsibility system in 1979 gave production a higher priority. Higher revenues in 1979, with fewer soldiers employed for farm production, are said to have stemmed in part from these early changes. Gradually, the importance of political goals faded and the importance of production and revenues in military-controlled agricultural areas increased, to the point where the reforms were clearly improving efficiency, output, and revenues. The evolutionary change was given more direction with Hu Yaobang as General Secretary of the CCP, and Yang Shangkun serving as Vice Chair of the Central Military Commission (by 1985).[17]

By the beginning of 1983, following reforms in civilian state industries, the Central Military Commission renewed its emphasis on (1) production, (2) taking advantage of the Open Door, (3) increasing personal responsibility, (4) increasing revenues, and (5) struggling to resolve numerous problems in military-run economic installations.[18] In 1984, the leadership gave the order to convert idle or underutilized resources to the production of civilian industrial machinery and consumer goods.

The following year marked an even broader strategic shift, militarily and financially. With reforms and crises gripping the Soviet Union and relations with the United States at least lukewarm, in 1985 the Chinese Central Military Commission changed from a strategy of protecting against "early, full-scale, and nuclear attack" to one of civilian support during a time of relative peace. By June, Deng Xiaoping unveiled a plan to the Central Military Commission to reduce the military further by one million men, down to around 3 million from around 4.2 million. Over half-a-million people with civilian job skills had to be placed in new jobs or newly reorganized bureaus.

Concurrently, the government began its first real austerity drive and rectification campaign of the reform period. This would foreshadow later "rectifications," all of which suggested that military control of for-profit business centers can lead to inefficiencies and abuses. Side effects include inefficient business practices, work incompatible with military professionalization, and threats to stable, clean government (see also below).

The 1985 economic crackdown in military circles was designed in part to improve production methods for export, and in part to close or reform bankrupt, poorly run, or illegal operations. Yet the macroeconomic context—inflation, government deficits, and rising competition for state-run firms—also must have been critical. In any case, in the 1985 crackdown, some 695 military-run enterprises and companies were said to have been shut down, along with the commercial and trading operations of 3,384 military officers and staff. The military also closed 600 economic joint ventures between military and civilian entities. No figures are given on the *percentage* of military firms shut down. But judging from the information provided on the number of military firms in existence in the first half of 1985, this appears to have been an austerity crackdown on a very large percentage of firms.[19] At that time, the military ran over 4,000 factories and mines and over 1,000 industrial and service companies and outlets. Further, it had opened trade with a dozen foreign nations.[20]

Yet Deng Xiaoping decided that the problems of military management paralleled those of business management elsewhere in the state sector. The answer was not privatization and the total separation of government and business functions, but rather further budgetary and managerial autonomy and a further blending of public, semi-public, and private organizations. As a consequence of the broad shift in thinking and manpower, the idea of defense conversion and civilian-use products proceeded full-force.

Also in 1985, the General Logistics Department was ordered to release transportation resources and supply depots, rail lines, ports, and airfields for use by civilian and local enterprises. Unused barracks, warehouses, oil depots, and real estate were also loaned or given to civilian organizations, and military trucks began hauling goods to market (see also below).

The military had always engaged in the production of non-military goods, but in the mid-1980s, with China's growing domestic consumer market and export trade, the military concluded that civilian products were its best hope for profits in an environment of decreasing support. According to one source, the military's total production of civilian-use goods in 1986 was said to be worth 4 billion yuan, with 630 million yuan in profits and taxes, representing some 32.3 percent of all military production revenue.[21] The emphasis was on a drive into civilian markets, and again, the goal was more production, more exports, more revenue, and more profits.[22] Several sources list increased exports of military-produced goods as a particularly important goal for the military and all defense-industrial organizations.[23]

In July 1986, the State Council and CCP jointly decided to transfer management of four major defense industrial bureaus (in charge of the nuclear industry, aerospace industries, ordnance, and airplanes) to joint management by the State Council and the military. The dramatic change was described as a means through which defense conversion could proceed more smoothly and rapidly (see also below).[24]

Meanwhile, by 1987, despite "rectifications" and mergers, the People's Liberation Army still directly controlled some 3,700 factories and mines, with 170,000 employees all geared toward civilian-use production responsible for one-third of total military profits.[25] Counting all production, civilian or otherwise, the military controlled some 242 chemical factories, 575 agricultural farms, 16 husbandry (stud) farms, and 11,500 smaller-scale factories, mines, service outlets, and economic work units of one kind or another. Altogether, these projects are said to have employed some 670 thousand workers, and received some 2.4 billion yuan in revenues—seven times more revenues than in 1978.[26]

By the late 1980s, the expansion of "tertiary capital" ventures—meaning enterprises involving foreign capital investments, foreign joint ventures, or foreign-owned subsidiaries—also began in earnest. The military participated in nearly 7,000 ventures involving foreign capital or earning foreign capital through exports by 1987, providing work for 45,000 employees and earning around 25 percent (over 600 million yuan) of total military profits and taxes (around 2.5 billion).[27]

II. Defining the Military-Industrial Complex

The "military-industrial complex," defined broadly to include both men in uniform and civilian defense bureaucracies, industrial bureaus, and research centers, plays a vast role in China's domestic economy. Under reform, it can be said to include the following components:

- All military and paramilitary bodies, including the PLA, the PAP, and the reservists (altogether, perhaps 5.6 million people);[28] and any civilian bureaus and civilians who work on maintaining the bases and residences of these soldiers.

  Within the military, the General Armament Department (GAD) is of particular importance to the management of the military-industrial complex. The GAD has extensive authority over the defense industries' research, development, production, procurement, installment, and management of weaponry. It is one of a handful of economic "super-ministries" with vast funding and responsibilities in the second half of the 1990s.

  The importance of the General Logistics Department should also be noted. It manages all military logistics and (at least until recently) many profit-seeking centers under direct military control.

- All farms, factories, transportation facilities, and communications facilities run directly by the military, and all military-controlled enterprises, managed directly by the military through the General Staff, the General Logistics Office, or lower-level bodies in regional and divisional commands. These "work units" and business organizations are far less significant to the national economy than the former ministries of defense industries, and the government has vowed to close down or (more likely) redistribute the enterprises to other civilian bureaucracies. Yet around 10,000 production units still employ at least 800,000 full-time civilian workers and staff at the time of this writing. Further, none of the open reports suggesting imminent "closure" of enterprises has yet detailed exactly which kinds of production units will be closed. Meanwhile, the farms, transportation, and communications work may consume a significant percentage of the workday of men in uniform.

  In the summer of 1998, Jiang Zemin ordered the military to close its many business interests to clamp down on corruption,[29] but it is too early to know how, or if, this order will be carried out.

- Ministries of National Defense Industries. These ministries have been distancing themselves from the military since the beginning of the reform period, and organizationally they now fall under the State Council, not the Central Military Commission or other defense organizations. Some ministries also successfully earn free-market profits.

  Yet while these ministries are now more civilian in command and focus, some offices still focus on military contracts. For example, one electronics subsidiary of the Ministry of Information Industries is the

China National Electronic Import-Export Corporation, or CEIEC, which produces cryptographic systems, radars, mine-detection equipment, fiber and laser optics, and communications technology with obvious military applications.[30] Some industrial bureaus rely on economic and technical assistance from military strategists at GAD, the National Defense University, and other defense organizations. Also, some bureaus (e.g., the Ministry of Ordnance Industries) still receive a larger percentage of their revenue (although no longer a majority) from military orders.

- All civilian organizations and bodies with *primarily* military foci, such as the National Defense Office of the PRC State Planning Commission and the Ministry of National Defense. The jurisdiction of the Ministry of National Defense, which is a branch of the State Council, remains unclear in China's National Defense Law of 1997. Some Chinese sources argue cynically that its primary purpose is to have a means to liaison with parallel civilian bodies (e.g., the U.S. Department of Defense) in other countries.[31] But it is speculated that the Defense Ministry is legally responsible for procedural matters, such as overall planning of contacts between the armed forces, as well as the government and the formulation of laws and regulations. It also studies China's defense needs and lobbies for them within the Chinese State Council.[32]

- Other civilian organizations and bodies with *some* military foci. There is no room here to expand the point, but it should at least be noted that some of the research contracted out by civilian planning organizations to civilian research and production organizations ultimately may be designed for military application. For example, the State Science and Technology Commission (SSTC) is a civilian body under the State Council that carries out long-term planning for information-related projects, and some of these have an obvious defense application. The SSTC publicly announced the National Medium- and Long-Range Program for the Development of Science and Technology on April 7, 1992, which covered both civilian and military technologies that China hoped to develop in the subsequent three decades, including microelectronics, photo electronics, biochemicals, communications, aeronautics, nuclear technologies, high performance computers, air-to-surface and surface-to-air observation, and modern telecommunications.[33] Generally, one should remember that most research on military technologies carried out in China is *not* listed as part of the defense budget (see also next chapter).

- All national defense science and technology institutes, such as the National Defense University. In 1985, the military industry's science and technology research centers produced only 220 million yuan in civilian products, but by 1995 they produced 4 billion yuan worth, with products in industries ranging from nuclear energy to satellites, shipbuilding, and civil aviation. Defense production is quite dispersed, with few dominant players, and even at the very sophisticated level of research centers associated with the defense industrial bureaus, there are as of yet few real giants.[34] Also, the greater part of the production of these bureaus is in civilian goods; the goal is to have these institutes producing around 10 billion yuan of civilian products by the year 2000.[35]
- Some of the plants, physical structures, and businesses located on national defense economic regions and military industrial zones.[36]

III. Economic Activities Directly Controlled by the PLA and The Army's Quixotic Struggle for Profits

Thoroughly blending military and civilian functions has been a prominent goal throughout the reform period. It is labeled in Chinese sources as " 'civil-military compatibility' (*junmin jianrong*)—our strategic thought on national defense development."[37] The idea of civil-military compatibility implies the need for simultaneous economic and military development, both to increase defense technological capacity and to ensure that prosperity becomes a defense priority.[38]

The military *directly* "participates in and underpins" national economic construction in many ways. First, the military aids in the production of farming, grazing, and fishing. One secret source claims that in all, the military cultivated four million *mu* (over 265,000 hectares) of agricultural land in the 1990s; of this, 85 percent is mechanized, supposedly double the national average. It is possible that this makes the military farms more competitive than ordinary farms in terms of productivity, although, like traditional communes, they are probably also less diversified and provide fewer profit incentives than small-scale farms. Still, it appears that some 930,000 *mu* of this cultivated land (almost one-fourth of the total) is bringing cash crops to the market.

Agricultural work also includes large construction projects. In the past decade, to support agricultural development, China's armed forces supposedly have dredged more than 500 rivers, built 200,000-odd kilometers of irrigation channels and dams and dikes, dug more than 1,000 reservoirs, and reclaimed wasteland and leveled land of over two million hectares, "thus laying a foundation for bumper harvests."[39]

Another six million *mu* of land is managed or used by the military, for everything from oil fields to grazing cattle. The navy, meanwhile, is employed to augment fishing industries. It works in many ways to achieve this broad goal, from repairing fishing boats to training technical personnel and setting up production plants.[40] The navy is also employed for other maritime development. Early in the reform period, one reason for a noticeable "naval renaissance in China" was "the emphasis on improving China's economic system," which encouraged the rapid build-up of the merchant marine to fuel development along the coast. "China's naval renaissance was induced by a confluence of decisions and events which turned the country away from its traditional continentalist philos-ophy to one which was decidedly more maritime in nature. . . . Between 1970 and 1980 nearly ten million dead-weight tons of merchant ships were either purchased or built by the Chinese."[41] More recently, naval ships have been employed to haul cement for civilian construction pro-jects, import foodstuffs from one region to another, and transport bulk cargoes not easily handled by other haulage means.[42]

Second, the military participates in economic construction by contin-uing to join major national and local engineering and industrial con-struction projects, helping with the finance, physics, and manpower of the operation.[43] Sources claim that during the reform period, the military has devoted some 400 million workdays to help build 12,000 key provin-cial construction projects. This comes out to about one week per soldier per year, working exclusively on industrial construction projects. These man-hours aided in the construction of over 2,000 kilometers of rail lines and roads, 500 energy projects, 260 bridges, 340 tunnels, 30 civil air-ports, and 40 marine ports. The PLA has also built peers, canals, tunnels, telecommunication networks, and oil fields.[44] Many military-owned or managed construction projects appear to have a direct economic payoff, with such products as raw energy and services via satellite networks sold to over 50 countries and territories.[45] To provide one example of a promi-nent project: Starting in 1993, 200,000 soldiers helped to renovate the north-south rail lines running from Beijing to Hong Kong.[46]

While one week of labor per soldier per year expended on industrial construction would not have a debilitating effect on combat capability, this statistic excludes the agricultural labor and construction projects listed above, any business activity, any relief efforts, and any medical work. It also appears to only include new projects, not repair work on roads, water, gas, and power lines, or beautification projects. These took up another 100 million workdays under reform.[47] Further, the 400 million work days apparently refers only to key construction projects at the provincial level. Another source says that from the beginning of the reform period, the military has participated in more than 180,000 national and regional engineering and construction projects, or 15 times more projects. The number of hours expended on these far more numerous, but apparently less prominent projects, is unknown.

Again, the military also has opened up many facilities previously considered secret or off limits, especially from 1984.[48] Further, military hospitals rapidly redefined their missions, and now serve millions of civilian patients.[49]

The extent to which the military maintains a commitment to Third Line regions is not clear; but as in the 1950s and 1960s, development projects in poorer areas remain prominent in Chinese propaganda.[50] While the production capacity of the military is almost certainly greater on its bases and production facilities in China's richest areas, it almost certainly remains more dominant (considering the size of military production as a percentage of all production) in poorer areas.

Development projects in poorer areas (especially Inner Mongolia, Xinjiang, Qinghai, and Tibet) are billed in idealistic and philanthropic terms, but clearly they also are designed to promote domestic stability (a kind of strategic goal) by improving local economies plagued by poverty.[51] In the 1990s, coastal areas occupy only around one-eighth of the territory the army must defend, but they house over half of all enterprises and more than 60 percent of China's industrial production. Hence, one military source from 1991 argued for the need to correct destabilizing regional imbalances by stimulating more interregional coordination of military industrial construction. The source lobbied for the idea that the number of joint ventures between coastal military enterprises and military enterprises in Third Line regions should be increased.[52] In terms of relief efforts in poor areas, the military claims to have helped to move almost one million people in over 20,000 poor areas out of poverty through various projects.[53]

Third, the military participates in the construction of Special Economic Zones and open areas, with a hand in electric stations, railroad stations, highways, airports, and wharves in Shenzhen, Zhuhai, Xiamen, Haikou, Dalian, and elsewhere. In the early 1980s, when Shenzhen's boom began, the military employed some 60,000 soldiers working on 160 construction projects to build an airport and an electric power station, hotels, retail outlets (including the city's Friendship Store), textile plants, and the most important civilian government offices of Shenzhen City.[54]

The military even runs its own special administrative zones. By 1993, it ran perhaps 120 high-technology zones of one kind or another. Through the mid-1990s the PLA worked to gradually increase this number and the number of firms and technical personnel employed in high-tech industries. There is a clear hope that emphasized civilian markets in these zones will eventually fuel improvements in defense ordnance and technology, but in the foreseeable future the goal is simply increased marketization and profitability.[55]

Fourth, the military is employed to combat major forest fires and aid in providing all other types of relief from natural disasters. During the reform period, the PLA supposedly participated in emergency rescues and disaster relief efforts on more than 100,000 occasions.[56]

Fifth and finally, the military is employed to "build socialist energy and civilization." This includes waging campaigns in minority regions supporting the value of unity in civil-military relations and in relations between the Han and the national minorities.[57] This also includes the construction of relevant public works projects in minority regions (e.g., schools).

Generally, all military-controlled factories also worked to turn themselves into corporations, or branches of corporations, through the late 1990s. Until a decision by Jiang Zemin in the summer of 1998, calling for the closure of military-run businesses, the military struggled to create corporate structures and earn profits in virtually every type of industry that one can imagine: In addition to military bases (often *on* military bases), the military's holdings by 1998 included electronics factories, pharmaceutical plants, mines, energy plants, hydroelectric projects, transportation development projects and roads, research centers and schools, broadcasting stations and publishing houses, hotels, department stores, and retail outlets. A rectification campaign first planned in 1992 and carried out in 1993 apparently closed or merged some 40 percent of all military businesses, but by 1993 one isolated source claimed that there were still over 6,200 enterprises controlled directly by the army.[58]

Some sources suggest much higher numbers (8,000 to 15,000) of businesses controlled by the military by the second half of the 1990s; but an exact number of army businesses may not exist even in closed sources, because there is no standard procedure for counting the number of businesses or defining them. For example, there were said to be over 100 enterprises in Shenzhen directly run by the PLA in 1992, but there were also several hundred other economic offices or organizations in some way registered under military numbers or tied directly to the military. Further, Shenzhen has housed the headquarters of one of the largest military conglomerates, named Triple Nine, or 999.[59] Was this conglomerate counted as one enterprise or dozens? One could ask a similar question concerning any military conglomerate. China Xinxing Corporation, founded in 1984 by the General Logistics Department, controlled more than 100 factories employing 10,000 workers in the early 1990s.[60] Again, was this counted as one company or one hundred?

At lower levels of organization, some branches of military bureaus no longer answered to the center or reported profits and earnings there, so the military has had difficulty tracking all of its holdings. Even those that have been controlled directly from the center by the families of high-ranking officers and staff were still encouraged to work toward profitability, not toward a centrally enforced, grand strategy. Businesses therefore created subsidiaries, holding companies, and offshore trading and foreign exchange organizations that military planners did not plan. This kind of activity is corrupt if handled illegally, and the justification for struggling to close all military businesses in 1998 was corruption and associated problems with smuggling.[61] Yet the legal basis of the military's corporations was always vague, and it is not clear which courts should regulate their dealings.

At the time of this writing, some military businesses are very large (e.g., Xinxing, Triple Nine), and there is no clear relationship between chain of command and the size of the business. That is, those businesses that are controlled at the highest level of military authority are not necessarily the largest. Nevertheless, the PLA General Staff Department controls at least six corporations that are relatively important players in China's military-industrial production, including the Poly Group (in Chinese, *baoli*) which is a major arms trader.[62] The PLA General Political Department directly controls at least two relatively large companies.[63] The PLA General Logistics Department controls the largest number of businesses, including Xinxing Corporation Group (a very large, diversified holding company) and Triple Nine (*san jiu* or 999) Enterprise Group (another holding company). The different services (air force, navy, second artillery, and land forces) also control their own corporations.[64]

In 1992, the military listed over 200 businesses as either large or medium-sized. Many branches of the military managed at least one large business, as table 3.2 (from one isolated, uncorroborated source) demonstrates.

Table 3.2   Number of Large and Medium-Sized Enterprises Controlled by
Various Branches of the Armed Forces, 1992[65]

Branch enterprises	Large enterprises	Medium-sized enterprises
General Staff	4	23
Political Commissars	2	1
General Logistics	37	30
Airforce	8	19
Navy	6	21
Second Artillery (*arpao*)	1	1
Shenyang Military Region	2	18
Beijing Military Region	1	7
Lanzhou Military Region	1	4
Chengdu Military Region	0	13
Guangzhou Military Region	0	11
Jinan Military Region	0	10
Nanjing Military Region	0	8
Total number of large and medium-sized military-controlled enterprises	62	166

This source suggests that the military's larger firms by the 1990s were spread out all over China, and that the military has been more successful in some fields than others. For example, by the end of the eighth five-year plan, the army may have opened something like 370 pharmaceutical plants with around 40,000 employees.[66]

Overall, the evidence suggests the vast majority of firms controlled directly by the PLA have been small, and several sources have described these businesses as crippled by numerous weaknesses: Many have a low technological base, are led by people without much knowledge of the market, and manufacture few or no leading products. Successes in medicinal products can be contrasted with weaknesses in textiles, where the military's many firms are not considered industrial leaders.[67]

Indeed, many firms directly controlled by the military appear to be little more than isolated factories with limited revenues and even more limited profits. At the beginning of the 1990s, of the 831 military-run enterprises in the wealthy and well-connected Nanjing Military Region, 90 percent had annual profits of less than one million yuan (around U.S. $120,000). Only seven of 831 firms were listed by China as "middle-grade" (*zhongxing qiye*).[68]

By the 1980s, the army exported products to over 50 foreign nations, and the development of exports had clearly become a focus of the developmental program of the Chinese military-industrial complex.[69] However, export earnings, while growing in importance, also appear to be low in businesses run directly by the military. The total exports of army organizations in 1991 was said to be worth U.S. $177 million, again according to one isolated source.[70] This was the best year up until that date in the history of the military businesses, and around double the 1987 figure (provided in yuan, above). Hence, a particularly adverse import-export situation in the post-Tiananmen years of 1989 and 1990 had apparently been corrected by this time. Yet if this figure is accurate, then several large, Western corporations earned more in exports than China's entire army did at the beginning of the 1990s. Perhaps exports have risen much higher in recent years, but the PLA would even then be crawling up from a low base.

Chinese estimates of total profits and taxes (*lishui*) earned by corporations owned by the military are a secret, but in 1993, the military may have produced 34.0 billion yuan worth of products annually, with profits and taxes totaling 5.75 billion yuan (less than a billion U.S. dollars).[71] Profits have probably increased in more recent years, yet these figures are again not particularly impressive.

It is nevertheless clear that the production of civilian goods for profit, at least until recently, has been a prominent military priority: Despite the weaknesses of these isolated economic units, the military claimed throughout the reform period, until 1998, that they were central to the army's future.

More autonomous production of both military and civilian goods has translated into an increasingly important source of personal wealth for the cadres with civilian and military titles who manage these businesses and offices.

The military businesses also became an important manpower priority through the 1990s. Like their total earnings, the number of workers employed by the military in businesses is a state secret. However, according to military sources, the enterprises appear to have employed around 670,000 full-time workers in 1987, and to have participated in the training of more than a million soldiers in dual-use (e.g. military and civilian) skills. They are also said to have provided jobs for more than 100,000 family members of soldiers.[72] A more recent source suggests that by 1993, the military employed some 823,000 people in its enterprises.[73] If these two figures are even roughly accurate, this would mean that military businesses became highly significant from a staffing perspective; that is, while the size of the army—men in uniform—decreased, its corporate work force picked up some of the slack.

Jiang Zemin's July 1998 decision to distance the military from business was presented in the context of an anti-smuggling campaign.[74] Yet it is unusual that smuggling has, to date, been the sole problem with military businesses cited in most open sources. As stated above, smuggling is only one corruption problem among many, and corruption is only a subset of the many problems that these inefficient enterprises face. Further, it is unlikely that the vast majority of the enterprises had the resources to profit from very significant smuggling operations.

The decision to ban commercial activity in the military may lead to the closure of some of the most inefficient army businesses and the transfer of many others. The State Economic and Trade Commission (SETC) in September of 1998 is said to have established the National Office for the Takeover of Enterprises by the Army, Armed Police, and Law Enforcement Bodies. The sweeping mandate of this national office is to take over and manage the thousands of enterprises run by the PLA's four general departments, seven major military regions, the armed police, and law enforcement bodies. The office will also work to ensure that "there are laws to abide by" on delinking enterprises from the military. Meanwhile, enterprises run at lower levels of administration (e.g., by subordinate areas of military regions) will be taken over by economic management work units of provincial and local governments.[75]

But PLA businesses may prove to be among the most difficult in the state sector to reform in one way or another, regardless of who is eventually listed as their boss. Interested military personnel may work to hold onto the businesses officially or as de facto kingpins and continue to staff them with managers in their families.

It is not surprising that the General Political Department has had to launch educational propaganda and discussions on the newly acknowledged need for enterprise reform. Doubts have been expressed among those military personnel who are personally affected. "When relatives were laid off and had to wait for employment, and when a decrease in the family income became a realistic problem in their own lives, some officers and men would unavoidably have mixed feelings."[76]

IV. Further Defining the Military-Industrial Complex: On GAD

On April 4, 1998, central authorities announced the formation of the General Armaments Department (GAD), designed to be responsible for research, development, and production of weaponry for the army.[77] The GAD was formed from the former Commission on Science, Technology, and Industry for National Defense (COSTIND), General Staff Department (GSD) Armament Department, and some related General Logistics Department organs. It has beneath it Departments of Comprehensive Planning, Arms' and Services' Equipment, Army Equipment, General Equipment Support, and Electronic Information Technological Groundwork.[78] At the time of this writing, Cao Gangchuan, a member of the Central Military Commission, is director of GAD.

The GAD's predecessor, COSTIND, in turn had its origins in the PLA's National Defense Science and Technology Commission (NDSTC), which was the organ in charge of research and development concerned with advanced weapons, especially nuclear weapons, from 1958 to 1982.[79] In August 1982, in response to conflicts among the NDSTC and its competitors, including the National Defense Industry Office (NDIO) and Science and Technology Equipment (Armaments) Commission Office (STECO), these organizations were amalgamated to form COSTIND. According to Zhang Aiping (commissioner of the NDSTC from 1975), the rationale behind this move was to eliminate the disunity and partisan disagreements between these organizations, which had impaired their efficiency.[80]

COSTIND reported directly to the CMC of the Chinese Politburo, and served as the lead agency of China's defense industrial complex until 1998. It funneled money from the state budget to leading defense organizations and universities that design and build weapons systems. COSTIND also managed the effort to procure foreign military and dual-use technology, either through commercial deals or through espionage.[81]

GAD has swallowed COSTIND, and it brings even more military bureaucracies under its control. Its creation was designed to avoid bureaucratic redundancies, further centralize and rationalize weapons procurement, and further increase the clout of this "superministry."

Is the GAD a military organization, run primarily by officers, seeking to promote defense modernization? Or is it a civilian organization, taking orders from the State Council (as COSTIND did from 1986 to 1998), and seeking to promote defense conversion and the financial interests of autonomous industrial ministries that have broken from military control? As with COSTIND, GAD should be considered a little of both, but the most recent reform and amalgamation of this bureau may have further complicated its dual, somewhat contradictory mission. COSTIND was a unit under the State Council that was supposed to assist and coordinate the involvement of other State Council commissions and ministries in defense production. Yet it reported directly to the Central Military Commission (CMC), facilitating communication between military administrative offices and defense industries.[82] The reshuffling and renaming of this bureau may make it more responsive to the Central Military Commission, as it is in control of more military bureaus than in the past. Still, the contradiction results from the fact that the most important defense industrial bureaus that GAD supports are increasingly commercial.

COSTIND exerted some control over at least six defense industrial corporations, institutes, and associations,[83] and GAD presumably will continue to guide these organizations or at least many of their subsidiary offices. Are the organizations directly controlled by GAD primarily profit-seeking, or are they strategic organizations with goals tied narrowly to China's defense objectives? The answer is again both. For example, of the organizations formerly run by COSTIND, China Xinshidai Corporation has been oriented toward many advanced technologies, while Xiaofeng Technology and Equipment Corporation is more narrowly focused, with special interests in computers, testing equipment, and robotics of interest to military planners.[84] Outside military strategists argue that the industries in which these businesses compete are important for China's defense future, but COSTIND struggled to manage these and other businesses as profit-making centers, largely producing civilian products that may never have significant defense "spin-offs." The leaders of GAD are hoping for further production of high technologies that might be useful from a strategic perspective, but they have vowed nonetheless to treat "economic effectiveness as the key."[85]

China's military institutes, similarly, are funded by GAD and other bureaus to advance China's military strategy, military technology, and military training. Yet the economic pursuits of these institutes are often determined more by comparative advantage, profit-making goals, and access to the market than by strategic objectives. For example, by 1995, there were nearly 100 joint ventures at military industrial institutes with foreign organizations, and over 60 military institutes had been granted foreign trading and exchange privileges, making up some 25 percent of all research institutes in China with such privileges.

The joint ventures and foreign trade may have promoted equipment modernization, but they were primarily formed for any projects that seemed market-worthy. Further, the sixty organizations with foreign trade privileges used these privileges to manage relatively small, decentralized ventures that are unlikely to produce very prominent military technologies; the majority run on foreign trading contracts worth less than U.S. $1 million.[86]

V. The Ministries of National Defense Industries

More than GAD, the ministries of national defense industries have distanced themselves from military control. These ministries (focused on electronics, shipbuilding, ordnance, aviation, space, and the nuclear industry) answer to the State Council since July 1986, and the change from military to civilian authority was made to further the drive toward defense conversion.[87]

The industries are constantly being reorganized, but through much of the reform period, they have controlled profit-making corporations with investment structures that are independent of the military and to some extent even of the State Council. Thus, for example, China North Industries Corporation (NORINCO, a large arms producer) has been a kind of commercial subsidiary of the Ministry of Ordnance Industry, while some other very prominent defense manufacturers (the Great Wall Corporation, China Precision Machinery Import/Export Corporation) have been associated with the Ministry of Space Industry.[88]

Yet despite the defense conversion and "civilianization" taking place in these ministries and bureaus, most of China's weapons development has been coordinated and funded through them (with the help of GAD). Hence, a book discussing China's defense establishment cannot ignore the organization, funding, revenues, and expenses of these frequently revamped ministries.

Paul Humes Folta, in a book on defense industrial reform, suggests that five new economic priorities forced a change in organization in defense industrial ministries during the Deng Xiaoping period:

1. Defense industries were forced to do more to support economic construction.
2. There was a shift from heavy to light industry, which hampered weapons and other military equipment development.
3. Defense and civilian science and technology institutions were asked to emphasize practical innovations to fuel economic growth, not theoretical research.
4. There was an emphasis on "technological transformation" rather than "capital construction"; hence, existing floor space and equipment was to be used more, and more efficiently.
5. Cutbacks forced the defense industry into some competition with civilian industry both for resources and markets.[89]

As a result of these changes in priority and function, by 1982, civilians headed each of what was then six defense industrial ministries, and by 1985, their budgets fell under the direction of the State Council.

Since 1985, as the goal of defense conversion has become more prominent, China's defense industrial ministries have produced, in the words of one outside analyst, "whatever they could lay their hands on, such as electric fans and blankets, meat grinders, kitchen utensils, and even desks and chairs. Most of the products [have been] low-quality, low-grade items with little output value."[90]

The ministries' names have for the most part changed, sometimes more than once, to reflect their civilian status. Some new names are designed to ensure that these organizations will less resemble government offices of any kind, and more resemble pure corporations and conglomerates (e.g., the China Shipbuilding Corporation).

A number of internal joint ventures between domestic military and civilian industrial bureaus started up in the 1980s, further blurring the lines between the military-industrial complex and civilian administrations. These internal joint ventures include projects to produce everything from cars and aircrafts to nuclear power stations.[91] Some 2,000 joint ventures of every kind had formed by the end of the 1980s between defense industrial bureaus and civilian industrial bureaus.[92] To develop export-oriented products, many inland military-industrial organizations have also developed joint ventures with coastal firms.[93]

It is difficult to know exactly what percentage of production from the defense industrial ministries is geared toward civilian-use products. Official statistics differ in different sources, and it is not clear how any of the statistics are calculated. For example, are products sold by one business to another within a defense industrial bureau counted as civilian-use products? In any case, the statistics provided in table 3.3 clearly represent the trend.

From 1987 on, the value of the defense ministry's civilian production has been greater than the value of its military production, and new marketization efforts beginning in 1990 and 1991 appear to have accelerated the trend toward civilian production. This creates an obvious shift in priorities for China's military-industrial complex.

To what extent are these huge industrial bureaus (or state-run conglomerates) efficient competitors? Early in the reform period, analysts described the organization of the defense industries as "a set of separate vertical structures with little communication between ministries at all

Table 3.3   **Percentage of Goods Produced by Defense Industrial Bureaus for Civilian Use, Select Years**[94]

Year	Percent
1979	8-10 %
1987	~50 %
1990	62 %
1992	65 %
1994	80 %

levels down to the factory level, similar to the Soviet civilian and defense industrial model."[95] Efficiency and autonomy have increased since, but some of these conglomerates do not appear to be significantly more efficient than the average, even for Chinese state-run firms.

Sources of inefficiency have matched those for state industries generally, and include underutilized capacity; the backwardness of some products and sectors; rigid, vertical planning, in which each ministry has tried to ensure its own self-sufficiency from other ministries and industrial sectors; correspondingly poor economies of scale; lack of competition and overcentralization of decision-making; poor marketing, sales, and management; and secrecy that hides failures.[96]

The negative result is that through the mid-1990s, nearly 40 percent of defense industrial enterprises had no "pillar product" (*zhizhu minpin*) that earned profits. Of those that did, fewer than 20 percent were said to "truly have a product development capacity."[97] Hence, their products are viewed as having captured an insufficient share of the market.

Still, many of the factories of the defense industrial bureaus began with more educated staff and better equipment than most state bureaus. Moreover, reorganization efforts, joint ventures with domestic and foreign firms, and market pressures all have made these organizations far more efficient. Mainland analysts claim that in the defense industrial ministries, cooperation between military and civilian bureaucracies has saved between 25 percent and 50 percent on investment costs for the construction of products.[98] There is no evidence provided on how this cost-savings is calculated; does it include only the cost of investment, or does it mean the total cost after revenues of sales of civilian goods?[99] Either way, significant cost savings, if the information is accurate, may permit civilian and military contractors to receive much more value for each yuan spent on these defense industrial bureaus.

It is also clear that some defense industrial ministries, especially those concerned with electronics and shipbuilding, are reaping massive revenues from their civilian production. China's defense industrial ministries are officially predicted to reach sales levels of around one trillion yuan ($120 billion) by the year 2000.[100] This official figure is over ten times greater than official figures for current defense spending (see next chapter), and must be far larger than corresponding figures (although no up-to-date, exactly corresponding figures have been found) for businesses controlled directly by the army. So it is clear why the industrial side of the military-industrial complex has become a dominant concern of the government in peacetime.

Different industries have developed at different rates, with electronics being particularly successful at defense conversion. Yet by 1993, according to Mainland defense analysts, each of the six defense industrial ministries were producing goods primarily for the civilian market, including even the Ministry of Ordnance Industries, which appears more troubled than most of the others (see table 3.4).

As China moves away from a Soviet-inspired legacy of industrial production, many of its leaders favor a move toward dominant conglomerations of corporations like those found in Japan (*keiretsu*) or Korea (*chaebol*). Further, government leaders have turned specifically toward the largest defense industrial organizations as ideal candidates for further industrial dominance. While the advantages of Japanese- and Korean-style conglomeration can be logically argued (better economies of scale) and proven empirically (through Japan's and Korea's internationally recognized developmental successes), the recent economic troubles in both Japan and Korea may lead China to rethink the appropriateness of future Chinese *keiretsu* or *chaebol*.

Sections of the Ninth Five-Year Plan for the National Defense Science and Technology Industries (1996–2000) provide key information about the goals of each of the military industrial bureaus through to the millennium.[101]

General goals of the plan focus on civil-military conversion and enabling

Table 3.4 Percentage of Goods Produced by Defense Industrial Bureaus for Civilian Use, by Industry: 1993[102]

Industry	Percent
electronics	90.4
space (astronautics)	83
shipping	78.5
ordnance (*bingqi*)	76.3
aviation	73
nuclear	72

state industrial conglomerates to support themselves as much as possible, by means of high-tech production, more marketization of products, and more prominent entrance into service-sector industries.[103] More specific goals of individual ministries are briefly outlined below, to demonstrate the extent to which these ministries are becoming independent, profit-seeking, state-owned corporations increasingly free from military control.

Electronics

The most important official ministry in charge of electronics and defense industrial development has been reorganized and renamed many times. The former Defense Ministry of Electronic Industries is now being redirected under a newly formed "superministry," the Ministry of Information Industries (MII). MII was formed by the State Council in July 1998 and mainly comprises the former Ministry of Posts and Telecommunications and the former Ministry of Electronics. It also bunches together the State Radio Commission and a State Council Leading Group on "Informatization." Finally, the Ministry of Radio, Film, and Television and the network of the Ministry of Aerospace Industry also have been subsumed by MII.

MII primarily sells civilian products, and its many re-organizations clearly have provided it with increasingly civilian economic priorities and functions. Even some of its more secretive research institutes are now being transformed into more open corporations. But its defense origins and goals are clear from Article XI of the State Council's MII Provisions.[104] Within MII, at the time of this writing, there is still a "Military Electronics Industry Bureau."[105]

With the most recent reorganization of China's state-run electronics corporations and bureaus, many official statistics now group together electronics and information industries. The information industries broadly defined are said to account for some 15 percent of the Chinese GDP.[106]

In its various guises, the electronics branch of MII during the reform period has been the leading conglomerate of China's electronics trade, and it claims much of the national electronics market described above. It is by far the largest of the former defense industrial bureaus. Again, although MII's electronics branch is still labeled a defense industrial bureau in many Mainland reports (and at the time of this writing it is far from integrated with other branches of MII), over 90 percent of its electronics sales are said to be to civilian organizations. So it is difficult to measure in empirical terms the extent to which MII should still be considered part of the military-industrial complex.

In any case, for many reasons beyond civilian sales, the line between military and civilian goals of the electronics industry is almost impossible to draw. One source states that China's electronics development proceeds with the idea that "the market leads, and economic construction rules the battlefield."[107] Still, the same source also claims (perhaps too strongly): "The electronics industry grew under the military, and scientific research units fundamentally follow the construction needs [of], and develop under, military industries."[108]

Many electronic technologies under development or production are dual-use, military-civilian technologies. Examples include radars, communication technologies, guided aeronautics, and components for computer and information systems. Meanwhile, research for both civil and military technologies is carried out in the research centers (*yanjiu suo*) of the defense ministries, such as those focused on electronic industrial production.[109]

Hence, the roughly half a million employees working on electronics within former defense bureaus of MII can be listed as part of the military industrial complex, even though they are led by civilian appointees concerned more with profits and opportunities in the civilian economy than with military goals. Their profits—and budget—do not form part of military spending or revenue. Their goals can be described as supporting, but not determined by, military strategy.

Shipbuilding

China is now the third largest ship builder in the world behind Japan and South Korea, but its own assessment is that it "lags too far behind Japan and the ROK both in terms of size of the industry and in terms of technological capability." China imported well over U.S. $1 billion in ships from Japan and Korea in 1998, and domestic commercial owners apparently prefer Japanese and Korean ships to Chinese-built ones.[110]

China's stated strategy for improving shipbuilding is to make the industry more detached from the government and more commercial, and to concentrate (as with many strategic industries) on trade. Imports of foreign know-how, as well as foreign goods, are encouraged, and there are over 125 shipbuilding joint-ventures or wholly foreign-owned subsidiaries in China.

On the other hand, while other sectors of the economy are unambiguously liberalizing, with increased competition (caused by lower prices in Japan, Korea, and other countries hit by the "Asia crisis"), China has back-tracked on some trade-related reforms. In 1998, the State Council and the Ministry of Communications ordered shipping companies to purchase more domestically built vessels and implemented new trade barriers to imports.[111]

The China Shipbuilding Corporation, again a former defense industrial bureau, is the biggest player in the Chinese shipbuilding market. The value of civilian production by the China Shipbuilding Corporation during the eighth five-year plan (1991 to 1995) increased five times from the previous plan to total three billion yuan (around $365 million). Mainland analysts hope that by the year 2000 the China Shipbuilding Corporation will be producing 3 to 3.5 million tons of ships per year, comprising some 10 percent of the world's shipbuilding market, and approaching international quality standards. At this level of production, key facilities would be operating at roughly 80 percent capacity.

Yet despite successes in terms of pure output, profits on individual products tend to be modest or negligible, with the largest sale in recent years—a Norwegian, 150,000-ton oil tanker jointly produced in China, the largest single export product for China in 1996 as measured by revenue—worth only around 70 million yuan.[112] Some 35 products sold for 5 million yuan or more, with five products worth over 20 million.[113] These sales and many others have led analysts of China's shipbuilding industry to boast (inaccurately) that "the shipbuilding industry is the most important organizational section of the national defense industries."[114] While the Defense Ministry of Electronics was actually more important (and MII is now even more substantial and powerful), the China Shipbuilding Corporation is a more dominant player within its industrial sector.

These days, the majority of the production of the China Shipbuilding Corporation is probably for civilian rather than military contracts, but statistics vary widely on how quickly the shift has occurred. A few sources suggest that already in 1979, around 40 percent of the products of the military-controlled shipping industry were civilian-use products, and this jumped to 86 percent by 1987.[115] Yet one source claims that military production still comprised 80 percent, while civilian production comprised only 20 percent of the shipbuilding industry's total production as late as 1991. One of the tables above suggests figures somewhere in between. Statistical differences may be due to different ways of categorizing what is civilian: Orders for navy-owned merchant vessels that transport trade merchandise may be listed as civilian by some and military by others. Still, while the China Shipbuilding Corporation was still responsible for the production of naval ships and craft by the mid-1990s, even the more skeptical sources concur that by 1995, civilian-use production formed the large majority (at least two-thirds) of total production by the China Shipbuilding Corporation.[116]

Ordnance

Research into weaponry production increased during the reform period, and the Ministry of Ordnance Industries played an important role in the development of conventional military weaponry for the PLA. China managed some 150 ordnance lines (*bingqi gongye de shengchanxian*) by 1985, producing more than 3,000 items for sale, up from only 645 items in 1980. Between 1980 and 1985, the value of these goods quadrupled.[117]

Yet starting in the beginning of the reform period, the army successfully cut orders for large quantities of low-tech products made by the technologically primitive, scattered factories of the Ministry of Ordnance Industries. As a result, this ministry had to seek contracts from civilian organizations. In the 1980s, it began to produce bicycles and sewing machines, in addition to the usual combat equipment.[118] One set of statistics on the shift from military to civilian production in the Ministry of Ordnance is provided by an authoritative, domestic, open-publication source (focused exclusively on China's ordnance industry) (see table 3.5).

Chongqing's Jialing Automotive Plant is a particularly prominent example of a successful venture, formed by the Ministry of Ordnance Industries and a civilian bureau. The "Jialing Group" has 11 member factories and 200 distribution plants, and it had become the largest producer of motorcycles in China, with a capacity to produce some 300,000 per years.[119]

Because it is China's largest arms exporter, the Northern Industrial Corporation (NORINCO) is a more famous conglomerate internationally. It produces much of the PLA's heavy equipment, including tanks and self-propelled guns. The Defense Intelligence Agency lists as its responsibilities, or "markets," the production of armored vehicles, artillery, infantry weapons, small arms, ammunition, and radars.[120] On the civilian side, by the mid-1990s, NORINCO was also responsible for some 50 percent of Chinese motorcycle production and 30 percent of all minivan production. In fact, three-quarters of all minivans now apparently come from defense industrial sources, and NORINCO, one of many subsidiaries of the Ministry of Ordnance Industries, is the leader in that market.[121]

Table 3.5 Production of Civilian Products by the Ministry of Ordnance
Industries, 1979-1989[122]

Year	Number of enterprises directly under the Ministry of Ordnance Industry	Number of production lines (da lei)	Number of products (pinzhong)	Value of civilian production (in millions of yuan)	Civilian production as percentage of total production
1978	202	9	167	470	13.11 (%)
1980	192	13	417	690	20.30
1985	185	17	495	2,239	33.42
1986	185	17	556	2,396	39.42
1987	186	12	398	2,840	35.17
1988	157	13	505	4,147	46.76
1989	158	16	500+	4,330	59.31

The Ministry of the Ordnance Industries also calls upon an increasingly large army of cadres and technicians to develop and manufacture its products. Some 100,000 experts and technicians of one kind or another comprising roughly 10 percent of the total number of employees of the ministry were employed by the end of the 1980s.[123]

Despite successes, the defense conversion work of the Ministry of Ordnance Industries appears to have proceeded somewhat more slowly than for the electronics and shipbuilding industries. Further, the evidence suggests that this ministry is faced with more than the average set of problems.

In the ninth five-year plan, the ministry's goals still include "taking the military as the base," but it also seeks to reform management to produce a "smaller structure and higher quality level" (tanzi xiao, shuiping gao). Specifically, the bureau is hoping to rectify struggling ordnance industry enterprises, of which, it is suggested, there are many. Thirty-two unnamed enterprises controlled by the ministry are singled out bluntly as "enterprises especially in trouble" (tekun qiye).[124]

In terms of civilian production, automotive manufacturing is regarded as having the comparative advantage and the greatest chance for expansion of production and profits within the Ministry of the Ordnance Industries. Carving out a large, stable niche in car manufacturing is the "grim struggle . . . that will make or break" the bureau. The bureau's leaders are working to form a car-manufacturing conglomerate during the ninth five-year plan, comprising many smaller plants and research centers, that would improve the technological level, production capacity, and quality of the vehicles produced by the ordnance industry. They hope this would make the vehicles more competitive in the Chinese market and perhaps within neighboring, emerging markets.[125]

Aeronautics

According to Xinhua, "The degree of development of the aeronautics industry is an important mark for assessing the comprehensive national strength and the level of science and technology development of a country."[126] China is working to ensure that its national strength is up to standards by continuing the conversion of its Defense Industrial Ministry of Aeronautics from a bureau producing primarily military machinery to a re-named Aviation Industries Corporation of China (AVIC), which is a more diversified stockholding conglomerate, with autonomous investment authority.

Specifically, the leaders of the industry are struggling to achieve five overall goals to promote the success of their bureau:

1. Improving the quality of production of civilian aviation, in part through international joint ventures (e.g. for the AE-100).
2. Improving the quality of non-aviation products produced by this bureau, ranging from cars to refrigeration equipment, information products, and industrial machinery.
3. Producing U.S. $3 billion in exports by the year 2000, with $1.8 billion at a minimum.
4. Generating total sales received of some 89 billion yuan, comprising 9.7 billion yuan in profits and taxes by the year 2000.
5. Pushing relatively large increases in staff salaries based in part upon these successes.[127]

On the military side, China currently is working on some 20 different types of airplanes, including fighters, attack craft, bombers, and automated pilot planes. The U.S. Defense Intelligence Agency lists among the responsibilities of a subsidiary, the China National Aero-Technology Import-Export Corporation (CATIC), the production of aircraft and remotely piloted vehicles, including defense aircraft. Yet around three-fourths of the airplane models under development at the beginning of the 1990s were a decade or a few decades behind world standards, and only some of the work is on up-to-date models.[128]

If the ministry in charge of aeronautics is to become truly competitive as a business organization—apparently its primary goal—its future lies with the manufacturing of more up-to-date civilian products. One source claims that half of the enterprises run by the Ministry of Aeronautic Industries in the mid-1990s boasted at least one commercial success on the civilian market,[129] yet the ministry in its own assessment still has a long way to go to reach the highest world standards of defense and civilian aeronautic manufacturing.

Astronautics

Open sources list many activities and accomplishments of the Chinese space community in international cooperative projects, including joint space projects and commercial satellite launch services, and the use of applied satellite technologies in education, transportation, communications, and environmental protection. Early in the reform period, the development of intercontinental missiles, stealth missiles, and communications satellites were three projects at the top of the military's research and development agenda, and in part with the assistance of the Ministry of Astronautic Industries, prototypes or production had been completed successfully on all of these between 1980 and 1984.[130] Open sources also discuss the problems faced by China's space industry, including inadequate technological capabilities, small production scale and low efficiency, and Western constraints on imports.[131]

Beneath the Ministry of Astronautic (or Aerospace) Industries and its successor holding corporation, the China Aerospace Corporation (CASC), one of the more important enterprises has been the China National Precision Machinery Import and Export Corporation. The blending of civil-military affairs within the ministries of defense industries is illustrated by the list of products through which this corporation earns revenue: It boasts both civilian and military clients, both domestic and foreign, and produces all types of missiles, rocket engines, radars, precision machinery, optical instruments, medical equipment, household electrical appliances, tools, and fixtures.[132]

From 1995, the U.S. government identified 20 subsidiaries of the China Aerospace Corporation, including some that are relatively well known (e.g., the China Great Wall Industry Corporation, which launches satellites as one of its many activities) and others that are more obscure. The apparently dispersed, Third Line locations of many of these companies may demonstrate a problem for their future as significant players in domestic or international markets.[133]

The Nuclear Industry

Nuclear industrial research and production was comparatively well funded and advanced in the Maoist era for strategic reasons, yet under Deng Xiaoping the national defense ministry in charge of the nuclear industry was revamped as a bureau primarily concerned with China's energy needs. Official sources claim that the value of civilian-use goods in the nuclear industry increased three times between 1980 and 1985, as nuclear power became China's second most important source of energy, behind coal.[134] More recently, projects under construction during the ninth five-year plan include nuclear power plants at Tai Shan, in Guangdong, and elsewhere. New projects would generate some 6.6 billion watts of nuclear power by around 2001 to 2003, with further planned projects down the pipeline. In total, the ministry is hoping for a 20-billion-watt nuclear generation capacity by the year 2010.

The goal on total energy output from the ministry was apparently set by the State Planning Commission, a civilian body, not by the military.[135] The ministry is also hoping to increase production of civilian goods by 20 percent per year, with the help of subsidiary firms of every size, including some that are developing export markets.[136]

In sum, the evidence suggests that the defense industrial ministries and their successor bureaucracies and corporations have done all they can, short of privatization, to earn profits in any field. In an atmosphere of only slowly increasing defense budgets and decreasing domestic procurements of many items, profits are most likely to be earned through the civilian economy and through exports. During the sixth (1981-1985) and seventh (1986-1990) five-year plans, China invested approximately 4 billion yuan in projects aimed at promoting "defense conversion." Perhaps another 10 billion yuan was invested during the eighth five-year plan (1991-1995), and the numbers continue to rise.[137]

The results have not strengthened the military, but they have helped to make China's state industry more successful, autonomous, and internationally significant. Scattered reports suggest that by 1996, total profits and taxes of defense industrial organizations exceeded (perhaps greatly exceeded) 50 billion yuan, or U.S. $7 billion.[138] The government, in any case, is billing China's defense conversion almost universally as a success:

As a result of technical transformation and newly built projects under the direction of the national industrial policy, approximately 450 production lines are now operating in the defense industry at a certain economic scale producing civilian consumer goods. . . .

Today, [defense industrial] enterprises have the capacity to produce more than 15,000 products for civilian use in over 50 categories, including telecommunications goods, energy and communications products, textiles, light industrial goods, medicines and medical apparatus, and engineering and building materials. Outputs of some products account for a substantial proportion of the national totals. For example, automobiles account for 9 percent, motorcycles 60 percent, railway cargo transport trains 26 percent and fully mechanized coal cutting equipment 24 percent. In addition, the national defense science and technology industries have used military facilities and technology to develop and produce civil aircraft, including the Yun-5, Yun-7, Yun-8, and Yun-12, and have cooperated with a foreign [U.S.] company in producing the MD-82 and MD-90 large passenger planes; the industries have also developed and produced the Galaxy-II supercomputer capable of doing 1 billion operations per second and its application software, the 300,000-K7 Qinshan Nuclear Power Station, shuttle oil tankers, multi-function container ships, large air-cooled container ships and other new and hi-tech products. Between 1984 and 1994, China launched 11 satellites for civilian use. Newly launched communications satellites have increased satellite television coverage in China to 82 percent. . . . Satellite remote sensing technology has produced great economic benefits in national construction.[139]

National defense industrial bureaus may have hosted three times as many "skilled engineering technicians" (*gongcheng jishu renyuan*) as in civilian industrial bureaus through the late 1980s.[140] As a result, these bureaus now produce technology that is frequently up to world standards. One source lists as the defense industrial ministries' most impressive, high value-added products geared toward the civilian market: textile machinery, special-use vehicles, drilling and exploration equipment, "high-grade light-industrial products," medical products, electronic devices, laser and infra-red products, and sea exploration and transportation equipment.[141]

All of these products are churned out by profit-seeking enterprises, domestic and international joint ventures, and limited-stock companies. The defense industrial bureaus have cooperated extensively with foreign partners in developing products for civilian use. By 1994, they boasted over 300 Sino-foreign joint ventures.[142]

VI. Problems with the Profit-Centric Focus of the Defense-Industrial Complex

The decision to push the Red Army and defense organizations into a hunt for profits may have helped to avoid the kind of military budgetary crises that have plagued other countries (especially Russia) in the post-communist era. Perhaps as a result, China's Communist Party leadership presented this decision in an almost unchanging positive light, until 1998.

Yet a number of problems emerged directly as a result of the decision to keep defense organizations in a semi-public, semi-private limbo, under the loose direction of the Central Military Commission and, in the case of defense industrial organizations, the looser direction of the State Council. These problems are already helping to lower military effectiveness and morale and to compromise civil-military relations. Eventually, if the military businesses are not closed (as is now, apparently, the goal), and if the defense industrial organizations are not privatized, the failures of these organizations are likely to cancel whatever temporary budgetary and factional victories may have been gained from reform policies toward them.

Ordnance is peculiar in that one must produce more than one needs, and store and maintain it, in case of war, when it will be in sudden, overwhelming demand. Hence, one must proceed with sales step-by-step, and only sell what is considered true surplus. Yet if the military command and the central leadership are in charge of contradictory tasks, e.g. expensive procurement and storage on the one hand, and sales and profits on the other, which will they choose as a priority? With official salaries for generals running at only a few thousand yuan (a few hundred U.S. dollars) per month, and reported revenues on military industries running in the billions of yuan, choosing the former, defense-driven task may not be easy. Under current policies, it also may not be legally required or even encouraged.

Many other conflict-of-interest problems arise from China's unusual policy, particularly if the PLA-run businesses remain even indirectly under PLA control. These businesses are urged to form joint ventures or sell stock to organizations and individuals based in places that China perceives as potentially hostile. These include the U.S., Russia, Japan, and Taiwan. If a general's family is in control of a business that is engaged in a large joint-venture project with a hostile nation, and leaders are considering war against that nation, will the general advocate fighting or accommodation? If the business partnership is healthy, the financial incentive toward accommodation would be clear, regardless of the strategic priorities of the central leadership.

The Chinese government admits to over 300 Sino-foreign joint ventures established in China with Chinese defense industrial ministries.[143] Organizations controlled directly by the military are also struggling to set up joint ventures, from hotels to manufacturing plants, and the army may have directly established a few hundred joint ventures by the early 1990s.[144]

The government also may be exporting defense industrial products to countries that are potentially hostile. From the 1980s, the largest firms struggling to export conventional arms have been China North Industries Corporation (NORINCO) for armaments, China Shipbuilding Trading Corporation (CSTC) for naval craft, China Aviation Technology Import-Export Corporation (CATIC) for military aircraft and AAM's, China Precision Machinery Import Export Corporation (CPMIEC) for surface-to-surface tactical missiles, and China Electronic Import-Export Corporation (CEIEC) for communications gear.[145] Defense organizations have created or helped to create other companies and conglomerates, including the China Nuclear Industry Corporation (*zhongguo hegongye zonggongsi*), the China Armament Industry Corporation (*zhongguo bingqi gongye zonggongsi*), and, by the early 1990s, other aviation and shipping corporations. China sells to both normal and pariah states. However, it frequently lacks heavy competition, and it is a more dominant arms exporter in countries whose markets have been shunned by Western governments, or when selling unconventional materials. The U.S. government imposed sanctions on CPMIEC and the Great Wall Corporation (both under the Ministry of Space Industries) in 1991, after intelligence reports provided powerful evidence that these two companies had sold missiles to Syria.[146] China's supplies of goods and information used in the production of unconventional weapons to friendly Pakistan also may have helped to fuel a nuclear competition in South Asia that is not in China's long-term interest. China allegedly provided Pakistan with blueprints for a bomb, as well as highly enriched uranium and tritium. It may also have provided scientists and key components for trigger magnets and other nuclear weapon delivery components.[147] Further U.S. sanctions were imposed on China for its sales to Pakistan in 1993.

Both the General Staff Department's Equipment Department (GSD/ED) and the General Logistics Department also control their own private corporations, which use the factories under their jurisdiction to produce weapons for the PLA and goods for export. Again, the GSD/ED controls

Poly Technologies Inc., a major corporation at least loosely affiliated with the China International Trade and Investment Corp. (CITIC), one of the first corporations established under Deng Xiaoping's reforms and still one of the largest and best connected.[148]

It is unclear how China's government would legally control sensitive sales by these military corporations or defense industrial organizations. In October 1993, the Poly Group denied the company's involvement in the sale of M-11 missiles to Pakistan with claims that it cannot export strategic weapons without the approval of the PLA General Staff.[149] While this may be true, China to date has publicized no legal mechanism by which it discourages sales—although its signature on the Non-Proliferation Treaty is one legal mechanism that at least delineates some illegal nuclear sales. Meanwhile, China's export regime appears to encourage virtually all exports, including missiles to Iran and ring magnets for use on nuclear devices to Pakistan. Neither is it clear if the same legal regime that was supposed to apply to Poly (the PLA-owned corporation that sold the ring magnets) would apply to companies owned by the Ministry of Ordnance Industries or other defense ministries more distant from the PLA.

Conflicts of interest can plague any arms-exporting economy. For example, the United States also provided weapons to Iraq in the 1980s when this may not have been in U.S. long-term interests. But regulatory problems and conflicts of interest are magnified when defense organizations (which should be concerned primarily with defense) directly or indirectly manage the profit-seeking organizations within an economy that will benefit from exports.

The many real estate and tourist ventures now controlled by the military might also have led generals to defend profitable locations, not strategic locations. The Third Line defense strategy may have been strained, in part, by the rush to invest in rich coastal provinces and Special Economic Zones, rather than in inland areas once regarded as the key to China's strategic defense policies. Apparently, in some cases entire plants belonging to the military-industrial complex were moved from Third Line, land-locked regions to the coast.[150]

The goal of profits may also have generated low morale among soldiers and worker-relatives of soldiers. The objective of a general is to properly provide for his soldiers and staff, and to employ at least the minimum number of soldiers required for the defense of strategic locations. The aim of a manager struggling to sell stocks or merchandise, by contrast, is often to keep salaries as low as possible without affecting the quality of production, and to fire employees perceived as unprofitable, including soldiers and technicians who may have been hired for reasons having nothing to do with profits. The general-manager also has an incentive to employ soldiers in civilian, rather than military, tasks. These tasks may have nothing to do with those that would promote combat readiness. Still, if such tasks (e.g. farming) save money or produce income, they may become more important than military training in the daily life of the soldier.

Defense bodies are in a unique position to exploit road, rail, and air for organizational or personal profit, and military-maintained monopolies are a problem that, military sources admit, have eroded civil-military relations. Some sources have singled out monopolistic coal mines in Shanxi Province, and transportation services in Guangdong Province, as particularly obstructionist to the proper functioning of the market. Civilian managers, meanwhile, may be tired of paying for Red Army labels to gain approval to open businesses (e.g. publishing houses) in order to be able to compete with government-run organizations.

Some defense industrial organizations are aided by long-standing monopolies in some sectors. The China State Shipbuilding Corporation is said to own all Chinese shipyards and shipbuilding and marine equipment firms.[151] It has begun to separate itself from the army but not from the government. As a result, some government leaders will have an incentive to block any trust-busting measures. Further, while China seeks to transfer army businesses in part to crack down on government smuggling rings, with shipping industries dominated by an already internally transferred company, this measure may not solve the problem. Further shifts toward power for the China Shipbuilding Corporation (for example, if the navy provides this bureau with control over naval businesses) may enhance smuggling rather than block it.

Many products from military-industrial organizations struggle to compete with civilian products, even though their traditional line of goods may have no market outside the socialist plan. Any financial support for military or defense industrial businesses that are failing represents an obstacle for a nonstate organization struggling to compete, often without support, in the same business. And the Soviet Union's experience demonstrates that if these publicly controlled organizations take away from civilian technological development, the effect will be perilous in the long term. While organizational reforms in defense industrial organizations especially should help to alleviate this potential problem, some Mainland critics still feel that China's economy remains unbalanced: It is a country that has nuclear weapons and satellites but is technologically backward in other respects by world standards.[152]

Corruption and lawlessness in military circles is on the rise, in part because the hunt for profits drives the defense establishment's uniformed and civilian staff into illegal activities. Again, a campaign against illegal activities in the early 1990s led to the closure of hundreds of military trading organizations, and more than one-third of military enterprises were said to be shut down, reorganized, or in one way or another rectified after a crackdown in 1993. But the problems are far from solved.

In addition to smuggling, the military reports many illegal practices with stock fraud, the selling of army registrations and advertising rights, impersonation of officers for profit, piracy on the high seas, money laundering, black-market peddling of military-produced or military-controlled products, and Mafia activities. None of these activities are good for civil-military relations, and—as in the case of alleged PLA involvement in piracy of a tourist boat filled with Taiwanese on Qiandao Lake—some threaten the interests and reputation of China internationally.

Military officers and staff are spending money on many allegedly business-related fixed assets (massage parlors, restaurants, saunas, expensive cars), which may neither earn profits nor have any defense application. Instead, they are projects built for the luxurious lifestyles of the officers themselves. All defense expenditures are supposed to be accounted for and geared toward the defense goals of China's government and military, according to a PRC Law on National Defense, proclaiming these goals in 1997.[153] One can assume that the legal stipulation was in response to aberrations in practice.

Hence, while most Chinese sources support China's defense conversion efforts, some suggest that the contradictory roles of defense industrial factories, especially those controlled directly by the military, have led to compromised objectives and lax discipline. In the words of one Mainland defense analyst: "Today, the army's social burdens are truly overbearing. The army is an ordnance team; it needs to be always ready for war. It ought to give a few leather factories, textile mills, and steel plants to local [government] offices to manage. It shouldn't be managing factories, or social issues (with the exception of those in outlying regions); it should simply reduce the number of organizational personnel whose tasks are unrelated to fighting battles."[154]

As a result of many managerial problems, military businesses and perhaps even the majority of defense industrial bureaus have lost more money than they have earned. One-third of all state industries are said to lose money, and, because of the legacy of the Third Line program, the military and defense bureaus appear to have more businesses in poor areas than is generally true in national bureaus. Poor regions are where state industry losses are highest. In bad years—1990, for example—more than one-third of military-run industrial enterprises reported deficits, apparently more than the average for state-run firms generally. Defense industrial bureaus and army firms also have to "re-tool" factories designed for different markets, and the process appears to be difficult, even for the most successful firms. For example, NORINCO, the most prominent company of the Ministry of Ordnance Industries, was said to be losing money in the early 1990s because it had difficulty shifting tank and artillery plants to civilian production.[155]

VII. Conclusion

The decision to separate defense industrial bureaus from the military was probably an intelligent one. It is, in a sense, a move on the road toward the privatization of several large economic organizations. It would no longer be a huge jump at this point for the China Shipbuilding Corporation, or the businesses until recently run by the Ministry of Electronics, to became private conglomerates. They are already functioning as semi-privatized companies, with government support and appointees but autonomous management structures.

The much more recent decision, in 1998, to create a General Armaments Department, is also a logical means to simplify the Chinese procurement process. With COSTIND and defense industrial bureaus responsible to the State Council, and the army to the Central Military Commission, a lack of coordination on armament procurement was perhaps inevitable. A unified bureau may help to improve the management of procurement, although it is far too early to tell the overall result of this change.

Some other "reforms" have been steps in the wrong direction, taken for the wrong reasons. While the decision to close military businesses may alleviate some problems, a further decision to privatize former defense-industrial bureaus would place China's defense management on sounder footing. Until that decision is made, the central leadership is likely to be distracted away from the strategic goals outlined in chapter one. Indeed, under current conditions, it may be impossible to isolate defense goals from profit-making goals, or to implement any truly new "grand strategy."

It was hoped that more autonomy for the military and defense industrial organizations might promote higher profits. Yet more autonomy without privatization—and without a clear separation of government, military, and business functions—may simply mean loosened command and control.

CHAPTER 4

Trends in Chinese Defense Spending and the Illusive Goal of Modernization

A currency that has never been completely convertible, the continued existence of nonmarket inputs and outputs, and deliberately opaque information are among the most obvious problems that plague analyses of China's defense budget. Analyses of historical changes in defense spending are further hampered by incomplete information not only about components of defense spending but also about changes over time in how the components are calculated and presented.

The information that does trickle out from official Mainland organizations on current and past defense spending is often intentionally distorted. At the top, Chinese military strategists have traditionally employed secrecy or deception to hide strengths and, especially, weaknesses. Further, high-ranking officials themselves may lack key details or be the victims of deception perpetrated by lower-level administrators. Standardization at certain levels of military administration and in regional bureaucracies is admitted to be woefully incomplete, and at every planning level there are incentives to exaggerate both needs and victories. Deliberately misrepresented data can result in new allocations for allegedly troubled factories that are actually swimming in civilian contracts. Distortions can hide profits from tax bureaus, attract skilled technicians and staff, provoke transfers of unwanted surplus labor, or conceal gross mismanagement and corruption.

Despite the quagmires, this chapter employs both open and internal circulation Chinese sources to chart changes in the defense budget that may have helped to promote strategic modernization, leading to a leaner, more specialized army, with more advanced weaponry and more efficient logistics.

The chapter concludes that a restructuring of funds and limited increases in funding have helped to promote some defense modernization. However, China has been unable to promote changes that Chinese military planners regard as essential.

Historically, the direction of defense budgets is tied almost entirely to domestic conflicts. Indeed, students of international security might find that many of China's budgetary shifts, ignoring domestic affairs, appear counterintuitively to head in the *wrong* direction: Spending surges and declines except during the Korean War appear to be only tenuously tied to any international tensions.

There is no evidence that the budgets have a greater international logic under reform. Defense budgets are still largely inward-looking rather than focused on international security goals or objectives; funds are poorly spent on outdated forces and projects; funds for technologically advanced special force units and crucial defense industrial projects are still lacking; and a great deal of money and effort is wasted by socialistic management structures.

I. Analysis of Historical Trends in Defense Spending

Official figures on China's defense budget from 1950 to 1995 are culled and calculated from three statistical yearbooks and provided in table 4.1 and figure 4.1.

While defense spending trends frequently change directions, a close look at the statistics in table 4.1 suggests one central plotline: In a nation with an army founded to achieve a national liberation, domestic factors far more than international ones determine the course of China's defense spending. With the exception of the period of the Korean War, the history of Chinese communist defense spending is a history of domestic political struggle (see figure 4.1).

In 1949, as the communists struggled to destroy residual Guomindang resistance on the Mainland, military spending encompassed 40 percent or more of all government expenditures,[2] and spending remained high during the Korean War. Officially acknowledged military expenditures as a percentage of overall national budgetary expenditures then demonstrate a decline until 1989, when spending picked up again. Yet even before 1989, changes in defense spending are more of a roller coaster ride than a gradual slope downward, with slope changes fueled by internal discord.

Defense spending as a percentage of national expenditure peaked in the early 1950s (43 percent in 1951, at the height of the Korean War).

Table 4.1 Official Figures on the Defense Budget 1950-1995[1]

A.	B.	C.	D.	E.
Year	Gross expenditure on defense (billions of yuan)	Percentage of national budget	Defense spending increase from previous year, (percentage)	Defense spending increase from previous year inflation adjusted (percentage)
1950	2.8	41 (%)	—	—
1951	5.3	43	89 (%)	68
1952	5.8	33	9	9
1953	7.5	34	29	26
1954	5.8	24	-29	-32
1955	6.5	24	12	10
1956	6.1	20	-7	-7
1957	5.5	18	-11	-13
1958	5.0	12	-10	-10
1959	5.8	10	16	14
1960	5.8	9	0	-4
1961	5.0	14	-16	-35
1962	5.7	19	14	10
1963	6.6	20	16	23
1964	7.3	18	11	15
1965	8.7	19	19	22
1966	10.1	19	16	16
1967	8.3	19	-22	-20
1968	9.4	26	13	13
1969	12.6	24	34	35
1970	14.5	22	15	15
1971	16.9	23	17	17
1972	15.9	21	-6	-6 *(continued)*

Despite continued poor relations with the United States and heightened tensions in the Taiwan Strait from 1954 to 1958, China's defense spending, adjusted for inflation and as a percentage of the national budget, decreased rather precipitously during the mid-1950s. At this time, China's former revolutionaries were focused on many industrialization projects and central planning issues, including communization, which would dramatically expand the size and expenses of civilian governments.

China's international position grew much more dangerous during the Great Leap Forward with the demise of a Sino-Soviet alliance, and one would have expected this to have an effect on defense budgets. Still, for entirely domestic, political reasons, Mao's Great Leap Forward emphasized civilian over military production, and the official percentages of

Table 4.1 Official Figures on the Defense Budget 1950-1995[1] *(continued)*

A.	B.	C.	D.	E.
Year	Gross expenditure on defense (billions of yuan)	Percentage of national budget	Defense spending increase from previous year, (percentage)	Defense spending increase from previous year inflation adjusted (percentage)
1973	14.5	18	-10	-10
1974	13.3	17	-9	-10
1975	14.2	17	7	7
1976	13.4	17	-6	-6
1977	14.9	18	11	9
1978	16.8	15	13	12
1979	22.3	17	33	30
1980	19.4	16	-15	-22
1981	16.8	15	-15	-18
1982	17.6	15	5	3
1983	17.7	14	1	-1
1984	18.1	11	2	-1
1985	19.2	10	6	-3
1986	20.1	9	5	-1
1987	21.0	9	4	-3
1988	21.8	7	4	-14
1989	25.1	8	15	-2
1990	29.0	8	16	13
1991	33.0	10	14	11
1992	37.8	10	15	9
1993	42.6	9	13	-1
1994	55.1	10	29	6
1995	63.7	9	16	1

spending devoted to defense, after dropping precipitously in 1958, did not regain former levels until 1962. Especially in 1961, the famine in the countryside and the fall of Peng Dehuai each helped lead to dramatic declines in military spending—the largest declines after adjusting for inflation in China's postrevolutionary history.

Defense expenditure again jumped dramatically upward by 1968, to 26 percent of national budgetary expenditures, and border clashes with the Soviet Union are an obvious international source of tension at this time; yet the temporary budgetary increases (and the border clashes themselves) were above all the result of domestic issues, including political turmoil during the Cultural Revolution; the increased prominence of Lin Biao and military bureaus over civilian leaders and bureaus; and the

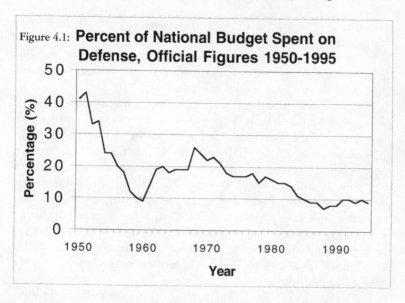

Figure 4.1: **Percent of National Budget Spent on Defense, Official Figures 1950-1995**

growing need for a military solution to suppress urban dissent in China's major cities. Indeed, the most dramatic defense budgetary increases after the Korean War occurred in 1969, the year that the army suppressed red guard organizations throughout China and began to organize the exodus of college and middle school students from cities to the countryside.

As the Soviet Union reacted to tensions and blustering threats from China with massive increases in forces on the Chinese border, creating a genuinely destabilizing troop presence through the first half of the 1970s, China's defense spending actually decreased (as a percentage of the budget, in gross terms, and adjusting for inflation). While relations with the United States improved during the 1970s, the trend is again primarily the result of domestic policy considerations, including the fall of Lin Biao and the complicated dynamics of the last half-decade of the Cultural Revolution.

A massive increase in spending from 1977 to 1979 coincided with Deng Xiaoping's struggle to secure power, employing the military as his base. The first year in which Deng's power seemed secure, 1979, was a rare period in which international tensions (the Soviet Union's invasion of Afghanistan and especially China's failed attack on Vietnam) were at least as significant an influence on defense spending as purely domestic concerns (Deng's payback to generals who helped him secure power, the renewed fear of popular dissent and the decision to crush the Democracy Wall movement).

Yet after 1979, the normal pattern re-emerges. Defense spending declined through the early and mid-1980s, largely in order to promote Deng Xiaoping's domestic economic priorities.

If military modernization was one of the four modernizations, why did defense spending apparently decline, after inflation in gross terms, and as a percentage of the national budget, in the 1980s? A book published by the Contemporary China Publishing House, *The Chinese PLA*, outlines the theoretical underpinning for the overwhelming emphasis on butter over guns in military budgets during the first decade of the reform period: International power is not achieved primarily through nuclear capability, army size, alliances, or diplomacy. Instead, its primary source is a nation's economic base. Economic development is power development. One source lists the centrality of economic construction as nothing less than Deng Xiaoping's primary contribution to Chinese strategic thinking on "military sciences" (*junshi kexue lilun*).[3]

The economics is power formula meant that even military spending would be directed toward internal development goals, as opposed to international security concerns, to an extent not seen since perhaps the 1930s. Further, military spending would be considered far less important than spending on civilian bureaus specifically geared toward economic management and construction.

In order to correct the economic deterioration that took place under the Cultural Revolution and reverse the consequent "backwardness of China's production power," the military would be asked to work single-mindedly to promote China's overriding concern under reform, economic development:

> The CCP Central Committee and the Central Military Commission decided that under China's current, contradictory development stage, the military would operationalize a strategy of military construction which took the goal of national economic construction as the central element; promoted military construction to serve the overriding public interest of national construction; acted under, employed our strength for, and continuously strove to support, socialist [economic] construction as our central goal.[4]

Early in the reform period, a Work Conference Instruction on All Military Logistics, April 1978, involving the highest military authorities, already mapped out a reform program for the new era. It would borrow from a 1953 slogan on "serving the nation, serving the army," to create an army more concerned with construction and modernization in peacetime.[5]

From 1984, the goal of defense conversion—employing defense factories and tools for civilian, market production—became far more prominent (see also chapter three); and in the 1990s it has been promoted to an unprecedented degree. Some Mainland strategists would treat all military resources as national defense resources that should be exploited for defense conversion and national development. "Taking defense conversion as the goal" means employing "military production, military industrial technology, military equipment, and military personnel"—every input of the military-industrial complex—to promote the goal of economic development.[6] In sum, domestic economic construction needed the highest percentage of resources that was feasible, and in budgetary allocations defense bureaucrats promoting genuine security and weaponry programs were forced to take a back seat until 1989. Even outside observers skeptical of most Chinese military proclamations concede that military spending probably did decline in the 1980s, perhaps precipitously in the first half of that decade.

During a time of unprecedented international peace, at the dawn of the post–Cold War era, a final spending turnaround occurred in 1989, with increases that countered inflation. Increases in real terms continued in the first half of the 1990s, as the Soviet Union, the primary international threat to China, collapsed. Clearly, this turnaround was not the result of increased international threats. What caused it?

The most dramatic overall spending increases followed in the wake of Martial Law in Tibet, the Tiananmen Massacre in Beijing, Martial Law throughout China, and the rise of Jiang Zemin, an outsider to military circles. When Jiang Zemin became Deng Xiaoping's General Secretary and handpicked successor just after the Tiananmen Massacre, he personally wielded few sticks that he could use against the military, and he surely felt that it was in his interest to provide military leaders with carrots.

Other reasons promoted by official sources for the spending increases, especially pronounced in the early 1990s, are provided below; but the timing of the most recent upward trend suggests that it is at least in large part the result of fears of domestic instability and personal jockeying for power. This does not put a very professional, modernized varnish on defense spending, a central pillar of China's military planning.

II. Components of the Official Defense Budget:
Reading Between Opaque Lines

At the time of this writing, in 1999 defense spending is slated at just below 105 billion yuan (around U.S. $12.6 billion), a slightly sharper than average increase of 12.7 percent over 1998's figure.[7] Sun Zhiqiang, Director of Finance in the General Logistics division of the PLA, states that the higher than average rate of increase is due to the decision to close military businesses, which will allegedly have a negative effect on military logistic capacity in the short term. Also, there is a continued effort to ensure that the military budget and military living standards keep up with increases in the national budget and living standards in China generally.[8]

China has not invented a uniform way to present what this stated budget is supposed to consist of, and most Mainland discussions of the subject obscure as much as they reveal. According to a 1995 "White Paper on Defense," 34 percent (18.8 billion yuan) of the defense budget at that time consisted of living expenses, principally salaries, food, and uniforms. Another 34 percent was consumed by maintenance activities, said to include military training, construction and maintenance of facilities, water, electricity, and heating. Finally, 32 percent (17.5 billion yuan) was spent on research efforts, including tests, purchases, maintenance, transportation, and storage of equipment.[9] The categories were not changed in a 1998 White Paper, but the percentages allegedly spent on each category were excised from this more recent document.[10]

The 1995 White Paper lists many obvious categories of possible expenditure but is otherwise not particularly helpful. Why is maintenance listed twice? When listed under research, does this mean exclusively the maintenance of research facilities? Why should the storage of equipment be listed under research rather than maintenance? More importantly, what percentage of the budget funds each branch of the armed forces? Why doesn't the purchase of foreign equipment, including expensive technology imported from the Soviet Union/Russia, appear anywhere on this list? Does the budget include expenses for the militia, the People's Armed Police, reservists, or the Ministry of Defense?[11]

Assuming the White Paper correctly lists total living expenses of PLA soldiers (the paper's most clear-cut category), further assuming that the living expenses category excludes all civilian defense personnel, and further that there were around 3.2 million soldiers in 1994 (as claimed), the White Paper suggests that China spent some 490 yuan per month per soldier, or around U.S. $700 per year at the official exchange rate, by the middle of the 1990s.[12] This figure does roughly match the cost of unskilled industrial labor in the Chinese countryside for that year; yet it is difficult to estimate an average salary and benefits package based upon this estimate of living expenses. One Mainland source, moreover, suggests a figure for living expenses that is almost three times higher.[13]

Other sources provide further (incomplete and contradictory) clarifications. According to a recently published "PRC Law on National Defense," defense expenditures are said to include national debt issued for defense projects and scientific research and production costs for defense projects. This includes all land, material, and capital employed to produce and develop defense hardware. Yet there is no mention of how debt is incorporated into the data, nor of which specific bureaucracies are part of the defense budget. Finally, it is not clear if "defense expenditures" as defined here are equivalent to published defense budgets. This document also does not discuss purchases of foreign hardware.[14]

Sometimes sources offer data to back a lobbying effort and sometimes, apparently, just to contribute logical information to the open discussions of the subject. Still, all open sources are heavily censored, and they rarely provide any statistics that would breathe life into the analysis.

Another Mainland source, for example, would split the official budget into two broad divisions: "construction" (*jianshe*) and "consumption" (*xiaohao*). "Construction" includes equipment purchases, airports, wharfs, defense depots (*guofang dongku*), barrack construction, equipment for battle (*zhangbei zhendi*), and other long-term fixed construction expenses.[15] Consumption expenses include equipment maintenance, upkeep of installations, machinery management expenses, and finally living expenses of personnel. These categories are interesting only in that Chinese authorities have repeatedly stated the wish to limit the amount of money spent on maintenance, including living expenses of soldiers, and to increase the amount spent on new construction, including research, development, and production. Yet this article only points to a common goal without telling us the extent to which it has been realized.

A fourth Mainland source on China's national defense economics breaks defense spending into four basic categories:

1. soldier support and related military expenditures, including:
   * daily activities and exercises (*richang huodong*)
   * training

- equipment and military materiel
- living expenses

2. national defense scientific research, including
   - basic research
   - weapons manufacturing

3. national defense basic construction, including
   - national defense industries
   - national defense transportation
   - national defense resource exploitation and production
   - civil defense engineering projects

4. other (no explanation)[16]

The largest expenses are said to be the living expenses and training of soldiers; otherwise we are provided with no information on the size of any of these categories. One curious aspect of this list is that it includes "national defense industries"; if this is a reference to the national defense industrial ministries, then its presence on the list is surprising. These ministries are now independent of the military and are almost never listed as part of the defense budget. It is also worth noting that imported weaponry, again, is not deemed worthy of mention on the list, nor is maintenance and upkeep, said in most sources to be a burdensome expense indeed.

Yet another Mainland source lists the following components of military spending:

- equipment manufacturing (*zhuang bei yanzhi*)
- purchases (*gouzhi*)
- maintenance (*weixiu*)
- military facilities, constructions, and defenses (*junyong sheshi jianshe yu weihu*)
- military materials and supplies (*junyong wuzi gongying*)
- living expenses of officers and staff (*guanbing shenghuo*).[17]

Again, there is no evidence that the budget is actually calculated with these categories in mind, and like other lists above, this one appears to exclude foreign imports (unless this is part of "military materials and supplies"). This list and others provide cumulative evidence, but by no means prove, that foreign imports are wholly excluded from the stated defense budget.

A source focused on defense development strategies lists four broad components of military expenditures: (1) living allowances for soldiers, (2) education and scientific research in military sciences, (3) maintenance of facilities, and (4) ordnance, equipment, and installation purchases and construction costs.[18]

One purpose of the article is to lobby for relatively less money spent on soldiers, and relatively more on research and development. People's War is a strategy that is never mentioned, and the rhetoric again demonstrates how far China has moved from this strategy of the Maoist past.[19]

There is some information on the cost of soldiers that matches the information in the White Paper, and the spending categories closely match those in the fourth source listed above. Yet little more can be garnered from this document on actual expenses and how they are calculated.

The most worthy recent unclassified English-language effort to plunge into the morass of conflicting information and estimate the defense budget and its components is carried out by Shaoguang Wang in *The China Quarterly.* He cuts and pastes from disparate, open Chinese sources (some listed here) and then divides stated defense-related expenditures into three broad categories: the official budget; defense-related outlays in other budgetary categories; and extra-budgetary revenues. Within the official defense budget, he finds or calculates information on no less than 11 specific categories:

1. personnel—pay and fringe benefits, pensions, etc.
2. procurement—weapons and equipment from domestic and foreign sources
3. maintenance of weapons and equipment
4. scientific research—in military sciences, military medical research, testing and evaluating weapon systems
5. maintenance—power and other utilities; allowances for business trips; special allowances and other running expenses
6. operations—intelligence; meteorological observation; topographic survey, the provision and management of housing, medical care, and other services
7. construction—military buildings, facilities, and other national defense works
8. education and training—military academies, training equipment and installations, operational costs of training
9. stockpiling strategic defense materials
10. combat costs

11. miscellaneous—foreign affairs; money awards for surrendered military personnel of enemy; other

Wang's categories, while more detailed than those in Mainland sources, may be unrepresentative of the accounting methods used by the government when actual defense outlays are calculated. Further, Wang has clearly culled these categories from a variety of sources, and some information could easily be excluded or counted twice. Indeed, Wang is forced to assume that categories in some sources can be compiled or subtracted from categories in others to calculate information that is otherwise unavailable.[20] The discussion above helps to show why such calculations may be inaccurate.

Nevertheless, Wang does gather information from an impressive collection of sources, and while many analysts on the subject are still at the starting gate, he at least rounds the track and draws the following conclusions: Personnel probably does comprise roughly one-third of the official budget, as stated; procurement comprises perhaps another 25–27 percent; repair and maintenance of weapons 12–14 percent; and finally military research in the official budget (carried out directly by the PLA and its institutes—a minority of all defense-related research) comprises another 3–4 percent. Because the PLA needs to pay roughly 30 percent of its own expenses with goods from farms and factories, Wang concludes that this official budget reflects only 70 percent of actual expenditures even for listed items; and again, Wang is aware that many defense-related expenses are listed or hidden elsewhere in annual national budgets printed by the State Council.[21]

While one hesitates to draw conclusions from obviously incomplete information, what is most interesting about the Mainland sources cited above and the one published in the West is that they frequently list personnel and maintenance costs as the highest costs in the defense budget. The evidence suggests that these costs are indeed cutting into China's defense modernization effort. Cumulatively, they also tend to suggest that key spending components, such as imported arms, are not included in the official budget.

III. Extra-Budgetary Funding and Revenues

At China's National Defense University, officers are apparently taught that China's official defense budget is the actual budget for all defense appropriations, including even foreign imports such as those from Russia.[22] If it is true that this is what officers at the lower ranks are taught, then there are two possible reasons: One is that even officers at lower ranks are left intentionally uninformed about military allocations and logistics, and hence the application of strategy in the army for which they work. This in itself has implications for China's capacity to implement any strategy. A second possibility is that the official defense budget genuinely does cover the majority of the defense allocations that are directly controlled by PLA organizations, as opposed to other defense-related bureaucracies (e.g. State Council defense committees and defense industrial bureaus, the People's Armed Police, etc).

Either way, independent analysts almost all conclude that China's stated defense budgets leave out many items that are clearly related to the defense of China. For example, Shaoguang Wang, cited above, would estimate that China's budget in 1994 exceeded stated budgets by more than 50 percent, if one adds extra-budgetary expenditures ultimately spent on defense. Items not listed in the budget probably include much of the research and development expenditures for new weapons and equipment; expenditures for the reserves, local militias, and the People's Armed Police; subsidies for the production of weapons provided to official organizations not subordinate to the military; and earnings from the PLA's businesses and arms sales.[23]

Official U.S. organizations, foreign governments, and autonomous consulting groups place yet higher figures on Chinese defense spending. Two Central Intelligence Agency (CIA) reports cover defense components that are comparable to those included in the U.S. defense budget, and conclude that China's military expenditures run to approximately twice their published claims during various studied years of the reform period.[24] A recent White Paper on Defense published by Taiwan states that China's defense budget is almost exactly three times higher than is claimed on the Mainland—and roughly 3.5 times the defense budget of Taiwan (NT$268 billion in 1997).[25] The U.S. Arms Control and Disarmament Agency (ACDA), meanwhile, attempts to analyze the budget with purchasing power parity (PPP) estimates, and concludes that in U.S. dollar terms, China's defense expenditures of every kind exceeded U.S. $51 billion in 1991.[26] Compared to the official defense budget measured at official exchange rates, this ACDA figure is around a dozen times greater.

The Washington-based Defense Budget Project would consider all of these estimates still too low. While the official 1994 PLA defense budget totaled around $6 billion in U.S. dollar terms at official exchange rates, the Defense Budget Project, adding extra-budgetary expenses and apparently employing dramatically high PPP estimates, raised the value of the Chinese budget massively, concluding it could range between $92 billion and $143 billion.

Such a high budget would permit the PLA to afford aggressive weapons, such as a multitude of new aircrafts, and this poses "a challenge to the U.S.," according to analysts at the Defense Budget Project, the Heritage Foundation, and others.[27]

Such a high budget would also enable China to falsify the analysis of a sluggishly modernizing military presented here. However, exaggerated PPP estimates can tremendously distort China's strengths, capabilities, and successes, and the DBP estimate appears to be a gross exaggeration. Obviously, few U.S. analysts would swap an F-16 or a Trident submarine for their Chinese equivalent. Similarly, if Chinese soldiers and militia earned the same salary as the average U.S. private, China would have fired a great deal more of the PLA's surplus laborers in the past decade. And even if low domestic prices enable the Chinese to buy more for less domestically, this does not mean that the PLA has a war chest in U.S. dollars to secure from abroad what it cannot manufacture at home. Yet clearly, all of these sources are counting many important items that the Chinese government does not include in its official defense budgets, items that may be critical for accurate assessments of defense spending trends.

Extra-budgetary Funding

One topic discussed frequently, but never defined or itemized in any Mainland source this author has read, is the military's financial debt, or "debts" (*fakuan*), at various levels of administration. Again, when national debt is issued for planned defense industrial projects, this supposedly appears in the defense budget. Yet military logistic bureaus clearly borrow money for factory investments and perhaps for many projects and programs. This may mean, de facto, that the military overruns its official budgets, perhaps substantially, every year.

Since there is no discussion of the size of the debt or debts, it is impossible to assess the significance of this problem or its influence on China's actual defense budget. However, this begs the question: If strategic investments by military-run businesses, for example, turn out to be foolish from a financial perspective, yielding losses rather than projected profits, how is this calculated? While many military businesses and factories have been closed or reorganized (and now all of them may be closed or transferred to civilian bureaus), there are no reported bankruptcies among military businesses. There is no evidence on who bails out businesses or failing factories; how the bailout is budgeted; or when, if ever, de facto bankruptcies appear on balance sheets.

Losses resulting from inflation or unplanned cutoffs of subsidies; cost overruns on military exercises such as the expensive exercises in the Taiwan Strait in the spring of 1996; or unplanned repairs on collapsing facilities may also comprise what is referred to blandly as "military debts."[28] If so, cost overruns, especially in years of high inflation, may be substantial, and this is an item that is rarely included in any estimates, official or independent, of the Chinese defense budget.

From 1991, the Central Military Commission and General Staff worked to reform the financial management of national defense to place it in some legal framework. One of the primary problems they hoped to address was the need for "legalization" of the national defense debt.[29]

It is probably justified that vast industrial organizations formerly controlled by the military are not currently listed as part of the defense budget. Again, after 1985, after major changes in strategic thinking on national defense construction, the management of the nuclear industry, the aircraft industry, ordnance, and aeronautics industries (formerly the Second, Third, Fifth, and Seventh Bureaus of Industrial Machinery) ceased to be controlled by the PLA and fell under the direction of the State Council.[30] Most of their production now comprises civilian goods sold to civilian customers. On the other hand, research, production, and development for defense contracts is carried out in these bodies, on government contract, for military use. Because these organizations are now controlled by the State Council, it would be very easy for China to list a host of defense-related expenses as part of the State Council budget—if authorities chose to list them at all.

In addition to the national defense industrial ministries mentioned above, subsidized research, raw materials, production, and services are probably provided to the military by so-called "base industries" (*jichu gongye*—meaning energy, mechanics, chemistry, forestry, construction), and other more distant industries in which the military participates (transportation, post, and telegraph). As more of these industries are controlled more and more by market forces, planners may find that defense budgets will need to be further augmented merely to pay for what was once subsidized (e.g. energy, free transportation to and from posts).[31]

Yet how much money is spent, for example, on research for nuclear weaponry and China's Second Artillery (missile) force? How is the money spent? What percentage of the bill is hidden in budgets for, say, the State Council's defense-related bureaus? The more secretive the budget, the more difficult it is to make claims based upon any official source that is not at the highest level of classification. China's nuclear weaponry and missile technology provide China with a comparatively cheap deterrent against attack by any power, no matter how great. But while these technologies are probably cheaper for China than advanced conventional forces, they are not free. China must have sunk a great deal of money into nuclear ordnance and missiles to produce prototypes and manufactured models in these fields—models that are more advanced than China's usual class of weaponry.

Many independent analysts employing itemized lists like those above conclude that the official defense budget does not cover the costs of *any* research and development of new weapons and equipment, except perhaps that which is carried out directly by the PLA's offices and institutes.[32] Until recently, COSTIND was the main unit filtering money from the Ministry of Finance to defense industries and bureaus (again, bureaus not listed as part of the military budget). As it was controlled in large part by the State Council, its budget was almost certainly not listed as part of the military budget. With the creation of the GAD as one of four military general headquarters (see also chapter two), it is not clear if the budget will now be calculated differently.

The Chinese government has repeatedly stated that arms imports are part of the defense budget, but the evidence makes these claims doubtful. During years of higher-than-average imports of high-budget items, there are no changes on official defense budgets or budget trends. For example, according to the Interfax News Agency, Russia supplied nearly $2 billion worth of Su-27 fighter-interceptors and S-300 PMU1 anti-aircraft missile systems from 1991 to 1993. In 1994, Russia and China signed an agreement on supplies of nearly $500 million worth of S-300 PMU systems and reached an understanding on the supply of four Russian submarines. They agreed in 1995 that Russia would supply 22 more Su-27 jets for a total of nearly $710 million. For $410 million, the same contract allowed China to domestically manufacture Su-27 SK jets. Russia would assist in an assembly line scheduled to produce 15 Su-27s a year. A total of 200 jets will supposedly be built before 2015. Russia has also signed a contract with China on the delivery of short-range Tor-M1 anti-aircraft systems. In February 1997, Russia signed another contract with China to supply Sovremeny class destroyers and Ka-27 and Ka-28 naval helicopters. Russia is also engaged in talks on the installation of anti-aircraft missile systems and advanced radar systems for Chinese naval vessels.[33] The Interfax News agency notes a "slowing down" of military deals with China in the mid-1990s, but suggests that Russia is trying to increase them. From the Russian perspective, the problem is that China is reluctant to pay the market price for the goods.[34] Still, at even somewhat-below-average market prices, the Su-27 fighters especially should have caused large defense budget increases, all other factors being equal. But there is no evidence that these big-ticket items influenced official spending claims.

Local militias, civil defense reserves, and the People's Armed Police (PAP) annual budgets also appear to fall outside the official defense budget. It is difficult to know how expensive these organizations could be, yet some of them are truly massive. For example, a book published by China's National Defense University on China's military reserves states that theoretically, according to China's "Law of Military Service" (*bingshefa*), all males between the ages of 18 and 35—around 150 million people, roughly the population of Japan—are supposed to qualify as reservists who could be called up in the event of war. Within this number, by around 1990, China had perhaps 800,000 retired soldiers still under 35 who could qualify as a reserve force of possible, genuine value to the military. Yet this same source states, without providing any numbers, that while the reserve force in China is 20 times the size of that of the United States, China spends on its reserves only 2 percent what the United States spends.[35] It is impossible to verify this statistic, but obviously if China really spends anything close to 1,000 times less per reservist than the United States (20 divided by 2 percent), it must not be buying the same product. Training and retraining, in particular, must be virtually nonexistent.

The People's Armed Police—staffed by several hundred thousand more employees who are assigned border and capital guard duties—may be of some importance in China's strategy if the nation were ever required to defend the capital, or some outlying minority regions, from domestic or foreign attack. Yet again, it is nearly impossible to put a price tag on the cost of this bloated but poorly equipped organization.[36]

Regardless of their cost, the contributions of reserves, the PAP, and local militias to the defense of China would be minimal against a technically competent and well-equipped opponent. The employees of these organizations would be even more useless in an offensive attack waged by China. Hence, even if we struggle to include these organizations as items in the Chinese defense budget, we can conclude that as defense outlays they may suggest weakness more than strength. They burden the government with added, bloated, socialistic payrolls and bureaucracies and represent part of the Maoist heritage of People's War that Chinese reformers have been trying to shake off.

Extra-Budgetary Revenue

Military analysts study the Chinese army's extra-budgetary revenue to assess whether there are pools of extra funds lying around for defense outlays outside the official defense budgets. Since 1984, China has been struggling not only to make military bureaucracies more efficient, but even, in some cases, to make them profitable.

The most obvious source of extra-budgetary revenue for the Chinese military, and the one listed most frequently in independent analyses of China's defense budget, is arms sales. Yet Chinese arms sales appear to have declined in the late 1980s, and they may not have recovered in the 1990s. The International Institute of Strategic Studies provides estimates for the cash value of Chinese arms sales in table 4.2.

During these years, the United States, the Soviet Union/Russia, the UK, and France were all bigger players in the international arms trade, and in 1991, China was also passed by Germany to place sixth on the world charts.[38] Also, while the General Staff, General Politics, and General Logistics bureaus all control businesses that sell arms, the majority of Chinese arms merchants, including the biggest one—the Northern Industrial Corporation (NORINCO)—are not directly controlled by the military.[39]

Problems for Chinese sales include the demise of the Soviet Union, after which Russia flooded the market with higher quality weaponry; the completion of the Iran-Iraq War, which was profitable for China; and a

Table 4.2 China's Arms Sales[37] (in constant, 1995 U.S. dollars)

Year	Value, in millions	Percentage of world arms exports
1987	2,460	2.9
1988	3,750	4.9
1989	3,240	4.7
1990	2,300	3.8
1991	1,550	3.6
1992	1,180	3.3
1993	1,150	3.2
1994	740	2.3
1995	630	1.7
1996	584	1.5

growing technological gap between Chinese arms and what Western armies are willing to sell at the end of the Cold War.[40]

In all, in an article published in 1996, Paul Godwin estimated the maximum value of all Chinese arms sales (including those not controlled by the PLA) at around U.S. $1.5 billion annually.[41] Clearly, if this is the total value of all sales, the army, as only one important player, would receive only a percentage of the revenue and would earn far less than that sum, directly, in profits. Shaoguang Wang estimates that the profits that directly accrue to the PLA might be as low as U.S. $40 million annually.[42]

Another source of funding for China's army is its military businesses that produce civilian goods. It is the conclusion of this author that these businesses always lost more money than they made. Further, their profits have rarely channeled back into investments that from a national security perspective could be considered strategic. More details on these businesses can be found in the previous chapter, but the discussion can close here with the conclusions found in one military source, which suggest that true competition for civilian-use products on the market requires technology, skills, and capital resources. These are not always present in military-run industrial units; the military's technological industrial enterprises are moving into the market slowly; the capital is not flowing for them to invest. Thus, "many work units are presently receiving definite pressure."[43] It is no surprise that Jiang Zemin is working to close these units.

A final source of funding is military-run farms. Thirty percent of military region and military unit budgets are supposed to be funded by the military regions themselves, through farms and enterprises run by soldiers or their dependents. In recent years, 60 percent of all army companies supposedly raise 70 percent of their own meat and vegetables.[44] Still, the Xinhua news agency in 1994 listed the total profits from the PLA's 600 farms in 1993 at 700 million yuan (or around U.S. $85 million).[45] If this statistic is accurate, then farming is not a particularly big business. Either way, if too many hours of a soldiers' day are wasted in the fields, rather than in training or on tours of duty, these farms would only decrease, rather than increase, China's fighting power.

This section concludes with the lamentations of a military analyst who analyzes "revenue outside the [military] budget" (*yusuanwai shouru*). He asserts that aside from a small portion that might go toward paying living allowances and welfare of employees of work units, much of the budget is not returned to military or central planning organizations to pay off debts or to carry out any national plan.[46] It is unlikely that many military bureaucracies are profitable, and those that are have probably succeeded specifically because they have broken from the control of central planners. This means that they re-channel their revenues not into a "grand strategy," but rather into their own isolated, petty businesses and factories, with profit as the primary, or perhaps exclusive, concern. While the military controls a handful of large businesses producing civilian goods (e.g., Triple Nine), it should be reemphasized that the majority of its businesses are tiny and technically backward.

IV. Recent Spending Trends:
Toward a Modernized Force Structure?

For China's army to achieve "First World" military capabilities and a sharper focus on international security concerns, it would require not only a larger economic base and (eventually) increases in defense funding but more importantly a major shift in priorities. On a strategic level, Chinese analysts appear especially concerned that much of the military budget is wasted on masses of poorly trained, unnecessary soldiers, who would simply be mowed down or isolated far from any battlefield if deployed against a force employing up-to-date high-tech weaponry. On a managerial level, Deng Xiaoping hoped for the reform of military economics, primarily moving from a wasteful system—criticized as excessively reliant on Soviet models—to a more market-oriented system that, during peacetime, would emphasize the production of civilian-use goods.[47] Some marketization has occurred, and some dual-use technology has been developed. However, military strategists are surprisingly open in their complaints about the extent to which many managerial reforms have succeeded in practice.

Strategy and Defense Expenditure

Arguments on the strategic need for troop cuts complement arguments about the economic and budgetary need for troop cuts. A quotation from a 1975 military proclamation promoted by Deng Xiaoping, entitled "The Military Must Be Rectified" (*jundui yao zhengdun*), states: "The number of soldiers has greatly increased, so the military expenditures are now greater in the national budget, and a great deal of the money simply goes to paying for food and staple products."[48]

In the discussions over troop size since 1985, the cutting of one million soldiers or more has been specifically tied to the desire to invest in "new scientific and technological improvements in military weaponry and ordnance,"[49] and it must have provided at least a modicum of new funds for this purpose. However, the still-bloated size of China's army, more than any strategic concern, is probably the single most important reason that defense spending cuts could not be sustained, and were reversed, in the late 1980s.

The most important problem in military circles cited in Chinese sources by the late 1980s was one of remuneration. While the national economy and living standards rose throughout the 1980s, living standards may have fallen for army employees. Inflation for all retail prices from 1979 to 1991 exceeded 100 percent. It is difficult to obtain information on exactly how this affected the military and military living conditions, due both to secrecy and the large number of goods that the military produced and purchased at nonmarket prices. One source suggests that the nominal, total inflation rate for military expenditures between 1979 and 1991 may have been something like 60 percent.[50] While it is difficult to know how this compares with increases or decreases in the actual (as opposed to official) defense budget, numerous sources, including those prepared only for internal circulation, claim that the living standards of soldiers and civilian workers employed by the army declined in real terms in the late 1980s. Even with around one-fourth of the troops supposedly cut in the second half of the 1980s—providing more money per soldier-employee—it is therefore likely that living standards really did decline for the average soldier in the 1980s, and especially between 1987 and 1989.

The decline may have been precipitous for those stationed in large cities, where the inflation was highest. Further, the salaries of officers in particular appear to have declined, at least in comparative terms. One article states that in 1985 military cadres' salaries were approximately 20 percent higher than those for local officials. Now, although local civilian officials hold lower administrative ranks (as local rather than national cadres), their salaries are rising much more quickly with the increased wealth of some local governments.[51]

Housing and benefits for military personnel may also have deteriorated. One internal circulation article claims that while housing investments in state-owned industry increased 2.5 times from 1981 to 1991, investment in the construction of military housing from 1979 to 1993 remained unchanged.[52]

Meanwhile, in order to ensure that civilian support personnel are technically qualified, the military bill for civilian employees may be increasing even if the number of these employees is decreasing. Without specifying the source of its statistic or exactly what it is supposed to include, a *PLA Daily* article on logistic support services suggests a bill for salaries of *civilians* employed directly by the military. "Military organs or undertakings at all levels still employ hundreds of thousands of staff and workers at the moment and have to pay some 3-4 billion yuan to these personnel every year as living expenses, or even more with housing, medical, or welfare benefits factored in."[53]

Another internal circulation only source published in 1990 by China's National Defense University provides the most definitive explanation of why it has been difficult for the army to alleviate the burden of soldiers' salaries and living expenses from expense accounts:

1. Inflation hit staple products harder than it did some other items bought and sold by the military; hence, cost of living adjustments to compensate for inflation wiped out much of the savings made from restructuring army production and reducing army size.
2. While more soldiers "left retirement" to pursue second jobs and contribute to military and nonmilitary production, the burden of retired soldiers on military expenses was high and growing.
3. While military budgets remained low, the expense of paying for soldiers and their families—maintaining primary schools for their children and so forth—increased or remained quite high, apparently due to higher standard of living expectations.
4. While the number of soldiers was reduced, there was a somewhat greater reliance on a volunteer force and on cadres with technical expertise and training. As the quality of the force improved, so did its cost per soldier.[54]

A new ruling in 1993 suggests a possible result of the decline in living expenses. That year, China ordered all male residents of Beijing aged 18 to 21 to register for military service, curbing its tradition of voluntary registration. Apparently, young people today are more preoccupied with education and commercial jobs, and the change demonstrates the difficulty that the military has attracting capable people.[55]

One cannot assume, therefore, that a change in defense spending trends in the late 1980s represented a change in China's strategy or international security goals. The larger budgets were designed in large part to correct imbalances that permitted military employees of every rank to be paid comparatively less. At the very least, it is clear that lower-ranking officers and soldiers were informed that the defense spending increases resulted not from any new strategic design but rather from the need "to make up for, or partly make up for inflation."[56] It is also clear that vast quantities of new funds in the early 1990s were indeed quickly siphoned off to improve salaries and to feed and house millions of military employees and retirees. Again, this suggests the military, de facto, pursued an unreformist policy: "First secure a living, second secure equipment" (*yibao shenghuo, arbao zhuangbei*).[57]

Many internal sources do accept the need for more cuts, but in the short term, even the decommissioning of staff will not be free. As of July 1998, China is developing a "social security system" for armed servicemen.[58] The costs that will result from this nascent insurance scheme for the army are as yet unknown.

Improvements in China's military technology and particularly in its weaponry are regarded as of critical strategic and tactical importance, as are related increases in research and development. In 1988, Deng stated, "The next century is the century of high scientific and technological development."[59] In addition to securing more money for living expenses, defense-spending increases in the 1990s did permit more procurement of airplanes and ships, and it permitted further investments in strategic missile forces and staff. These increases are described as "continuously useful to the stability of the armed forces."[60]

And if military lobbyists have their way, of the money spent on development, more will go to weapons research and prototype development, with comparatively less to mass manufacturing and weapons procurement. Purchases of weapons are said to have risen from 7.5 percent of the official military budget in 1950 to 33 percent in 1970,[61] yet advocates of this reform would apparently stop or reverse the trend, if it has not already reversed, to allow China to pay for generational advances.

Funding for research institutes throughout China, including those run by the military, also appears to have increased, and it is clear that China struggled to raise the amount of money spent on military research in the first decade of reform.[62] Some sources claim that research funds for defense industrial projects also increased in the early 1990s.[63]

Yet without reliable statistics, it is impossible to monitor the extent to which the proposed shift from manufacturing to research has been achieved in practice. On the one hand, recent changes in expenditure away from manufacturing and procurement appear to have made the National Defense Ministry of Ordnance Industries less profitable than some other national defense industrial bureaus. This ministry is said to suffer from cuts in orders, and it has been slower than other bureaus in making up for the loss with civilian contracts. The problems of this bureau and other changes noted here suggest a shift away from procurement.

Yet this does not necessarily imply a significant shift toward research and development. Moreover, much of the research and development carried out by Chinese defense organizations is not of a very strategic nature, even when it involves the ordnance industrial ministries. So-called strategic investments frequently focus primarily on economic objectives, including civilian product development. Strategic objectives include, for example, the possibility of dual-use production development that would allow military spending and economic growth to be complimentary.[64]

In addition, if research really comes at the expense of production and procurement, this obviously has important opportunity costs. While the PLA wishes to reduce maintenance costs that are regarded as excessive, if procurement is limited, it must maintain outdated ordnance. Currently, the army is said to be forced to adopt an adage to describe the excessively long active life of its equipment: Before the equipment is truly regarded as defunct, it must be "new for ten years; old for ten years; repaired and patched up for another ten years."[65] If China wishes to waste less time and money repairing old systems, it must eventually not only research but also build new ones.

In any case, outside analysts of China's military research and development question whether the budget is sufficient to fund significant modernization. Two Western analysts estimate China's total research and development budget annually at around U.S. $2 billion, and conclude: "Given the poor state of Chinese defense R&D overall, this support amounts to little significant investment in the long-term health of the sector. The increasingly costly nature of advanced military R&D further limits the potential impact of these investments. . . . The PRC's defense R&D base is deficient in several areas of technology considered to be on the cutting-edge of weapons development, including microelectronics, computers, avionics, sensors and seekers, electronic warfare, and advanced materials. In many disciplines, Chinese technological development has stagnated."[66]

Some Chinese analyses essentially concur with this assessment. The 14th central committee's five year plan and its 2010 long-term goals emphasized defense modernization focused on high technology, yet one source suggests that this effort has so far been compromised by social commitments—such as paying for a large workforce, schools, hospitals, and pensions—that have nothing to do with military modernization.[67]

Beyond correcting for inflation, some sources suggest that early 1990s budgetary increases were designed to promote China's strategic capacity to fight regional wars under high-tech conditions, and they did help to pay for new (but unspecified) air and sea power procurements that would advance this goal.[68] One military source echoes others when it promotes more development of coastal regions, and more autonomy for individual coastal regions, in order to develop both the economies and the level of talent required in a regional war under high-tech conditions. Specifically, it promotes more development of high-tech capacity and weapons capacity in coastal regions; more development of civil-military relations and exchanges of products to promote strength in these regions; and more development of experts with technical skills in these regions in order to modernize the forces. A concentration of research and development in major cities, along the lines of the economic reform program generally, would help to promote military modernization.[69]

Military sources also advocate improving the situation in "poorer outlying regions" (*jianku bianyuan diqu*).[70] The recommendation on minority regions is in part to make forces stationed there more specialized and capable in the rough terrain, but in large part simply to improve living standards of soldiers in comparatively poor regions and harsh climates.

Finally, to fight regional wars, China is also increasing the proportion of resources devoted to air and naval forces.[71] Yet again, it is not clear to what extent apparently increased funds for naval and air force modernization have genuinely increased China's capacity to fight the kinds of regional battles it could face in the foreseeable future. Some Mainland analysts, lobbying for more money, argue that the increased funds of the 1990s, while necessary, have not yet resulted in substantially improved fighting capacity for China's navy or air force. Some of China's disputed Spratly Island claims, for example, encompass uninhabitable reefs hundreds of miles from the Chinese coastline in the South China Sea. In internal circulation only documents, China's self-assessment of its naval forces is that they still primarily comprise small vessels, with limited capacity far from the Mainland.[72] In general terms, many open sources claim that the power and responsibilities of the Chinese navy despite increased budgets, are not up to the task of protecting China's great seas and coastlines.[73] Meanwhile, closed sources decry the airforce as even weaker.[74]

Managerial Changes and Defense Expenditure

Some managerial changes during the reform period have improved the efficiency and strategic value of military expenditures. However, managerial problems in defense ministries have led to severe problems of budgetary mismanagement, highlighted in many open and closed Mainland sources.

One highly significant change under reform is the decentralization of budgetary authority. This change has been promoted both to improve management and to increase China's ability to fight regional, high-tech wars. In 1978, the CMC issued a "Decision on the Rectification and Support of National Defense Financial Work," which decentralized the financial management of many departments. In 1985 the military promoted the slogan "united leadership, separate work responsibility" (*tongyi lingdao yu fengong zeren xiang jeihe*) designed to push the decentralization effort further.[75] Now vocational work departments have more ability to spend on investments, including profit-making ones, that they feel are most justified in their units; and lower-level finance departments are increasingly responsible for accounting and financial supervision at their level.

Managerial decentralization of budgets appears to be increasing in recent years. In 1991, the decision was made to further push separate work management and the dual-track system where vocational departments and finance departments at each level receive more responsibility over the allocation of resources.[76] One source suggests that the 14th Central Committee meeting in particular promoted "regional pluralization" (*duoyuanhua*) in the armed forces. This involves both the "decentralized" (*fensanxing*) financial authority across regions, and also, to some extent, decentralized strategic investment decisions, where mountainous regions, desert regions, and regions with extensive coastlines would have more power to assess their logistic needs and manage them.[77]

According to one source, further changes are necessary to prepare China for regional, high-tech war. The effect of high-tech war on economic planning relates first to the speed with which a high-tech war will begin and progress. The highest technology adds to the element of surprise, and it also means that a war can break out or develop rapidly across a wide span of territory. The economic implication is that resources must be ready in advance and must be mobile, so that they can be distributed when and where they may be quickly needed. A second effect is that the resources, including human resources, should emphasize quality, and this means experts in high technology and in material production matter more than ever. Third, while this kind of war may be quite expansive, it may be of a limited duration and with limited objectives. The military would therefore have to have a distribution network set in place before the battle that could be drawn on quickly. Employing the military for civilian construction in peacetime therefore makes sense as a strategic decision as well as a practical one. Should war break out, the military would have a larger production base to quickly draw upon. Fourth and finally, economic resource investments will need to be more agile and directed, but at the same time they cannot be aimed at just one area or element of war, as conflicts may be quite encompassing and may change rapidly.[78]

To promote China's high-tech capabilities, the military also must accept a regionalism that pays particular attention to the defense needs of coastal areas that are central to Chinese production. This is the very opposite of Mao Zedong's Third Line strategy, which emphasized inland areas, and because this particular conclusion is often implied but rarely stated, a long excerpt on the subject of regionalization and budgetary management is provided here:

> Regional war under high-tech conditions demands that the military economy is protected in an effective, appropriate, and timely fashion. As a result, the military resources must be distributed to the most powerful sites, where they can be most vigorously secured. The regionalization and "directionalization" of military economic resource distribution would also take into account the nation's economically uneven development. Hence, it has become suitable to put into practice the regionalization of our military economic resource redistribution system. Presently constructed military economic regions would, by means of regionalization (*quyuhua*), be rendered more effective.[79]

> Military economic regional construction should follow the special characteristics of each region's economic resources and what each would need to secure in wartime. According to our nation's economic development situation and the new era in the strategic direction of military sciences and responsibilities, we can push for northeast, northwest, southeast, and southwest regions that would form comparatively independent military economic regions. . . . Every military economic region's resource distribution should stress its special characteristics: A northeastern economic military region's distribution of resources could stress securing the economic resources for a team of soldiers that would fight a war in the extreme cold; a northwestern economic region could stress ensuring the resources for a regional war in a high plateau and desert area; a southeast military economic region's resource distribution could stress naval war and beach landings (*dengji*); and a southwest military economic region's resource distribution would stress securing the economic [capacity] to fight a war

in high plateau and mountainous regions. Each military region would work together and come to the aid of the other, providing a comprehensive security force.[80]

Some of these conclusions are obvious and must always have been considered. One would not provide naval resources to the land-locked northwest. Yet the evidence on China's force structure is that currently, resources are distributed somewhat evenly across regional divisions, and bureaucratic power games are more important than regional needs in determining how money is spent. It is not surprising that this analyst would abandon such a model and push China further toward diversification and decentralization. The emphasis on naval war and beach landings for a southeastern region is particularly interesting, and has implications for the maintenance of China's claims on the Spratly Islands and Taiwan.[81]

In addition to regionalization, recent management reforms in the 1990s, especially after decisions at the 14th Central Committee meeting, have increased the focus on marketization. Under Jiang Zemin's stewardship, China appears to be searching more earnestly for "a system of national defense expenditures under socialist market conditions" with an emphasis on the word "market." This means an increased effort to define "rights of ownership" (*suoyou quan*) at lower levels and (at least until 1998) to enhance "the profit motive" (*liyi zhuti*) in military industrial enterprises and factories.[82]

One authoritative book on China's national defense economics suggests that the combination of personnel reforms and marketization experiments has made national defense industries much more efficient.[83] Another claims that by the 1990s, joint civil-military national defense construction, civilian spinoffs, and more effective management have made possible capital investment savings of 40 percent or more.[84]

Increased efficiency and cost savings, if genuine, may permit the military to receive much more with each yuan spent.[85] Yet while most Mainland sources are naturally positive toward the successes of China's logistic and management reforms, it is difficult to get more concrete statistical information on whether any of the reforms have dramatically enhanced the quality of management over forces or weapons development. And Mainland authors working for the military themselves provide surprisingly frequent, scathing assessments of the army's financial management after formulaic praise for improvements in the reform era.

Deng Xiaoping's effort to enhance quality over quantity and research over development and procurement is indeed a shrewd shift in focus, and worthy of the praise it has attracted from Mainland analysts. Still, some sources admit that moving on the road toward quality is not the same as arriving there. According to one source, China still has a long way to go and is struggling to improve quality for four reasons with budgetary implications: (1) The emphasis is still on "living standards first, equipment second" (*yibao shenghuo, arbao zhuangbei*). (2) Capital is wasted on the maintenance or replacement of old and backward ordnance and equipment and old installations that are "dragging back the hind legs of defense modernization." (3) Many parts of the army have been left far behind in the effort to improve technology, mobility, or warfighting, with little money or time spent on modernization of many units. (4) Extensive army work in "unemphasized directions and regions" (most likely meaning landlocked, poorer areas) hinders the creation of an appropriate overall layout for army production.[86]

And after hailing the reforms of the 14th Central Committee as positive and significant, one military analyst suggests at the same time that many of the results of the recent pluralization effort have been negative: Decentralization, for example, implies some loss of central control over budgets, great irregularities in the methodology of budgetary allocation, and other problems that cut into Jiang Zemin's stated goal, as chairman of the Central Military Commission, to promote centralized command and "security power."[87]

Another analyst focusing on the distribution of military expenditures registers complaints that largely focus on the problems of decentralization. Methods are by no means standardized across regions and localities; the old system has a clear influence on the reformed system, with overlapping, excessive, and ineffective organizational links between central and lower authorities; and military expenditure distribution standards are weak in many respects. China is slow in its response to emergencies, because stability of allocation across regions and bureaus is the central attribute of military expenditure. Budgets do not properly account for developmental and inflationary imbalances across regions, rendering some regions comparatively poor and others richer, for no strategic reason. There is inordinate complexity in the distribution of military expenditures, and the distribution of funds, generally, is said to be "insufficiently fair."[88]

While there is an almost total censorship of the empirical evidence for the conclusions of another article on army financial management,[89] the point of the article is apparently to oppose further decentralization: Only through increased centralization—the opposite of current budgetary reforms—can China create a unified picture of procurement and development strategies; limit corruption; and neutralize the narrow focus on the personal interests of office managers heading sub-sections of every corner of the armed forces. If the military does not want budgetary "leaks" and "loopholes" (*loudong*) to dig a giant "cavity" (*da kulong*) in military finances, through waste and corruption, some unity of authority is regarded as essential.[90]

Four other analysts from the General Logistics Department highlight related problems. The military still has three primary financial systems rather than one, leading to disjointed leadership and management: The General Logistics financial system (*zonghou caiwu xitong*), the General Staff equipment financial structure (*zongcan zhuangbei caiwu xitong*), and the enterprise production financial structure (*shengchan jingying caiwu xitong*). Next, there are separate systems within each branch of the armed forces: The air force has its own three large financial systems; there are separate systems for construction enterprises, research, aviation, and so forth. Then each military region has its own logistic financing department, and these regional offices suffer from particularly poor regulation of finances, according to this source. In addition, there are separate financial structures to manage real estate and other issues. Finally, outside the budget, the military enterprises operate with their own independent policies on financial expenditure.[91]

This source continues its eye-opening laundry list of legal and administrative woes:

> Presently, the General Logistics Finance Department serves as the head financial management office reporting to the Central Committee; yet it organizes its work on the annual defense budget without law, even without any powerful macroeconomic regulation, supervision, or management. The result of this is that, first, it weakens the capacity to regulate national defense expenditure on a macro-level, crating contradictions. Second, some departments and work units, using their own financial rights and powers, do several things that they shouldn't do—buying several things they shouldn't buy—lowering the effectiveness of any efforts to straighten out the process.[92]

New rules have been issued to govern financial management, yet they are usually "decisions" (*jueding*), "regulations" or "stipulations" (*tiaoli*), not "laws" (*fa*). This weakens their force. This source and others mention a "Decision on Improving and Promoting Army Financial Management" (*guanyu gaijin he jiaqiang jundui caiwu guanli de jueding*) that was passed in 1991; but this again was not a law.[93] In some respects this decision also may have complicated administrative structures rather than simplifying or improving them.[94]

Another primary problem with the implementation of many reform goals on budgets and marketization is a severe lack of capital. How can one carry out defense conversion, for example, at a time when the military is struggling to cut support for outdated units? Other problems, such as weaknesses in management and structure, are said to be closely tied to the question of funds. Better trained managers and more modern plants require capital.[95]

On the marketization effort, one article makes the point that the military's capacity to develop real market price indices is weak, due to its "independent, sealed off, special" environment, in which the majority of the accounting ledger still consists of government-funded consumption.[96] Generally, marketization is not the same, and may not be as successful in the long run, as privatization. In any case, some problems with the analysis of Chinese military budgets clearly stem from China's own problems in monitoring military cash flow.

It is not surprising that regulatory structures, weak throughout China, are particularly powerless when combating mismanagement or corruption in the military, a particularly powerful, secretive, and complex bureaucracy. To reform the system, the four analysts from the General Logistics Department quoted above would continue the decentralization of financial authority, yet also enhance macroeconomic regulation of the entire structure. Specifically, they suggest that enhanced regulatory authority should be given to the CMC Financial Management Department (*zhongyang junwei licai bumen*).[97] Yet even with continued efforts at reform, regulation of the military is likely to be weak for decades.

Perhaps it is fair to blame the mismanagement of defense economics at the most general level, on 40 years of Soviet influence. Two Mainland analysts would do exactly that, and further argue that Soviet-style mismanagement can only be corrected through a transformation combining enhanced market socialism with increased reliance on law. Unfortunately, no predictions are made as to how long such a transformation might take.[98]

V. Future Directions

The future direction of China's defense funding and defense financial management depends primarily upon political will. Most defense analysts are in agreement about the problems, but even in the 1980s and the first half of the 1990s, with Deng Xiaoping firmly in charge, solutions were slow in coming. Now, with a military outsider, Jiang Zemin, at the helm, it is not clear that China will have the internal political will to throw off the legacy of excessive force size, backward technology, and socialistic management.

Chinese propaganda sources such as the New China News Agency seek to present Chinese military spending as tiny by the standards of great powers, and representative of the minimal needs of a large developing nation. The truth is more complex. Defense spending is not as low as China pretends, and more importantly, it is by no means representative of China's needs: A good deal of the money is wasted.

One can sum up the discussion with the recommendations of one internal circulation only source cited above, which discusses a broad "Strategy to Rectify the Structure of Our Nation's Defense Expenditures": Resources must be shifted from staff and maintenance into a third, critical category of expenditures, labeled simply "development." Money must be taken from ground forces and poured into the navy and airforce. The military needs more funds for technological research and development, and less for the immediate production and procurement of large quantities of outdated hardware. And finally, with respect to ordnance as well as manpower, quality and technological modernization must take precedence over quantity and production for the sake of production.[99]

Yet will these goals be achieved? Defense funding increases in the early 1990s were accompanied by moderate shifts in focus, but without far more radical strategic and managerial changes, in Paul Godwin's words, the Chinese armed forces may be "condemned to prolonged and indefinite modernization."[100]

CONCLUSION

China and the Balance of Power in the Asia-Pacific Region

China's leaders hope to jettison archaic military conceptions, and new strategic priorities are indeed reforms. Still, this study emphasizes that China's overhaul of its armed forces has a long way to go. Its new strategy is neither strikingly original nor fully implemented. China's force structure, meanwhile, is dragged down by a Maoist legacy of obtrusive overstaffing. The problem of army surplus particularly plagues the land forces, but the entire PLA is suffering from the same disease. Organizationally and financially, China's military faces parallel problems of irrational management, hidden deficiencies, deficits, and waste.

The cynic would say: It is one thing to draw conclusions on China's currently incomplete hegemonic capabilities from the relative safety of the ivory towers of Europe or America, but have China's next-door neighbors drawn the same sanguine conclusions? Or instead, are China's neighbors rapidly arming themselves to counter a perceived threat—perhaps justified—from the world's most populous nation and the world's largest army?

This conclusion takes a comparative look around the region to see what has driven security doctrine and military force modernization elsewhere in East, South, and Southeast Asia. A review of the security policies and military modernization efforts of regional forces demonstrates that many regional leaders indeed look toward China with a somewhat wary eye. On the other hand, they rarely regard China as a significant, immediate threat to their states or their long-term objectives. Instead, when authorities look beyond their shores for potential adversaries, they rarely feel primarily threatened, or even substantially threatened, by China. China is not powerful or aggressive enough to have inspired enmity or fear. In fact, China's leadership has successfully convinced most regional authorities that its intentions under reform are primarily peaceful, and China's relations with its neighbors are probably better than they ever have been in the postwar period.

Of course, if China does not behave as a great power, neither do the leaders of other regional, developing states. Most of these leaders regard internal threats to domestic political stability as their most infernal dragons to slay. They organize their militaries accordingly.

This conclusion posits that despite limited military modernization in Mainland China, a clear balance of power has been maintained in Asia. Indeed, a comparative analysis of regional developments negates the idea that China is hegemonic or could in any way dominate its neighbors. This is first because of weaknesses in China's modernization effort, outlined above. It is second because so many of the other nations of the region, even in the current financial crisis, have themselves become more wealthy and secure with a successful, introspective focus on development. Indeed, even if China's power is increasing, the words and deeds of China's neighbors suggest that they feel *more* secure and confident vis-à-vis China than they have felt in decades.

I. Regional Overview

East Asia's much-cited arms race of the 1990s demonstrated some contradictory trends, and unusual elements of the apparent race should be highlighted briefly. It is curious, for example, that imports of fighter planes to the region actually declined from 1988 to 1993.[1] These are the years when China's military spending began to increase, when China was relatively unstable politically (just after the Tiananmen Massacre), and when regional integration efforts appeared at a temporary nadir. Despite these causes for concern, this was not a period when China's neighbors were consumed by fears of Chinese instability or power-projection.

It should also be noted that defense spending increases and decreases for East Asia as a whole are exaggerated by exchange rate fluctuations that have been dramatic in recent years. When the Japanese yen was high against the dollar, it appeared that the region as a whole was in an arms race; the collapse of Asian currencies had the opposite effect, regardless of the fact that threat perceptions and strategies may have changed only incrementally. These apparent changes in spending against the U.S. dollar tell us little about what militaries are up to domestically and why. Finally, the Asian financial crisis that spread through the region in 1997 almost surely slowed whatever race there once was.

Yet Asia did experience military spending increases in the 1990s. East Asia became the most lucrative regional market for arms exports outside the Middle East. In 1997 alone, Thailand received a small aircraft carrier from Spain, Taiwan the first batch of 150 F-16s and 60 French Mirage 2000 combat planes; Indonesia the first of 24 Hawk 109/209 advanced combat-capable trainers; Australia 33 Hawk advanced trainers; and Vietnam six Su-27s, to add to its previous supply, from Russia.[2] The total number of missiles delivered to the Asia-Pacific region increased from 1984 to 1986 and from 1989 to 1991. Over 3,000 missiles were delivered every year on average. Japan, South Korea, Indonesia, Singapore, and Thailand all have imported Harpoons, the most capable anti-ship missiles.[3] New naval vessels other than Thailand's aircraft carrier include Japan's manufactured and acquired super-modern fleet of destroyers, including American Aegis, the first of which was commissioned in 1993. China, Japan, South Korea, and Taiwan all acquired new submarines in the 1990s.[4] Indonesia, Singapore, and Thailand in the early 1990s were among the leading importers of tanks and other armored vehicles, from China, the U.S., and Germany.[5]

What accounts for the spend-fest?

China's military modernization may have convinced some of a "China threat" that needed to be answered. On the other hand, the causal relationship could have been the other way around. According to Renato Cruz de Castro, "China's naval force modernization cannot be adequately explained without looking at its regional context. . . . China's modernization program is a response to the more advanced arms modernizations being implemented by its two neighbors, Taiwan and Japan. . . . China's build-up of its naval and air forces is occurring within an emerging arms race in Northeast Asia."[6]

While China may have been provoked in part by external factors, and other nations by China, internal factors are perhaps more critical sources for the arms race. Panitan Wattanayagorn and Desmond Ball list, as "some determinants of regional acquisitions," nearly a dozen sources for regional weapons purchases in the 1990s. Factors that could all be characterized as domestic (although they are sometimes framed differently in their article) include self-reliance goals by regional government leaders, hoped-for civilian spinoffs from defense modernization, the desire to enhance national prestige, systemic corruption that permits arms transfers for personal gain, newly invigorated efforts by many nations (not just China) to lay claims on disputed sea resources, and the accessibility of comparatively cheap arms for purchase during a regional economic boom (until 1997) at the end of the Cold War.[7]

It should also be noted that discussions of an arms race tend to focus specifically on fighter planes, submarines, nuclear weapons, destroyers, and other ordnance that would be unwieldy if used for domestic control. Yet more general discussions of defense spending increases should also focus on non–arms-related purchases. The most crucial reason of all for general defense spending in Asian emerging markets may be a desire to increase control over a domestic citizenry through the threatened or actual use of force. And aside from the ordnance purchases, general increases in military spending have helped governments to build and maintain domestic bases that are staffed with comparatively large numbers of army and paramilitary troops that rarely leave home.

For a more complete picture of regional military policy and military budgets, one needs to look briefly at individual cases. To what extent do nations' actions demonstrate fears of China's emerging power? The discussion begins with an analysis of the most powerful nations in Asia and ends with a discussion of more vulnerable nations and territories.

II. Russia

While Russian defense spending is decreasing, as a former superpower, Russia has spent, and still spends, far more on "power projection" than other states with Far Eastern, Asian borders. Still, the land force (which is now primarily stationed at home) and the paramilitary forces (which largely deal with domestic problems) comprise over 80 percent of Russia's military (see table C.1).

It is clear that while some far-right nationalists in Russia would rattle sabers against a potential "yellow peril," the primary security concern of Russia is not external, nearby competitors like China, Japan, or Germany

Table C.1   Size of the Russian Armed Forces Circa 1997[8]

Army	420,000
Navy	220,000
Nuclear	149,000
Air force	130,000
Paramilitary	583,000
Total	*1,240,000*

but rather entirely internal threats of secession or revolt like Chechnya, or threats of turmoil caused by an economic meltdown. To some extent Russia also worries about threats outside of Russia but within the former Soviet Union. Many of these threats have grave implications for Russian borders or Russians abroad.

Fortunately, threats at home or within Soviet borders may be decreasing. The war in Chechnya that officially ended in August 1996 flared up again in the fall of 1999, yet the regular armed forces have seen only limited military action elsewhere (e.g., Tajikistan) in the second half of the 1990s.[9]

Meanwhile, Yeltsin recently has been uninterested in or unable to stop defense spending cuts. Defense still comprises around one-fifth of Russian government spending. Yet the federal government cannot collect the taxes required for any budget, so the amount that actually goes to the military is far less than what is earmarked.[10] July 1997 decrees announced consequent cuts in the authorized number of armed forces personnel and mergers of large bureaucracies (e.g., the Strategic Rocket Forces, Space Commands, and anti-aircraft missile units; the Air Defense Force and the Air Force). Conscription is supposed to end by the year 2005, as the Russian forces outside of Russia and in the eastern sectors are dramatically reduced.[11]

Spending on Russia's Far Eastern forces matches the general trend. Japanese intelligence suggests that Russia's Pacific Fleet has been reduced to half its 1985 size and that, given its current size and organization, its mission is defensive. Japanese analysts have also concluded that troop levels of the Far Eastern army have been reduced by 178,000 since 1992, and that the number of Russian military personnel on the Northern Islands has been reduced to 3,500 in 1995.[12]

The Russian forces are plagued by shortages of skilled manpower, desertions, and munitions and equipment depletions. Some sources conclude that Russia has lost its ability to conduct warfare beyond former Soviet territory.[13] The research and development budget has been drastically slashed, and it has become difficult to modernize weaponry. Because of these budgetary troubles, regardless of the parliament's decision on ratifying START II, Russian nuclear capabilities will probably remain at the levels indicated in the treaty until 2005.[14]

All the same, the majority of Russia's leaders recognize that they have little to fear from rising powers in the East. Russia's strategic nuclear forces in the Far East region include ICBMs, strategic bombers deployed along the Siberian railway, and nuclear submarines equipped with ballistic missiles, including Delta III-class nuclear submarines carrying SLBMs. The Russian Far East houses medium-range bombers and sea- and air-launched cruise missiles. Russia's Pacific Fleet, mainly based in Vladivostok and Petropavlovsk, consists of some 675 ships, including 60 major surface ships and about 65 submarines (45 of which are nuclear). Generally, troop levels and readiness have decreased substantially, but the ordnance and technology are still impressive, as are the quality and size of the regional forces (26 army divisions with approximately 220,000 personnel). Some forces are continuously being modernized. Oscar II class nuclear powered cruise missile attack submarines are now being deployed by the Pacific fleet, for example.[15]

Russian forces are frequently portrayed as war-weary; another way of putting this is to say that they have significant combat experience, in comparison, for example, to Chinese forces. At the time of this writing, the Russians are still fighting a war in Chechnya, and still have thousands of troops in Tajikistan despite a limited peace agreement reached in June 1997.[16] Russian forces have also been sent to Moldova and Georgia. Russia has a limited force in Armenia, and some tiny contingents of civilians and observers to support military modernization or internationally sponsored programs in Africa, Cuba, and Vietnam. Russia has been participating in UN missions in Angola, Bosnia, Croatia, Iraq/Kuwait, the Middle East, and the Western Sahara.[17]

In sum, despite growing internal weaknesses, Russia's military is not only very well equipped but also relatively experienced. Under such circumstances, what is Russia's perception of "the China threat"?

Relations with China have not been better since the 1950s. Russia and China signed a series of agreements in 1994 and 1995 that delineated the land border, reduced China's armed presence along the border, led to more exchanges of information on military activities, promoted more military technology exports from Russia, and reinforced mutual no first-use nuclear policies. Also of particular importance for regional security were the Agreement on Confidence-Building in the Military Field in Border Areas, signed in Shanghai with China in April 1996, and another agreement on conventional force reductions (between China, Russia, Kazakhstan, Kyrgyzstan and Tajikistan) signed in Moscow a year later. The first agreement limits military activity and requires multilateral observation of all significant military actions within 100 kilometers of the borders of these nations. The second agreement covers all of China's northern border with other states and requires signatories to have no more than

130,400 military personnel in an area 100 km-wide on their side of the border. The only state that at this point maintains border forces approaching this density is China. So to the extent that anyone feared Chinese northward advances, China's implementation of the terms of this document should allay their fears.[18]

Russian exports of arms increased around 60 percent between 1992 and 1997, to around U.S. $4 billion per year. This represents an increasingly important source of foreign currency for Russia, and the many important sales to China—of Russia's best ordnance—are evidence that Russia is somewhat unconcerned about the China threat.[19]

III. Japan

Japan since World War II has progressed away from militarism and the kinds of domestic problems of military interventionism that plague many developing world nations. This is evidenced by the tiny size of the forces that could in any way be compared to paramilitary forces in other states of the region (such as China's People's Armed Police or militia units). IISS puts the coast guard and some Ministry of Transportation personnel in a paramilitary category, for lack of a better one, and comes up with a paltry total of 12,000 troops, all noncombatants.[20] Japan is plagued by economic crises, but from a military perspective it appears entirely free from the problems of military professionalism in organizationally troubled, developing world autocracies like China's, or those of many younger democracies.

Meanwhile, over half of the Japanese Defense Agency's budget is occupied by maritime and air defense forces, while a minority (around 42 percent) goes to the ground self-defense forces.[21] The Japanese force resembles a standing army less than the forces of any nation in the region.

From the mid-1980s to 1997, the United States successfully dragged Japan toward more defense spending. However, these increases began as a counterweight to the Soviet Union's eastern forces, and they were never primarily in response to a perceived China threat. With the fall of the Soviet Union and the implosion of the Japanese bubble economy, Japan's 1997 defense budget was the lowest budget in U.S. dollar terms for five years. This mainly reflected exchange rate fluctuations that had previously inflated the value of Japanese programs. Still, overall, Japan's defenses remain expensive compared to those elsewhere in the region. This is because of high labor costs, comparatively high costs of development and procurement in an atmosphere of limited production and strict restrictions on exports, and higher burden sharing at U.S. bases than in many other countries hosting a U.S. presence.[22]

The Japanese land forces (the Ground Self-Defense Forces) are small but well equipped compared to others in the surrounding region (Russia's, North Korea's, China's). While they have not seen real combat since World War II, they have participated in disaster relief operations and UN peacekeeping operations abroad.[23]

Comparing Japan's navy (maritime self-defense force) to others worldwide, it is somewhat impressive numerically: Japan now has the fifth largest navy in the world,[24] staffed by 42,500 soldiers. China's navy has seven times more soldiers, but Japan's navy mans 58 surface combatants, against China's 54. Its naval technology (AEGIS ships equipped with up-to-date anti-air defense missile systems to protect territory and trade routes) also tends to be of superior caliber.[25]

Since 1983, the navy's missions have expanded:

> The major step taken by Prime Minister Nakasone regarding defense policy involved Japan taking an active role in the Japan-U.S. alliance. In concrete terms, the United States had asked Japan since 1983 to assume primary responsibility for three sectors of defense in Japan's adjacent waters: control of the seas south to the Philippines and Guam; the ability to mine and blockade the passages from the Sea of Japan to the Pacific Ocean; and the building of an air defense screen across the Japanese islands to interdict Soviet aircraft. In response to these, Nakasone took steps to alter Japan's essentially passive security policy. The Nakasone years were marked by the extension of Japan's maritime defense zone from 200 to 1,000 nautical miles southeast of Honshu, joint U.S.-Japan planning on sea lines of communication (SLOCs) defense, and the participation of Japan's Maritime Self-Defense Force (MSDF) in RIMPAC exercises with the U.S. Navy. Nakasone also scrapped the post-1976 policy of limiting the nation's defense expenditures to less than one percent of gross national product (GNP).[26]

The Japanese air force (air self-defense force) employs only 44,100 soldiers, ten times fewer than China's air force. Still, its 368 combat aircraft could pack a very mean punch. Japan's technological edge in aeronautics is impressive. It has early warning radars and AWACs, F-1s, F-15s, F-16s, jointly developed FS-X fighters based on the F-16, and other modern American or American-designed military planes. And since 1981, the mission of the Japanese air force also has grown. "U.S. requests for Japan to deploy refueling aircraft and over-the-horizon radars in order to protect sea lanes to a distance of 1,000 kilometers were initially rebuffed by the Japanese government as potentially offensive, but finally accepted in 1981."[27]

Unlike some Western countries that invest 5–15 percent of their national defense expenditures on research and development (R&D), Japan invested only 3 percent on R&D in the mid-1990s.[28] Yet Japan's unparalleled manufacturing base would obviously be a plus if it decided a build-up, or a more active defense, was for any reason necessary. A Japanese defense White Paper states that tanks deployed by Japan are manufactured by over 1,000 companies.[29] The coordination effort for such complex ordnance could be handled as successfully in Japan as in any country in the world, and much more successfully than in China. Also, the reason Japan manages to limit spending on research somewhat is its continued close security relations with the U.S. after the Cold War. Further, while Japanese research budgets are not very high in percentage terms, they increased in the late 1980s and 1990s, and they are comparatively impressive: "Two decades after launching its 1976 National Defense Program Outline (NDPO), Japan has emerged as one of the major investors in military R&D and now spends more than any other non-nuclear weapon state except Germany."[30]

Why does Japan maintain a powerful deterrent, complete with the most up-to-date non-nuclear ordnance, and why does the U.S.-Japanese security relationship continue to be strong, if Japan has no perceived enemies? According to Japanese government sources, "After the end of the Cold War, the Security Treaty's role to deter expansion of the East Bloc vanished. But the overall environment around Japan has not changed, making Japan's possession of an independent defense system unrealistic." In addition to protecting Japan, the U.S. alliance helps "to ensure the U.S. commitment in the Asia-Pacific region." Also: "Without the Security Treaty, Japan would need to establish an impeccable defense system on its own to cope with every form of emergency. This would mean an excessive economic burden and, above all, it would raise suspicion from the world, especially Asia."[31] This document is careful to avoid an extensive discussion of any particular threat and suggests that spending increases are designed primarily to cement a stable relationship with the United States, which lobbied strongly for the increases during the Reagan and Bush years. But what about China?

Japan and China are on rather good terms in recent years, and Japan regards China primarily as an important trading partner, not a military threat. The White Paper's summary of the military situation around Japan does not discount China as a potential adversary, but in its list of countries whose militaries warrant concern by the Japanese Defense Forces, Russia's military is listed first. China's and then North Korea's follow. According to this document, Japan sees North Korea's unstable domestic situation and its nuclear and ballistic missile development efforts as militarily the largest unstable factor in the region. With respect to China, this document suggests that the military modernization has proceeded gradually. Still, as China is struggling to secure "key points for sea operations centering on the Spratly Islands," it is said that China's naval and air modernizations should be watched closely.[32]

The relationship between China and Japan hit a temporary stumbling block during the recently re-inflamed tensions over the Senkaku Islands dispute, with nationalistic demonstrations in 1996 in Japan and, in response, through much of the Chinese-speaking world.[33] Yet overall, the potential for war between these two nations, contrary to the opinions of some quoted in the introduction to this book, is almost nonexistent in the foreseeable future. As the two nations' economies become more complementary and linked, contemporary history suggests that the thawing of limited tensions will continue.

IV. North and South Korea

North Korea's troops are forever poised for a cross-border attack on the South, and North Korea maintains a giant army by world standards. The North's million-man army (1,055,000 soldiers, 923,000 or 87 percent of whom are in the land army) would be a daunting enemy for any nation. Even superpowers are threatened by its nuclear terrorism in the 1990s. So is North Korea a great power?

Even more than the Chinese force, the North Korean army is the army of a struggling developing country: It defends a crippled economy, a pariah government, and an unstable internal situation. It is preoccupied with unresolved border disputes. It works without an alliance of any kind, and with minimal trading capacity. It relies upon a backward production base to maintain an externally threatening, but also poorly balanced, primarily land-based domestic occupation force.

Clearly, North Korea's forces have been built up largely for internal political reasons, not due to fears of an external threat. They are equipped to plough no farther than the tip of the Korean peninsula, and their primary international purpose since 1950 has been the violent reunification of Korea on terms dictated by the North.

Meanwhile, China is the closest thing North Korea has to a friend, and in terms of the security threats that the North might face, China is surprisingly far from center stage. The only real threats to the North Korean government are all internal.

South Korea's army is staffed by 672,000 active soldiers, with 560,000 (83 percent) in the land-based army.[34] South Korea's sources of military security include extensive military appropriations and preparations domestically and, internationally, the cohesive alliance with the United States. With North Korea suggesting in isolated instances that it would no longer honor the Korean Armistice Agreement, while sending heavily armed soldiers to the Joint Security Area, it is no surprise that China is not highest on South Korea's threat list.[35]

While the land force is a higher percentage of overall armed force than might be expected from a peninsular, Newly Industrialized Country (NIC) with trading interests worldwide, South Korea's security problem leads the nation to amass almost all of the military power it can muster toward the northern front line. South Korea's capital, Seoul, is seconds in a supersonic jet from the demilitarized zone.

In September, 1996, the South Korean Defense Ministry produced a confidential blueprint for a "defense build-up" toward the year 2000, which offered ways to bolster the military after an evaluation of the security situation on the Korean Peninsula. The ministry also came up with its first mid-term (through to 2002) military build-up plan. This is almost certainly being revised in light of South Korea's financial crisis, but it still is revealing of the immediate goals and perceived needs of the Korean armed force.

The mid-term project called for a 12-percent increase in the defense budget annually from 1998 to 2002. The project included the purchase of more than eight P3C anti-submarine vessels and state-of-the-art radar systems for units guarding coastal areas. Under the project, the military also was to buy two early warning control systems, build two Korean-style destroyers, and purchase multiple launchers and U.S. ground-to-ground missiles.[36] Clearly, the purchases were primarily to safeguard waters around the demilitarized zone to protect against spying, raids, and attacks. Currently, South Korea's naval forces include over 200 ships, and around 500 combat aircraft, including F-16s.[37]

The United States stopped funding foreign military sales credits to South Korea in 1987, and over the next decade South Korean R&D budgets increased over six times in real terms.[38] By the mid-1990s, South Korea became one of the 10 largest investors in military R&D, and it was one of only three states known to be planning a significant increase in its military R&D budget just before the Asian financial crisis.[39] Meanwhile, some analysts argue that South Korea's economy has reached a level where it could develop its own nuclear weapons within a year if provoked by a successful nuclear weapons program in the North or (far less likely) by aggressive moves from China.[40] For the moment, its R&D appears to revolve entirely around conventional weapons.

Many of the pivotal reasons for the original creation of the South Korean alliance have changed or are disappearing. The Soviet Union disintegrated. The ROK is no longer weak and underdeveloped. The region as a whole has experienced sustained economic and political development, creating more symmetrical relations with the U.S. Russia and China have dramatically improved relations with the ROK.[41] Still, the U.S. Second Infantry Division remains in South Korea, as does the U.S. Seventh Air Force command headquarters. The UN still maintains a presence north of Seoul.

So while South Korea's security situation is tense, South Korea would be a terribly bitter pill for North Korea, China, or any nation to try to swallow. More importantly, China is definitively not the primary security threat, or even a growing security threat. Quite the contrary: Relations with China in the 1990s have improved dramatically. China continues to conduct military exchanges with North Korea. But after recognizing South Korea in the early 1990s, China also began military exchanges with the South. Consequently, there are reported to be six (increased from just one) military attachés at the South Korean embassy in Beijing. From the Chinese side, on December 7, 1996, a military group led by Major General Luo Bin visited South Korea and met with the Defense Minister, the Chairman of the Korean Joint Chiefs of Staff, and the Defense Ministry's intelligence chief. The two nations have also arranged naval visits.[42]

In short, at the end of the Cold War, the Chinese-South Korean relationship appears to be moving onto increasingly solid ground.

V. India

India, like China, is a struggling developing nation. Its military budget is on a scale similar to that of China's (around U.S. $8–10 billion annually in recent years, not counting nuclear and aerospace research). As in China, the budget is rising slightly, with scheduled spending in 1998/99 at around 412 billion rupees, or U.S. $9.8 billion.[43] As in China, the rise is primarily for domestic reasons and reflects the rising popularity of Hindu nationalist policies and goals. The budget also is somewhat similarly organized, with a huge land-based force of around 940,000 soldiers, compared to around 54,000 in the navy and 110,000 in the air force.[44]

The land forces frequently must enforce martial law in unstable territories. India also funds diverse paramilitary forces of almost three-quarters of a million people, and their primary purpose is also to manage domestic violence on behalf of the Indian state.

Indeed, India has no fewer than 12 paramilitary organizations:

> These . . . include the Coast Guard Organization and the Defense Security Force, which are subordinate to the Ministry of Defense. Paramilitary forces subordinate to the Ministry of Home Affairs include the Assam Rifles, the Border Security Force, the Central Industrial Security Force, the Central Reserve Police Force, the Indo-Tibetan Border Police, and the Rashtriya Rifles (National Rifles). The National Security Guards, a joint antiterrorist contingency force, are charged with protection of high-level persons (the so-called very very important persons—VVIPs) and are subordinate to the Office of the Prime Minister (also sometimes known as the Prime Minister's Secretariat). The guards are composed of elements of the armed forces, the Central Reserve Police Force, and the Border Security Force. The Special Frontier Force also is subordinate to the Office of the Prime Minister. The Railway Protection Force is subordinate to the Ministry of Railways. At the local level, there is the Provincial Armed Constabulary, which is controlled by the governments of the states and territories.[45]

India also boasts a second line of defense, composed of several citizen mass organizations. These include the Territorial Army (a voluntary, part-time civilian force), the National Cadet Corps, Civil Defense Volunteers, and Home Guards.[46]

India does have the capacity to project force beyond its borders, and it is clearly the greatest power on its subcontinent. But India's internal weaknesses mean that it is unlikely to become anything more imposing than a regional power anytime soon. Its need to focus on grating domestic security problems, including the maintenance of stability in the cities and outlying borders, is crippling from the perspective of power projection. Many army units are tied down handling insurgencies in Assam, Jammu and Kashmir, and Punjab. "Increasingly frequent outbreaks of communal violence . . . have necessitated the use of the army to restore calm."[47] In Jammu and Kashmir alone, human rights groups estimate that tens of thousands of people have been killed since 1989 in fighting between Indian military and paramilitary forces and Muslim separatists. And the situation appears, if anything, to be deteriorating. India's parliament in 1994 reiterated a vow to "liberate" and annex all of Kashmir, including the one-third currently controlled by Pakistan. More recently, India's Hindu nationalist government has placed Kashmir under the control of the Home Minister L.K. Advani, a Hindu militant who appears interested in attacks on Pakistan-controlled territory to weed out rebels. Meanwhile, since the late 1980s, veteran Afghan mujahidin have received support from Pakistan's Inter-Service Intelligence to wage an insurrection in the two-thirds of Kashmir controlled by India. The region also suffers from constant border volleys of rifle-fire between Indian and Pakistani troops.[48]

India's tensions with Pakistan and its lack of any more powerful allies or sponsors limit its ability to focus on security issues outside the subcontinent. Its strained civil-military relations and problems of military professionalism add further burdens to the nation's development. In the early 1990s, the chief of army staff, General Sunith Francis Rodrigues, repeatedly expressed his misgivings about the inordinate use of the army to deal with civil problems. He feared that such actions "increased the risk of politicizing the armed forces and reduced their battle readiness."[49]

Tactically and strategically, India's military is advanced by the standards of the subcontinent but not in comparison to China or any nuclear power other than perhaps Pakistan. Even its margin of superiority over Pakistan—its principal South Asian rival—has eroded. This is because of budgetary constraints, and because the armed forces are no longer able to obtain sophisticated weaponry at subsidized prices from Russia.[50] Now that both India and Pakistan have demonstrated their nuclear capacity (with tests and controlled explosions only several days apart in May 1998), the beginnings of mutually assured destruction may ensure that India will never fully subjugate its smaller adversary through military means.

It is perhaps not surprising, given India's difficulties at home and on its northwestern border, that China rarely figures into India's most significant security calculations. Admittedly, India's Defense Minister, George Fernandes, declared in May 1998 that he saw China, not Pakistan, as India's "potential threat number one."[51] But one wonders if this quotation was intended as an insult and provocation to Pakistan the very month that both South Asian states made the decision to publicly join the nuclear club. Either way, it appears that competition between India and China is only abating over the years, partly due to the end of the Cold

War, partly due to a sufficient balance of power, and partly due to similar economic priorities in both countries.

China managed to win a brief border war against India in 1962, and thereby gained control of a beautiful but otherwise somewhat useless and almost uninhabitable slice of the Himalayas. By contrast, these days, were China ever to try to encroach further upon India with threatening policies, it would face a far more experienced and well-equipped army.

While India's overstaffed army faces the many problems outlined above, it still is equipped with nuclear weapons. And unlike China, India's army has been receiving weaponry from Russia and other nations for quite some time. During the 1970s and 1980s, India purchased a great deal of Soviet weaponry, and also aircraft, submarines, and long-range artillery pieces from France, Germany, Sweden, and Britain. Simultaneously, it continued its efforts to expand and strengthen domestic capabilities to manufacture a range of weaponry that would maximize "self-reliance."[52]

Meanwhile, China and India are increasingly willing to de-emphasize the military component in their zero-sum debates over frozen borders. In November 1996, China and India signed the Agreement on Confidence-Building Measures in the Military Field Along the Line of Actual Control in the China-India Border Areas. This provides that each side should not engage in military activities that threaten the other side or undermine peace in the border areas. Further, each side should strictly respect and observe the line of actual control, limit the size of border defense and paramilitary forces, refrain from staging military exercises in close proximity to the actual lines of control, and provide warnings of any exercises in nearby regions.[53]

In recent history, India is actually much more ready to play an interventionist role in surrounding nations than China, and while it is rarely regarded in Western writing as a rising threat in need of containment, it behaves much more like a regional great power than China does. From 1987 to 1990, it accepted an invitation to help wipe out a Tamil opposition in Sri Lanka, and in 1988, the Indian army sent troops to the Maldives. Pakistan obviously considers India to be its primary security threat, and there are constant military skirmishes between the two nations in Kashmir. Unlike China, India plays a hegemonic security role in other nations that it practically surrounds (e.g., Bangladesh and land-locked Nepal and Bhutan). India has a major naval base hundreds of miles from its continental shores, at Port Blair in the Andaman Islands south of Burma. Unlike China, it also has an aircraft carrier to enhance its blue-water naval capabilities. And in addition to India's demonstrated nuclear capability, it has a missile-firing nuclear-powered submarine that it designed (based on Soviet models) at home.[54]

Finally, India has played a much larger role in UN-led peacekeeping operations than China has, and this has provided its troops with international experiences that Chinese troops lack. During the Cold War, India sent troops to the Middle East to diffuse Israeli-Egyptian tensions in a UN-led mission from 1956 to 1967 (at one time constituting the second-largest force in the mission), and it played a pivotal role in the UN's Congo Operation (ONUC) from 1960 to 1964 (providing one-quarter of the UN's manpower). Since the Cold War, India has provided military observers to UN missions in Iran/Iraq (1988 to 1990), Iraq/Kuwait (1991), Namibia (1989 to 1990), Central America (1990 to 1992), El Salvador (1991) and Liberia (1994). "Sizeable military contingents" have participated in operations in Cambodia (1992 to 1993), Mozambique (1992 to 1993), Somalia (1993 to 1994), Rwanda (1994), Haiti (1995), and Angola (1995).[55] By contrast, China did not participate in UN peacekeeping operations until 1990, and since then its military observers have not participated in any significant combat under UN supervision.[56]

There is a small chance that India and China could engage in border skirmishes before their almost uninhabitable border is wholly and definitively delineated. However, the chance of a more significant war occurring between these two states is as close to zero as it has ever been since China and India signed an agreement on confidence-building measures along the lines of actual control on the Sino-Indian border. In the future, these lines are very likely to be agreed upon as the permanent borders of the two countries. Meanwhile, for decades, neither state is likely to develop the power-projection capability to exert a hegemonic influence over the other. And while trade and diplomatic relations between China and India are not as developed as they could be, at the end of the Cold War they appear to be set on a long, upward trajectory.

There is no room here to fully analyze the purpose and military force structure of Pakistan, but suffice it to say that, largely because of an Indo-Chinese rivalry dating from the 1960s, Pakistan regards China as much more of a friend than a threat; India is the primary threat.

VI. Vietnam

Vietnam possesses an active armed force of 492,000 soldiers, of whom 420,000 (85 percent) are army. An additional 65,000 work in paramilitary support units. While China understandably wishes to maintain its territorial claims in the South China Sea, it has no apparent claims on Vietnamese land on the Indochinese Peninsula.

With Vietnam maintaining a very large regional force, that is very unlikely to change. Again, contrary to the opinions of some cited in the introduction to this book, China has no ability to exert hegemonic influence over Vietnam or to dominate Vietnam in any military sense, and there is no evidence that this has been a primary goal of the Chinese leadership or its military in the 1980s or 1990s.

Of course, Sino-Vietnamese relations are far from perfect. The behavior of the Chinese leadership toward Vietnam in 1979 was particularly violent and self-destructive. It can be understood only in the context of the corrosive influence of the Cold War rivalry of the superpowers in Southeast Asia, Vietnam's brutal aggression and invasion of Cambodia, Cambodia's self-destruction under China's ally, Pol Pot, and a Chinese domestic power transition, all occurring simultaneously. It is hard to imagine how a similar cauldron of trouble ever could be recreated.

Before China's 1979 attack on Vietnam, "Beijing's pride and prestige had been damaged by Hanoi's rough treatment of the ethnic Chinese community in Vietnam and by its toppling of China's ally in Kampuchea."[57] Yet China's pride and prestige could not have been placated by its performance in that war. China's political will after six weeks of bloody and unsuccessful forays was wholly sapped, and no Chinese objectives for Vietnam or Cambodia were achieved. In short, early in the reform period, if China had the aggressive ambitions of a great power in Southeast Asia, these ambitions were not fulfilled even on its own border with far-smaller Vietnam.

Since 1980, contemporary relations between China and Vietnam still have tremendous room for improvement. From a security perspective, Vietnam has fueled tensions with new (since the 1970s) territorial claims in the Spratly Islands, and China has fueled tensions with its apparent lack of interest in peaceful, international arbitration of any non-Chinese claims to these islands.

China and Vietnam suffered their first armed scuffle over the Spratlys in 1988, after Vietnam occupied disputed reefs (including Barque Canada, one of the largest in the Spratlys) with a military force in 1987. China responded with an increased naval presence and the occupation of other, previously unoccupied reefs. When Vietnamese warships shadowed Chinese investigative teams that clearly were backed by the Chinese navy, it was only then that a limited confrontation occurred, in which a Vietnamese auxiliary ship was the only boat sunk.[58]

In May 1992, Vietnam and China engaged in a further scuffle of unknown intensity in the South China Sea, due to conflicts over border disputes and contingent oil-drilling claims. And since April 1996, Vietnam and China are prospecting in overlapping waters in the southwestern Spratlys, with two exclusive (but overlapping) exploration contracts with two competing international oil companies.[59] If either company strikes a major artery beneath the sea, the stakes will rise significantly. Further scuffles would be almost inevitable.

Yet it is unlikely that aggressive naval maneuvers will lead to much more than scuffles at sea, away from populations, and South China Sea disputes should not cause a return to the levels of tension that existed between China and Vietnam at the beginning of the Chinese reform period. Also, it should be emphasized that China has behaved no more aggressively than Vietnam in their bilateral Spratly Island disputes, so Vietnam, apparently, feels less than dominated by China. China established the most significant offshore military base in the South China Sea, in the Paracels, around 170 kilometers off the Vietnamese coast. Yet this did not prevent Vietnam from maintaining its dubious historical claims, its occupation, and its control of over 21 islands and shoals in nearby waters.[60]

Generally, relations between China and Vietnam are improving dramatically for a number of reasons:

1. These are two of only four communist states left in the world, and they have adopted virtually the same strategies to reform and develop their economies. Vietnamese leaders clearly feel that they have more to learn from the Chinese reform effort than from Russia's more radical changes, and this appears to have contributed to the more positive opinions of each set of leaders toward the other. With similar reform efforts in both countries, trade links are also improving.

2. The end of the Cold War has dramatically improved the international context of bilateral relations between China and Vietnam. Vietnam established diplomatic relations with most countries by 1991 and relations with Washington several years later. On the Chinese side, the improvement in relations with the Soviet Union meant that neither Cold War adversary had a Cold War reason to fuel the Chinese-Vietnamese rivalries and hatreds.

3. Some also would cite "age-old, pervasive cultural links" (perhaps more emphasized by Chinese thinkers than Vietnamese ones) as a source of underlying strength in the bilateral relationship.[61]

Whatever the reasons, warmer relations between Vietnam and China have sparked more political, economic, and military contacts. Bilateral relations were normalized in 1991. In April 1994, Senior Lieutenant-General Dao Dinh Luyen, chief of the Vietnam army's general staff, met with Liu Huaqing, the Chinese army's second-in-command (directly subordinate only to Jiang Zemin) in Beijing.[62] This was one of the first friendly military-to-military exchanges that had occurred between the two states since the 1960s. More importantly, in November 1994, China reached an agreement with Vietnam to set up a joint working team for seeking a settlement on bilateral maritime disputes, and this was a small step toward peaceful settlement of the most contentious Spratly Island disputes.[63] Generally, trade relations between the two countries are better than they ever have been (and again, China is by no means "dominant," with Taiwan as Vietnam's largest trading partner).

VII. Taiwan

Taiwan has 376,000 in the armed forces, with 240,000 (64 percent) in the army. The paramilitary security groups (the National Police Administration, the Bureau of Investigation, and the Military Police) add another 25,000 officers to the total force.[64]

Generally, Taiwan maintains high defense spending and a large army for such a small island, and the reason is clearly to provide a deterrent against China. Taiwan also has a conspicuously high R&D budget, largely "to redress weaknesses caused by the reluctance of arms exporters to offend the Beijing government by supplying complete systems." Still: "Many of the projects portrayed as indigenously developed are actually licensed copies of foreign systems or assemblages of imported components, suggesting that Taiwanese military R&D is in effect a sort of technology laundering scheme." The best example is the Taiwanese fighter plane, the Ching-kuo Indigenous Defense Fighter (IDF), which is an F-16 "knock-off" that ceased to be funded when the United States approved the sale of F-16s to China. Taiwan produced 70 IDFs.[65] Taiwan's technological advantage over China in all fields except missiles and nuclear weaponry would help to ensure against surprise attack and would allow Taiwan to wage a terrible retaliation on China's airspace should the two sides come to blows.

China defines Taiwan as a renegade province. Taiwan's government has never attempted a Declaration of Independence or demanded a separate seat at the United Nations, and most of the world does not recognize

Taipei as the capital of an independent state. So Taiwan's de facto autonomy is at the very least awkward and insecure from the perspective of international law and the international system. Taiwan wholly lacks de jure independence from China.

Taiwan's security situation, consequently, is fundamentally different from the situation of any recognized state in China's neighborhood. China's developing world military is in a struggle to control its internal borders, and from a historical perspective, it is no surprise that this struggle for control includes Taiwan.

Yet despite Taiwan's dangerously insecure international status and its proximity to Chinese shores, China's political and military power has not reached the threatening point where it can confidently occupy, subjugate, dominate, or exert hegemonic control, even over Taiwan.

The weak position of Taiwan vis-à-vis China is clear: Taiwan is likely indefinitely to maintain a force that remains far smaller (currently, seven times smaller) than China's. Taiwan is also constrained in the level of support it might receive internationally. Certainly, if Taiwan provokes a cross-Strait crisis with a Declaration of Independence, the U.S. may walk from the scene and wait for the dust to settle. In the eyes of one analyst: "The U.S. position on Taiwan's status must be made clear to the Taiwanese. Taipei should be left with no ambiguity as to the U.S. position that only a peaceful, *mutually agreeable* solution between the two parties [China and Taiwan] is an acceptable basis for a change in the status quo. Unilateral moves by Taiwan toward de jure independence, including high-profile memberships in Inter-Governmental Organizations, do not square with present U.S. policy."[66]

Meanwhile, China's effort to maintain its claims over Taiwan is reflected in military as well as diplomatic action. In an infamous show of force in the spring of 1996, in advance of Taiwan's first direct presidential elections, China test-fired missiles and held live-fire war-games exercises off of Taiwan. The following September, China again conducted a joint military exercise in which its forces seized and defended an offshore island. The exercises, in the Shenyang Military Zone, involved the army, the navy, and the air force.[67] In all, China was said to have conducted seven military exercises practicing an invasion of Taiwan between 1996 and 1997. In addition to exercises in the Nanjing Military Region, which includes the territory on the Mainland closest to Taiwan, the Guangzhou and Jinan military regions have conducted landing and combat exercises on some islands, "using Taiwan's new generation military forces as an imaginary enemy."[68]

Generally, China refuses to renounce the option of using force against

Taiwan, stating that China would be provoked to take up arms on three conditions: a formal declaration of independence by Taipei, foreign intervention in Taiwan's internal affairs relative to the reunification issue, or Taipei's acquisition of nuclear weapons.[69]

According to Taiwan's White Paper, 80,000 troops of China's 31st Group Army are deployed in Fujian Province, and 260,000 others can supposedly be transferred quickly from emergency motorized forces or other strategic reserves in other military regions. The Chinese navy, meanwhile, might be able to employ hundreds of thousands of lightly equipped troops and the air force perhaps over a thousand fighter jets of varying quality for an attack on Taiwan. Most worrisome of all would be the Second Artillery Corps' Dongfeng-15 (M-9) and Dongfeng-21 missiles, "which can directly strike important political, economic, and military facilities in Taiwan." In all, the Ministry of National Defense (Taiwan) concludes alarmingly that "the Chinese Communists are capable of invading Taiwan."[70]

Yet China probably cannot bring Taiwan back under Mainland control through force. It is interesting that Taiwan's Ministry of National Defense finds the PRC capable of invading Taiwan, but not necessarily capable of capturing or subjugating Taiwan. China has essentially developed the capacity to destroy much of Taiwan with conventionally armed missiles and bombs. However, in the tragic event of a war across the Taiwan Strait, most or all independent analysts agree that Taiwan is sufficiently strong to stage an enormously powerful resistance against naval and air force operations from China. Despite the giant size of China's army, its navy, its air force, and especially its amphibious capability are simply not overwhelming for Taiwan. China also has yet to demonstrate that it is a sufficiently "revolutionary or profoundly disaffected power" to stage such an assault, except perhaps in the event of an outright Taiwanese independence declaration.[71] A Chinese assault would serve no purpose other than to kill civilians, destroy Taiwanese industry, and "teach Taiwan a lesson." Further, Taiwan's ability to destroy much of China's coastal industrial development is rarely analyzed by outsiders, because it is assumed that, while China might try to retake Taiwan, Taiwan almost certainly will never try to retake China through force. But in the event of a war, due to Taiwan's impressive air power, the destruction would almost certainly be a hellish two-way road regardless of who fired first.

The result of this ambiguous military situation (in effect, a sufficient balance of power) is that the status quo is likely to persist for some time to come. As long as the Mainland is led by authoritarians who are more or less successfully managing internal threats to their authority, it will never be in the interest of Taiwan to inspire the wrath of secure Chinese leaders and declare independence. Yet it also will never be in China's interest to attempt to subjugate rational leaders in Taiwan. Taiwan's own sources suggest that, despite the massive size of the Mainland army, only 80,000 soldiers are currently deployed by the 31st Group Army in Fujian Province.[72] For a three-million-man army, this hardly represents a threatening effort to stack forces near the Strait.

It also should be emphasized that while China and Taiwan are still technically at war, at this point the governments on both sides of the Strait are led by rational leaders who view development rather than territorial domination as their primary goal and basis of legitimacy. Chinese-Taiwanese relations therefore are generally improving, and there is reason to believe that the trend toward complementary, economically cohesive and politically stable interdependence will continue.

For example, senior negotiators from the two quasi-governmental organizations responsible for managing cross-Strait relations (Taiwan's Straits Exchange Foundation and China's Association for Relations Across the Taiwan Strait) met in China in mid-October 1998 and resumed direct contacts—suspended since 1995—aimed at reducing tensions and improving bilateral relations.[73]

China hopes to permit more cross-Strait trade and cross-border travel than is currently possible under Taiwanese law, with the goal of peacefully pulling Taiwan further under the Chinese wing. Perhaps the exercises off of Taiwan in 1996 could be portrayed as a stick, but since Deng Xiaoping formulated his "One Country, Two Systems" policy for Hong Kong, China has been primarily offering carrots to entice Taiwan's leaders and citizens toward closer relations.

For its part, Taiwan's parliament ended 43 years of martial law on the fortress islands of Qemoy and Matsu, just a stone's throw from the Mainland shores of Fujian and Mainland-controlled Xiamen Island, in the summer of 1992. Military garrisons remain on Qemoy and Matsu, but the move was a sign of the downgrading of overall tensions across the Taiwan Strait.[74] Taiwan also passed a Ten-Year Military Restructuring Plan in 1993 that was intended to improve the army's rapid response capability, but also led to reductions in the overall size of the army. "In the spring of 1997, Taiwan completed a plan to reduce total troop strength from 450,000 to 400,000 [including forces listed above as paramilitary] over a period of three years. The army is carrying out large-scale consolidation of military units and is planning to simplify the political commissar system that has existed since the time of Sun Yat-sen's nationalist revolution."[75]

This is not the behavior of a leadership fearful that it is on the verge of being attacked or dominated in any way. It is instead the behavior of a young but fairly wealthy and confident democracy—a democracy that is more fully demilitarizing its internal political environment.

VIII. Other Regional Forces in Southeast Asia

While comparisons with the forces of great powers like the United States are interesting (and many unfavorable Chinese comparisons are cited in this book), a more important and useful exercise would be to compare Chinese intentions and capabilities to those of other developing nations in the region. Is China becoming a great power in the eyes of leaders of smaller, Southeast Asian nations?

In fact, most are not terribly afraid of the "China threat." Further, a look at their militaries demonstrates many developing world similarities, albeit on a smaller scale, with the goals and structure of the Chinese military.

In Indonesia, Soeharto's successors have inherited a particularly large armed force of 461,000 spread out over ten military area commands (see table C.2).

At first glance, it is surprising that an archipelago would have a military that is so overwhelmingly (86 percent) land-based (counting the army and paramilitary forces), and so significantly stacked with paramilitary force (38 percent of the total). But on closer inspection, the Indonesian military's force structure and strategy predictably fits the pattern of most developing world militaries. The primary job of the military is to maintain stability in centers of state power, by keeping the average Javanese or Balinese citizen at bay. This effort is occasionally unsuccessful (1965, 1998). The military also has struggled to subdue active or simmering armed rebellions in the outer reaches of the nation (Fretilin in East Timor, the Free Papua organization, the Free Aceh movement).[76] As in many states of the developing world, at least one of these efforts has failed (in East Timor).

Table C.2   Indonesian Armed Forces, 1997

Army	220,000
Navy	43,000
Air force	21,000
Paramilitary police	177,000
Marine police	12,000
Total	*461,000*

Malaysia's armed force numbers 111,500, and 85,000 (over three-quarters) are in the army, a high percentage considering the peninsular and island geography of Malaysia. Malaysia also has 20,100 paramilitary personnel.[77] Since Malaysia jettisoned Singapore from the Malay federation, its most important military operations have included martial law enforcement and the prevention of riots against urban Chinese citizens and businessmen.

The Philippines has 110,500 soldiers (almost exactly the same as Malaysia), and some 70,000 (63 percent) work in the army, again, despite the fact that this is an archipelago nation.[78] The Philippines also has an active paramilitary force of 42,500 soldiers. In recent years, all significant security concerns have been internal: Domestic, disloyal oppositions consisting of the Bangsa Moro Army (the armed wing of the Moro National Liberation Front, or MNLF), the New People's Army (the communist insurgency), the Moro Islamic Liberation Front (a breakaway from the MNLF), and the Moro Islamic Reformist Group (also a breakaway from the MNLF).[79]

In February 1995, China and the Philippines each sent contingencies to patrol Spratly Island groups claimed by both nations. The incident was typical in that each side danced around the other and issued public proclamations on its inalienable rights to the islands; yet no gunshots were exchanged.[80] These militaries have some disputes to resolve, for example, on the question of who owns the uninhabited "Mischief Reef." But these kinds of questions are external to the primary business of both militaries.

Burma's army, meanwhile, is obsessed with the repression of its own population and the maintenance of control over far more popular opposition leaders. Burma is the country that provides the best case for listing China as a hegemonic or dominant power. China is clearly Burma's closest friend, to the extent that it has any, and security ties between the two countries are growing. The result is an extension of Chinese power into Burma and, by extension, Southeast Asia. But again, China is only a dominant trading partner in the north of Burma, along the Chinese border. And China's dominance primarily results from the fact that other nations, especially the United States, shun trade with Burma (especially military trade). Burma is simply too much of a poor, pariah state to attract support or interest in Western markets.

Further, some would argue that the primary danger of Chinese involvement in Burma is not that it upsets the balance of power vis-à-vis India or any other South or Southeast Asian power, but rather that China's involvement in Burma may destabilize Burma itself. China's presence could aggravate Burma's political problems by bolstering Burma's corrupt and xenophobic central leadership; or by leading to a destructive wave of anti-Chinese backlash, with riots from below against Burma's Chinese minority.[81]

So do Southeast Asian nations perceive China as a threat?

Generally, to the extent that the Chinese are feared in Southeast Asia, it is domestic Chinese citizens who are most feared. This is particularly true in Indonesia and Malaysia. Leszek Buszynski accurately identifies the more negative attitudes toward China that can be found in these countries, and some of his writing appears to demonstrate undue sympathy for what may be a view inspired more by racism than by history: "The problem of Southeast Asia's relationship with China arises from a discrepancy in capabilities and population size as well as history. Within Southeast Asia there is the belief that China regards the region as an area of influence with which relations should be structured hierarchically. As a mosaic of different cultures and ethnic groups, Southeast Asia lacks the political unity to resist the natural and historical tendency of the Chinese to push southward."[82] Is there merely a belief that China wishes to push southward and structure relations hierarchically, or is China actually pushing and enforcing its hierarchy?

Indonesia and Malaysia are singled out as particularly apprehensive not because of more prominent territorial disputes in the Spratlys (these are more salient with Vietnam and the Philippines) but because of their nations' uncomfortable relations with domestic Chinese minorities. Yet later in Buszynski's writing, he admits that even Indonesia and Malaysia might in the end perceive Japan as a bigger hegemonic threat. In July 1990, the Malaysian foreign minister claimed that Japan could replace the Soviet Union as the major threat to the region.[83]

While some in China might hope to control all of the resources in the South China Sea, China's actions in recent years toward securing these resources have been a wavering mixture of carrots and sticks. Sticks include limited scuffles with Vietnam and the Philippines, discussed above, and more generally the effort to improve naval capability to bolster China's power-projection capabilities. The carrots include more successful and sustained efforts to establish peaceful relations throughout the region and internationally, through bilateral and multilateral diplomacy. Most Southeast Asian nations are hoping that South China Sea claims will be settled multilaterally through UN judicial bodies or other international institutions rather than bilaterally, with China exerting pressure on smaller nations. These hopes seemed closer to being realized when China ratified the UN Maritime Law Treaty on May 15, 1996. While Chinese leaders view the seas as "the new high ground of strategic competition," this diplomatic breakthrough implies that they are moving, reluctantly, toward multilateral settlement as the best means to ensure that sea resources can be exploited quickly and in a sustainable fashion.[84]

X. Conclusion

In 1994, Colonel Xu Xiaojun, publishing in English for Western consumption in "China's Grand Strategy for the 21st Century," argued that the United States is the world's last remaining superpower, with more power to project in the Asia-Pacific region than any other nation. Japan, meanwhile, seeks the status of a major political power through trade, aid, and increased defense spending. Moreover, Japan's "obvious interest in sending troops abroad [has] caused widespread concern among Asian nations."

Does China also seek some kind of great power status? What is its grand strategy? "Developing its national economy is the centerpiece of China's grand strategy for the remainder of this century and the first half of the twenty-first century." If China succeeds in quadrupling its income levels from 1978 to 2000 and again from 2000 to 2050, argues Colonel Xu, it will then be only a moderately developed country—by today's standards—with an income of U.S. $4,000 per capita.[85]

China's defense minister highlights similarly unambitious goals for China's defense policy. "The basic goals of China's defense policy," according to Chi Haotian, "are to consolidate national defense, resist foreign aggression, defend the nation's sovereignty over its territorial land, sea and airspace as well as its maritime rights and interests and safeguard national unity and security."[86]

It is possible that all similar statements from China are designed simply for Western consumption, and that these apparently insecure proclamations serve as a decoy to distract us from China's *real* ambitions, expectations, and strategic goals. But the most obvious and consistent answer is usually the right one. In this case, the constant claim of Chinese leaders, in both external and internal reports, is that their primary concerns for China are domestic, and revolve around securing adequate economic wealth and political stability. The government's near monopoly on the domestic control of violence since the Cultural Revolution is almost unprecedented, and the geographic extent of its domestic control is historically far-reaching. It is not surprising that China's government is somewhat obsessed with the continuation of this temporally limited historical achievement.

China's military concerns, discussed throughout this book, result from the fact that China remains a much larger than average, but nevertheless still struggling developing country.

The U.S. security establishment regularly compares Chinese military power, strategy, and intentions to those of the United States, and many reporters and scholars do the same. While the exercise is important, informed U.S. analysts both within and outside the military rarely conclude that China will pose a significant danger to U.S. security interests anytime soon. The most ardent U.S. critics of China tend to be politicians, not military planners. Even beyond 2005, the U.S. military concluded in 1999: "China will continue to improve its regional force projection capabilities, but will not possess the conventional military capabilities to exert global influence."[87]

Of course, military planners need to consider not just probable developments, but also worst-case scenarios. *The 1997 Strategic Assessment* of the U.S. Institute of National Strategic Studies states that in a worst-case scenario, China's growing military strength "could embolden Beijing to resort to coercive diplomacy or direct military action in an attempt to resolve in its favor various outstanding territorial claims or to press other vital issues affecting the future economic and security environment of the region." Still, generally "Beijing shows no evidence of any willingness to allow its ties with Washington to collapse or evolve towards military conflict."[88]

In the 1990s China's decisions to sign and publicly support international bans on chemical and biological weapons, the Nuclear Non-Proliferation Treaty, and the Comprehensive Nuclear Test Ban Treaty have been well received in Washington. The two states' navies have also made friendly port visits to each other's naval bases, and in 1997, the United States and China agreed to establish a strategic partnership, with more bilateral exchanges of military information. At the Sino-U.S. summit of June 1998, Presidents Jiang Zemin and Bill Clinton agreed to not target strategic nuclear weapons at each other's countries. U.S. military personnel generally are reassured by these security dialogues and peaceful agreements (some admittedly more vague than others). Generally, despite recent U.S. investigations concerning stolen nuclear technology, relations between U.S. security forces and the Chinese PLA have never been better.

Relations with the rest of the world, including countries that are significantly newer and smaller, are also increasingly peaceful and defined through international laws and agreements. For example, China's troubles in its northwest territories are bad enough already, and the country's leaders appear uninterested in any further expansion of power into Muslim Central Asia. Agreements to reduce troops along northwestern borders and others on the Sino-Russian border are more of a peaceful concession by China (the largest armed force in terms of numbers) than by any other power.

The situation is also increasingly peaceful on China's southeastern borders. Further, recent rhetoric suggests that China is backing away from strict insistence on bilateral negotiations with weaker neighbors, and is more willing to accept the authority of multilateral bodies like ASEAN in Southeast Asian or South China Sea disputes.

In addition to the ASEAN Regional Forum (ARF), China has participated in the Conference on Interaction and Confidence- Building Measures in Asia (CICA), the Council on Security Cooperation in Asia and the Pacific Region (CSCAP), the Northeast Asia Cooperation Dialogue (NEACD) and other multilateral security activities.[89] According to a *PLA Daily* editorial: "Security dialogue and consultations, whether bilateral or multilateral . . . as well as strategic security coordination . . . will play an important role in preventing crises and checking the escalation of conflicts. The ASEAN regional forum serves as a successful example of this pattern."[90]

Some fear an impending "China threat," but ironically, China-watchers have reason to *hope* that China will, some day, emerge as a great power. In the process, China might become even more of a status-quo power, and even *less* threatening.

In the process of emerging, China would need to develop a more impressive legal system, a more liberal and successful economy, a more international and less mercantilist economic outlook, better relations between the state and working-class citizens, better relations between the state and national minority groups, a more professional and well-managed military, and better external relations in the Asia-Pacific region. All of these changes would contribute to the world's economic and political development and world peace, and this author, for one, would welcome them.

Unfortunately, they are unlikely to happen quickly. In the meantime, the collapse of the Soviet Union and other states with shaky foundations (e.g., Yugoslavia, Rwanda) present models of typical end-of-the-century security threats, or threats with a major security component. These include introspective ethnic wars; national or regional economic meltdowns; international refugee crises; organized and unorganized lawlessness; and national dissolution.

China's successes under reform are unprecedented—but that in itself should give one pause. Confucius said that the sun at high noon is a sun declining; is China at high noon? Either way, analysts of the China threat should consider that China's weaknesses, for decades, may be far more threatening than its strengths.

Notes

Introduction

1. Samuel S. Kim addresses the question of whether China should be considered a great power in Samuel S. Kim, "China as a Great Power," *Current History,* 196:611 (September, 1997), pp. 246-251. His answer is a qualified yes. For opinions on Chinese superpower, see Francis A. Lee, *China Superpower: Requisites of High Growth* (Houndmills, UK: Macmillan Press, Ltd., 1997); China is described as at least an emerging economic superpower in this source and in William H. Overholt, *China: The Next Economic Superpower* (London: Weidenfeld & Nicolson, 1993). For a journalist's view of Chinese superpower, see Karsten Prager, "China: Waking Up to the Next Superpower," *Time Magazine,* 147:13 (March 25, 1996) (http://www.pathfinder.com/@@skUlwAUA988z30nM/time/magazine/domestic/1996/960325/china.html).
2. Nicholas D. Kristof, "The Rise of China," *Foreign Affairs,* Vol. 72, No. 5 (November/December 1993), pp. 59, 65. For another source suggesting China is arming itself at a somewhat alarming rate, see Michael T. Klare, "The Next Great Arms Race," *Foreign Affairs,* Vol. 72, No. 3 (Summer 1993), pp. 136-152.
3. Gerald Segal, "China's Changing Shape," *Foreign Affairs,* Vol. 73, No. 3 (May/June 1994), pp. 43-58 (54).
4. Ross H. Munro, "China's Waxing Spheres of Influence," *Orbis,* Vol. 38, No. 4 (Fall 1994), pp. 585-605 (587, 594). It has been more than one thousand years since China successfully established hegemony over Vietnam through an occupation, and its military campaign against Vietnam at the beginning of Deng's reign was a lesson in dramatic failure. Still, the view expressed by Munro is quite popular; see also Gerald Segal, below.

Currently, India possesses a comparatively stable government, nuclear weapons, and a booming economy. Liberalization in both China and India has led to diplomatic breakthroughs between these two countries that are unprecedented and likely to last. Munro appears to overstate the case for India's weakness and its implications.

5. Gerald Segal, "The Coming Confrontation Between China and Japan?" *World Policy Journal,* Vol. 10, No. 2 (Summer, 1993), pp. 27-28.

6. Furthermore, "serious political tensions between China and Japan are certain, and military conflict is likely, if China's economic power continues to grow rapidly relative to Japan's." Roy bases his sensational conclusions on his interpretation of hegemonic theory and vaguely defined "international systemic pressures" caused by rising and falling power correlates. Denny Roy, "Hegemon on the Horizon? China's Threat to East Asian Security," *International Security,* Vol. 19, No. 1 (Summer, 1994), pp. 149-168 (149, 165, 168). See also Denny Roy, "The Foreign Policy of Great-Power China," *Contemporary Southeast Asia,* 19:2 (September, 1997).

7. Lee, *China Superpower,* p. 39.

8. Richard D. Fisher, "China's Purchase of Russian Fighters: A Challenge to the U.S.," The Heritage Foundation Asian Studies Center Backgrounder No. 142, July 31, 1996 (http://www.heritage.org/heritage/ library/categories/forpol/ asc142.html).

9. Alastair Iain Johnston, "China's Militarized Interstate Dispute Behavior, 1949-1992: A First Cut at the Data," *China Quarterly* (March, 1998), p. 1.

10. Richard H. Solomon, *Chinese Political Negotiating Behavior* (Santa Monica: RAND, 1985).

11. Steven I. Levine, "Perception and Ideology in Chinese Foreign Policy," in Thomas W. Robinson and David Shambaugh, eds., *Chinese Foreign Policy: Theory and Practice* (Oxford: Oxford University Press, 1994), p. 43.

12. Similar observations were made long ago in Samuel P. Huntington, "Patterns of Violence in World Politics," in Huntington, ed., *Changing Patterns of Military Politics* (New York: Columbia University Press, 1962), pp. 17-19.

13. *East Asian Strategic Review, 1997-1998* (Tokyo: National Institute of Defense Studies), 1998, pp. 113-114.

14. Jonathan D. Pollack and Young Koo Cha, *A New Alliance for the Next Century: The Future of U.S.-Korean Security Cooperation* (Santa Monica: RAND), 1995, p. xiii.

15. A good discussion of related issues is found in Robin Luckham, "Introduction: The Military, the Developmental State and Social Forces in Asia and the Pacific: Issues for Comparative Analysis," in Viberto Selochan, ed., *The Military, the State, and Development in Asia and the Pacific* (Boulder, CO: Westview, 1991), pp. 1-49.

16. The 1970 study, by Eric Nordlinger, is cited and critically reviewed in A.F. Mullins, Jr., *Born Arming: Development and Military Power in New States* (Stanford, CA: Stanford University Press, 1987), p. 5.

17. Huntington, "Patterns of Violence in World Politics," p. 33.

18. Efforts to measure the effect of military spending on growth are complicated by the fact that military spending can be funded through foreign loans or grants from outside powers, and by the fact that countries spending large amounts on their military probably do so after experiencing some modicum of economic success; otherwise, where would the money come from? A third problem not mentioned by A.F. Mullins is simply that macroeconomic theory would suggest *both* positive and negative effects from military spending, and these effects would be nearly impossible to isolate. For example, Keynesian, government spending programs of any kind can stimulate an economy toward growth; they can generate high deficits that create a long-term drag on growth; or they can do both. For a more detailed discussion, see Mullins, *Born Arming,* pp. 6-8.

19. A more complete discussion of the meaning of "military professionalism" is found in Harlan Jencks, *From Muskets to Missiles: Politics and Professionalism in the Chinese Army, 1945-1981* (Boulder, CO: Westview Press, 1982). See especially chapter one.

20. These words, in turn, are clearly defined by *The Department of Defense Dictionary of Military and Associated Terms* (JCS Pub 1-02). See also Michael B. Donley, "Problems of Defense Organization and Management," *Joint Forces Quarterly* (Summer, 1995), pp. 86-94.

21. Robin Luckham, "Introduction: The Military, the Developmental State and Social Forces in Asia and the Pacific," p. 3.

22. For example, in South Korea, Lee Yang-ho was fired as Defense Minister and arrested for taking bribes and leaking military secrets to South Korean companies in 1996. *Korea Annual, 1997* (Seoul: Yonhap News Agency, 1997), p. 93.

23. *East Asian Strategic Review, 1997-1998,* pp. 113-114.

24. Mohammed Ayoob, *The Third World Security Predicament: State Making, Regional Conflict, and the International System* (Boulder, CO: Lynne Rienner, 1995), p. 15.

25. "China must develop its own high technology. . . . In the 1960s, if China didn't have nuclear weapons, or a hydrogen bomb, or hadn't launched satellites, China simply would not have had the important influence of a great power, and it wouldn't have had the level of international prestige that it enjoys today." Deng Xiaoping, quoted in Huang Ruixin et. al., "Problems of Financial Management in Military Expenditure Optimization," *Military Sciences Economic Review* (*junshi jingji yanjiu*), 1995 (10).

26. The International Institute for Strategic Studies, *The Military Balance, 1997/1998* (Oxford: Oxford University Press, 1998), p. 178. Since 1990,

China has participated in or sent observers to six UN peacekeeping forces: the United Nations Truce Supervision Organization (UNTSO) in the Middle East, United Nations Iraq-Kuwait Observation Mission (UNIKOM), United Nations Transitional Authority in Cambodia (UNTAC), United Nations Mission for the Referendum in Western Sahara (MINURSO), United Nations Operation in Mozambique (ONU-MOZ), and United Nations Observer Mission in Liberia (UNOMIL). See "Text of Defense White Paper," Xinhua, July 27, 1998.

27. Lee, *China Superpower,* p. 40.
28. Michael Richardson, "East Asians Fear Rivalry for Nuclear Arms Might Drift their Way," *International Herald Tribune,* June 3, 1998, p. 5.
29. Academy of Military Science and China Military Science Institute, "Useful Explorations and Important Breakthroughs — A Summary of the Views at the 'Literary Forum on Studying Deng Xiaoping Theory and Exploring the Features and Laws of Governing the Military on New Terms,'" *PLA Daily (jiefangjun bao),* December 1, 1998, p. 6, in FBIS-CHI-98-363.

Chapter One

1. Harlan Jencks, "Ground Forces," in Gerald Segal and William T. Tow, eds., *Chinese Defense Policy* (London: Macmillan Press, 1984), pp. 65-66.
2. Rosita Dellios, *Modern Chinese Defense Strategy* (Houndsmills, UK: MacMillan, 1989), p. 1.
3. Kenneth W. Allen, Glenn Krumel, and Jonathan D. Pollack, *China's Air Force Enters the 21st Century* (Santa Monica, CA: RAND, 1995), pp. 22-23.
4. Paul Godwin, "Towards a New Strategy?" in Segal and Tow, eds., *Chinese Defense Policy,* p. 48.
5. June Teufel Dreyer, "The Role of the Armed Forces in Contemporary China," in Edward A. Olsen and Stephen Jurika, Jr., eds., *The Armed Forces in Contemporary Asian Societies* (Boulder, CO: Westview Press, 1986), p. 37.
6. Mel Gurtov and Byong-Moo Hwang, *China's Security: The New Roles of the Military* (Boulder, CO: Lynne Reinner, 1998).
7. Dreyer, "The Role of the Armed Forces in Contemporary China," pp. 26-7.
8. Georges Tan Eng Bok, "Strategic Doctrine," in Segal and Tow, *Chinese Defense Policy,* pp. 3-17.
9. *Ibid.*
10. Deng Liqun et. al., eds., *The Chinese People's Liberation Army, Vol. I* (Beijing: Contemporary China Publishing House, 1994), pp. 582-583.
11. *Ibid,* p. 439.
12. Harlan Jencks, "Ground Forces," p. 53.
13. Dellios, *Modern Chinese Defense Strategy,* p. 4.

14. *Ibid,* pp. 29-36.

15. "Chi Haotian Speaks on PRC Defense Policy." Xinhua, February 17, 1998, in FBIS-CHI-98-048.

16. John Wilson Lewis and Xue Litai, *China's Strategic Seapower: The Politics of Force Modernization in the Nuclear Age,* Stanford, CA: Stanford University Press, 1994, pp. 211-214.

17. Deng Liqun et. al., *The Chinese People's Liberation Army, Vol. I,* pp. 320-329.

18. *Ibid,* p. 296.

19. *Ibid,* p. 316.

20. Shu-Shin Wang, *Military Development of the People's Republic of China after the 1989 Tiananmen Massacre* (Taipei: Chinese Council of Advanced Policy Studies, CAPS Papers, No. 5: 1994), p. 106.

21. Dreyer, "The Role of the Armed Forces in Contemporary China," pp. 30-31.

22. "Army Implements Jiang's General Demand," Beijing Xinhua Domestic Service, July 29, 1997, in FBIS-CHI-97-211.

23. Deng Liqun et. al., *The Chinese People's Liberation Army, Vol. I,* p. 299.

24. *Ibid,* p. 306.

25. Su Ruozhou, "A Great Military Reform—Roundup of Strategic Changes in Our Army Building," *PLA Daily (jiefangjun bao),* December 18, 1998, pp. 1,2 in FBIS-CHI-99-018; "Deng Said Jiang Qualified Party Secretary," Beijing Xinhua News Service, August 8, 1997, in FBIS-CHI-97-220.

26. Deng Liqun et. al., *The Chinese People's Liberation Army, Vol. I,* pp. 312-313.

27. *Ibid.*

28. *Ibid,* pp. 304-5.

29. Wang, *Military Development,* p. 99.

30. "Nanjing Military Region Commander Chen Bingde on Military Theory, Reform," *China Military Science (beijing zhongguo junshi kexue),* 3 (August 1997), pp. 49-56, in FBIS-CHI-98-065.

31. Deng Liqun et. al., *The Chinese People's Liberation Army, Vol. I,* p. 297.

32. *Ibid,* pp. 297-8.

33. *Ibid,* p. 316.

34. *Ibid.*

35. Alastair Iain Johnston, "China's New 'Old Thinking': The Concept of Limited Deterrence," *International Security,* 20:3 (Winter, 1995/6), pp. 5-6.

36. Johnston doesn't leave us with a convincing sense of whether the idea of "limited deterrence"—discussed in some sources—has really gained ground at high levels, or is considered critically important at any level. Also, the concept is not particularly well defined by either the Chinese sources listed or by Johnston. Is there anything more here than the desire—expressed by some, budget permitting—for a flexible deter-

rent? Johnston admits that China has yet to implement this strategy, despite heavy investments in the missile force. The most important reason is probably that the strategy, although it would obviously enhance Chinese nuclear capabilities, is simply not considered to be worth the economic or political opportunity costs that would be incurred by executing it. China appears to be heading instead in a different direction, with efforts to develop better, longer-range missiles (including MIRVs) that can easily reach across the Pacific and thereby serve as a minimal deterrent against any superpower. The policy is an awkward mixture of minimal deterrence; intelligence, research, and development (e.g., the successful efforts to develop neutron bomb technology and employ supercomputers for MIRV advances); and peaceful efforts at diplomacy (e.g., the signing of the CTBC treaty). For more on limited deterrence, see Johnston, "China's New 'Old Thinking': The Concept of Limited Deterrence," pp. 5-42.

37. Again, see Dellios, *Modern Chinese Defense Strategy,* quoted above.
38. Deng Liqun et. al., *The Chinese People's Liberation Army, Vol. I,* p. 298.
39. *Ibid,* p. 297.
40. *Ibid,* p. 317.
41. Zhao Shuanlong, "The Initial Battle Is the Decisive Battle, and Preparations for Military Struggle in the New Period," *PLA Daily (jiefangjun bao),* August 18, 1998, p. 6, in FBIS-CHI-98-257.
42. *Ibid.*
43. "China: Nuclear, Chemical, and Biological Weapons and Their Protections," *People's Military Surgeon (beijing renmin junyi),* 40 (September, 1997), pp. 505-507, in FBIS-CHI-98-133.
44. *Ibid.*
45. *Ibid.*
46. *Ibid.*
47. *Ibid.*
48. Xu Yong, "Initial Discussion of Deng Xiaoping's Thoughts on Weapons and Military Equipment Construction in the New Period" *(deng xiaoping xinshiqi xuqi zhuangbei jianshe sixiang chutan),* in Li Lin and Zhao Qinxuan, eds., *Theory and Research on Military Economics in the New Era (xinshiqi junshi jingji lilun yanjiu),* Beijing: Military Sciences Publishing House, 1995. p. 101.
49. "Checking Information Warfare," *PLA Daily (jiefangjun bao),* February 2, 1999, p. 6, in FBIS-CHI-1999-0217.
50. Yu Huating and Liu Guoyu, eds., *High-Tech War and Army Quality Building* (Beijing: National Defense University Publishing House, 1995), p. 43.
51. *Ibid,* p. 45.
52. *Ibid,* pp. 45-6.

53. *Ibid,* p. 55.
54. *Ibid,* pp. 306-314.
55. *Ibid,* p. 43.
56. *Ibid,* p. 44.
57. *Ibid,* pp. 315-328.
58. The Scientific Research Branch of the National Defense University and the Army Command Study and Research Office, *Research on War Command under High-Tech Conditions (gao jishu tiaojian xia zuo zhan zhihui yanjiu),* (Beijing: National Defense University Publishing House, 1997).
59. *Ibid.*
60. *Ibid.*
61. *Ibid,* p. 4.
62. *Ibid,* pp. 8-9.
63. *Ibid,* pp. 1-11.
64. Qian Guoliang, "Studying Problems of Command with the Transformation of Land Offensive Battles," in *Ibid,* pp. 12-18.
65. The Scientific Research Branch of the National Defense University, pp. 19-25.
66. *Ibid,* pp. 26-31.
67. *Ibid,* pp. 39-43.
68. *Ibid,* p. 50.
69. *Ibid,* p. 88.
70. The third key listed in this essay is to employ automated systems and computers to a greater extent than they are currently employed. *Ibid,* pp. 87-92.
71. *Ibid,* pp. 93-96.
72. *Ibid,* p. 99.
73. *Ibid,* pp. 100-101.
74. *Ibid,* pp. 75.
75. *Ibid,* pp. 75-81.
76. *Ibid,* pp. 55-60.
77. Zhang Zhen and Su Qingyi, eds., *High Technology and the Modern Airforce* (Beijing: Military Sciences Publishing House), 1993.
78. *Ibid.*
79. Liu Mingtao et. al., *Missile War under High Tech War* (Beijing: National Defense University Publishing House, 1993), pp. 83-86.
80. *Ibid,* pp. 101-106.
81. "Nanjing Military Region Commander Chen Bingde on Military Theory, Reform," *China Military Science (beijing zhongguo junshi kexue),* 3 (August 1997), pp. 49-56, in FBIS-CHI-98-065.
82. Liu Yichang and Li Lin, "On Construction of Defense Economics under Market Conditions" *(lun shichang jingji tiaojian xia de guofang jingji jianshe), Military Sciences Economic Review (junshi jingji yanjiu),* 1996 (3), p. 14.

83. He Liming et. al., "Military Production and Defense Development Strategies," *Military Sciences Economic Review (junshi jingji yanjiu),* 1996 (12), p. 16.

Chapter Two

1. Deng Liqun et. al., eds., *The Chinese People's Liberation Army, Vol. I* (Beijing: Contemporary China Publishing House, 1994), p. 347.
2. Jiang An, "Who Holds the Gun?" *Straits Times,* April 13, 1997.
3. "PRC Law on National Defense, Fifth Opinion of the Eighth National People's Congress, Promoted March 14, 1997 and Endorsed by PRC 'Chairman' Jiang Zemin." Text released by Xinhua, 1997.
4. Deng Liqun et. al, *The Chinese People's Liberation Army, Vol. I,* p. 353.
5. *Ibid,* p. 340.
6. Cui Ning, "China: Hi-Tech Project Highlights 5 Areas," *China Daily,* April 3, 1996.
7. Huang Xiaofeng and Yao Zheng, "The Special Requirements of Electronic Warfare on National Defense Industrial Structures" *(xinxizhan duiguofang gongye jiegou de tezhu yaoqiu), Military Sciences Economic Review (junshi jingji yanjiu),* 1997 (2), pp. 22-23.
8. Richard A. Bitzinger and Bates Gill, *Gearing Up for High-Tech Warfare? Chinese and Taiwanese Defense Modernization and Implications for Military Confrontation Across the Taiwan Strait* (Taipei: Chinese Council of Advanced Policy Studies, CAPS Papers No. 11: September, 1996), p. 13.
9. These will reportedly not provide the precision or image clarity of Western satellites, but could still be used for defense purposes. Prepared Testimony of Richard D. Fisher before the Senate Foreign Relations Committee and the East Asian and Pacific Affairs Subcommittee, "China's Peoples' Liberation Army: Challenges for American Policy in Asia," Federal News Service, October 11, 1995.
10. Cui Ning, "China: Hi-Tech Project."
11. "Telecommunications: High-Speed Optical Fiber Computer Network Developed by Defense University," Xinhua, December 1, 1995.
12. Bitzinger and Gill, *Gearing Up for High-Tech Warfare?,* p. 13.
13. "More on Enhancing Defense Modernization" *(zai lun jiaqiang guofang xiandai huajianshe), Military Sciences Economic Review (junshi jingji yanjiu),* 1996 (4), p. 32.
14. Harlan Jencks, "Ground Forces," in Gerald Segal and William T. Tow, eds., *Chinese Defense Policy* (London: Macmillan Press, 1984), p. 61.
15. Authors at the National Defense University argue in one book focused on logistic modernization that high-tech war challenges logistics by threatening intelligence systems more than ever before; through the unprece-

dented speed of battles; by allowing battles to take place anywhere (deep inland, underwater, or in the stratosphere); and by diversifying the type of battle that China must defend itself against (conventional or unconventional, from electronic wars to "Star Wars" missile and anti-missile attacks). Yu Gaoda and Gao Wenyuan, eds., *High-Tech War Logistics* (Beijing: National Defense University, 1995), pp. 53-56.

16. Jiang An, "Who Holds the Gun?"
17. *Ibid.*
18. Paul Humes Folta, *From Swords to Plowshares? Defense Industry Reform in the PRC* (Boulder: Westview, 1992), p. 20.
19. "Text of Defense White Paper," Xinhua, July 27, 1998.
20. Folta, *From Swords to Plowshares?* p. 24.
21. The International Institute for Strategic Studies, *The Military Balance, 1997/1998* (Oxford: Oxford University Press, 1998), pp. 176-179.
22. Shu-Shin Wang, *Military Development of the People's Republic of China after the 1989 Tiananmen Massacre* (Taipei: Chinese Council of Advanced Policy Studies, CAPS Papers, No. 5: 1994), pp. 91-92.
23. "Text of Defense White Paper."
24. "More on Enhancing Defense Modernization" *(zai lun jiaqiang guofang xiandai huajianshe), Military Sciences Economic Review (junshi jingji yanjiu),* 1996 (4), p. 31.
25. *Ibid.*
26. "Text of Defense White Paper."
27. See, for example, "Jiang Zemin Criticizes Slow Progress in Army Reform," Ming Pao (HK), May 19, 1998, p. A12, in FBIS-CHI-98-140. See also Liu Hsiao-hua, "Armed Police Force: China's 1 Million Special Armed Troops," *Wide Angle (kuang chiao ching)* (HK), No 307, Apr 16, 1998 pp 42-47, in FBIS-CHI-98-134.
28. Liu Hsiao-hua, "Report on April Enlarged Meeting of CMC: Policy of Fewer But Better Troops Aims at Strengthening Reserve Service Units" *Wide Angle (kuang chiao ching)* (HK), May 16, 1998, in FBIS-CHI-98-161.
29. *Ibid.*
30. Nanjing Army Command Academy, People's Armed Forces Department, "Members of the Militia Must Undergo Military Training in Accordance With the Law," *Chinese Militia (zhongguo minbing),* February 9, 1998, pp. 28-30, in FBIS-CHI-98-119.
31. Wang, *Military Development,* pp. 91-92.
32. U.S. Department of Defense Report to Congress, "Security Situation in the Taiwan Strait," updated February 26, 1999. See http://www.defenselink.mil/
33. Deng Liqun et. al., *The Chinese People's Liberation Army, Vol. I,* pp. 360-365.
34. "Country Alert," *The Economist Intelligence Unit,* 8/25/97.
35. "More on Enhancing Defense Modernization," p. 31.

36. "Taiwan 'White Paper' Lists PRC Capabilities, Invasion Exercises," Taipei Lien-Ho Pao, March 25, 1998, p. 4, in FBIS-CHI-98-086.

37. "More on Enhancing Defense Modernization," p. 31.

38. In the conclusion of his book on the PLA, Harlan Jencks suggests that one possibly unprofessional element of PLA organization is Maoist decentralization and powerful regional command structures, which can make unified missions difficult, compromise organizational hierarchies, or detract from command and control. It would be fair to argue that, despite some command and control modernization, this problem still exists two decades after Jencks began working on his book. See Harlan W. Jencks, *From Muskets to Missiles: Politics and Professionalism in the Chinese Army, 1945-1981* (Boulder, CO: Westview, 1982), p. 263.

39. Deng Liqun et. al., *The Chinese People's Liberation Army, Vol. I,* p. 364.

40. U.S. Department of Defense Report to Congress, "Security Situation in the Taiwan Strait."

41. Wang, *Military Development,* p. 97.

42. Tai Ming Cheung, "Growth of Chinese Naval Power: Priorities, Goals, Missions, and Regional Implications," (Singapore: Institute of Southeast Asian Studies, 1990), p. 5.

43. "On Deng Xiaoping's Thinking on Military Expenditures" *(Deng Xiaoping Xin Shiqi Junfei Sixiang Chutan), Military Sciences Economic Review (junshi jingji yanjiu),* 1995 (8), p. 25.

44. See also [Navy Senior Colonel] Yan Youqiang and [Navy Senior Colonel] Chen Rongxing, "On Maritime Strategy and the Marine Environment," *China Military Science (beijing zhongguo junshi kexue),* 97:2 (May, 1997), pp. 81-92, in FBIS-CHI-97-197.

45. U.S. Department of Defense Report to Congress, "Security Situation in the Taiwan Strait."

46. Cheung, "Growth of Chinese Naval Power," p. 42.

47. *Ibid,* p. 32.

48. The International Institute for Strategic Studies, *The Military Balance, 1997/1998,* pp. 177-178.

49. Wang, *Military Development,* pp. 91-92. An earlier source lists only four main divisions in the early 1980s: the main surface force, a submarine force, a naval air force, and a coastguard force. The first three are evolving into a navy with regional responsibilities out to at least the limits of China's continental shelf and exclusive economic zone (ranging between 200 and 350 nautical miles). See Bruce Swanson, "Naval Forces," in Gerald Segal and William T. Tow, eds., *Chinese Defense Policy* (London: Macmillan Press, 1984), p. 90.

50. The International Institute for Strategic Studies, *The Military Balance, 1997/1998,* pp. 177-178.

51. Renato Cruz de Castro, "Interactive Naval Development of Three

Northeast Asian States," *Contemporary Southeast Asia,* 17:3 (December, 1995), p. 323.

52. Bruce Swanson, "Naval Forces," in Gerald Segal and William T. Tow, eds., *Chinese Defense Policy* (London: Macmillan Press, 1984), p. 85.

53. Cheung, "Growth of Chinese Naval Power," p. 42.

54. "On Deng Xiaoping's Thinking on Military Expenditures," p. 26.

55. Cheung, "Growth of Chinese Naval Power," pp. 19-22.

56. The thrust of his quoted comments to the air force was similar, stating that new money should be spent on research into new aeronautics technologies and prototypes, and that there could be fewer purchases of outdated models. "On Deng Xiaoping's Thinking on Military Expenditures," p. 26.

57. Cheung, "Growth of Chinese Naval Power," p. 53, footnote 108.

58. Swanson, "Naval Forces," p. 89.

59. John Wilson Lewis and Xue Litai, *China's Strategic Seapower: The Politics of Force Modernization in the Nuclear Age,* Stanford: Stanford University Press, 1994, pp. 229-230.

60. *Ibid,* p. 226.

61. Cruz de Castro, "Interactive Naval Development of Three Northeast Asian States," pp. 323.

62. *Ibid,* p. 324.

63. The International Institute for Strategic Studies, *The Military Balance, 1997/1998,* pp. 177-178.

64. Kenneth R. Timmerman, "The Peking Pentagon," The American Spectator, April, 1996 (http://www.security-policy.org/papers/96-D29at.html).

65. "Kohl to Make Rare PLA Visit," *South China Morning Post,* November 9, 1995.

66. Cao Min, "Hi-Tech Program Fuels Economy," *China Daily,* April 5, 1996.

67. Wang, *Military Development,* p. 83.

68. Cheung, "Growth of Chinese Naval Power," pp. 38-41.

69. Liu Huaqing, the former commander, has predicted that fewer than 10 percent of China's land-based missiles would survive a large-scale nuclear first strike. Lewis and Xue, *China's Strategic Seapower,* p. 230.

70. Chiang Shang-chou, "China's Naval Development Strategy—Building an Offshore Defensive Naval Armed Force," *Wide Angle (kuang chiao ching)* (HK), December 16, 1998, pp. 70-73, in FBIS-CHI-99-019.

71. Cheung, "Growth of Chinese Naval Power," p. 42, footnote 125.

72. Wang, *Military Development,* p. 92.

73. Military Balance, quoted in Prager, "China: Waking Up to the Next Superpower." *Time Magazine,* 147:13 (March 25, 1996) (http://www.pathfinder.com/@@skUlwAUA988z30nM/time/magazine/domestic/1996/960325/china.html).

74. IISS states that China's navy employs 18 destroyers and 36 frigates. See

The International Institute for Strategic Studies, *The Military Balance, 1997/1998*, pp. 177-178.

75. Taiwan's navy by the mid-1980s boasted 26 missile-armed destroyers and nine frigates. Cruz de Castro, "Interactive Naval Development of Three Northeast Asian States," p. 327.

76. *Military Balance*, quoted in Prager, "China: Waking Up to the Next Superpower."

77. Cheung, "Growth of Chinese Naval Power," p. 41.

78. Edward Neilan, "China Builds Aircraft Carrier," Korean Herald Asia Intelligence Wire, May 24, 1997; *The Economist Intelligence Unit*, October 3, 1997.

79. Cheung, "Growth of Chinese Naval Power," p. 37.

80. Prepared Testimony of Richard D. Fisher, "China's PLA."

81. "On Deng Xiaoping's Thinking on Military Expenditures," p. 26.

82. For example, from the same source: "In modern war, the role of the air force, more than ever, must not be underestimated; it is now possible, [working] independently from the air to achieve the strategic objectives of war." *Ibid.*

83. For example: "The sight of Polish cavalry charging the armored columns of the Wehrmacht in September 1939 would probably offer the closest historical parallel to a meeting in battle between China's air forces and the air power of China's close and unfriendly neighbor, the Soviet Union. Two decades of neglect have left the People's Liberation Army Air Force (PLAAF) in very poor shape." Bill Sweetman, "Air Forces," in Gerald Segal and William T. Tow, eds., *Chinese Defense Policy* (London: Macmillan Press, 1984), p. 71.

84. Bill Sweetman, "Air Forces," in Segal and Tow, eds., *Chinese Defense Policy*, pp. 71-84.

85. These numbers are provided by Shu-Shin Wang and Richard Fisher, respectively. Wang, *Military Development*, p. 92; Richard D. Fisher, "China's Purchase of Russian Fighters: A Challenge to the U.S.," The Heritage Foundation Asian Studies Center Backgrounder No. 142, July 31, 1996 (http://www.heritage.org/heritage/library/categories/forpol/asc142.html).

86. *Military Balance*, quoted in Prager, "China: Waking Up to the Next Superpower."

87. Fisher, "China's Purchase of Russian Fighters."

88. *Ibid.*

89. IISS lists number of SU-27s delivered to China at 24. The International Institute for Strategic Studies, The Military Balance, 1997/1998, p. 167. The *Economist* suggests that 48 Su-27s had been sold to China by March of 1997. "China Economy: Military Spending," *Economist*, March 8, 1997.

90. Bitzinger and Gill, *Gearing Up for High-Tech Warfare?*, pp. 10-12; 20; see also "China Economy," *Economist*.

91. Fisher, "China's Purchase of Russian Fighters."

92. China has publicly denied that it obtained information about the U.S. F-16 fighter via secrets transferred by Israeli officials or businessmen managing the Lavi fighter program. However, the allegations originated from Haaretz, a respected Israeli daily. See "U.S. Upset Over Israeli-China Deals," Reuters, June 6, 1995; "China Denies Report it Obtained U.S. Bomber Secrets," Reuters, December 8, 1995.

93. Wang, *Military Development* (Taipei: Chinese Council of Advanced Policy Studies, CAPS Papers, No. 5: 1994), p. 97.

94. Mure Dickie, "Models, Slogans, Cookery Herald China New Military," Reuters, July 28, 1997.

95. "On Deng Xiaoping's Thinking on Military Expenditures," p. 26.

96. Fisher, "China's Purchase of Russian Fighters."

97. *Ibid.*

98. Kenneth W. Allen, Glenn Krumel, and Jonathan D. Pollack, *China's Air Force Enters the 21st Century* (Santa Monica, Ca: RAND, 1995), pp. xiii.

99. *Ibid,* p. xiv.

100. *Ibid,* pp. xv.

101. *Ibid.*

102. *Ibid.*

103. Fisher, "China's Purchase of Russian Fighters"; *Military Balance,* quoted in Prager, "China: Waking Up to the Next Superpower."

104. Allen, Krumel, and Pollack, *China's Air Force Enters the 21st Century,* pp. xvi-xvii.

105. *Ibid.*

106. "On Deng Xiaoping's Thinking on Military Expenditures," p. 26.

107. Allen, Krumel, and Pollack, *China's Air Force Enters the 21st Century,* pp. xv.

108. The article suggests a two-pronged strategy to build up China's equipment in this competition. On the one hand, China would import new technology, and this is listed first. Yet afterwards, it is argued, China would need to have the technical capacity to produce its own high-tech equipment and weaponry in order to hold onto Taiwan. "More on Enhancing Defense Modernization" *(zai lun jiaqiang guofang xiandai hua-jianshe),* *Military Sciences Economic Review (junshi jingji yanjiu),* 1996 (4), p. 32.

109. "TV Series on Military Airplanes Completed," *Xinhua,* August 14, 1997.

110. "On Deng Xiaoping's Thinking on Military Expenditures," p. 26.

111. Lewis and Xue, *China's Strategic Seapower,* pp. 211-214.

112. Recent histories of China's missile development can be found in Wang, *Military Development,* pp. 80-82; Liu Mingtao et. al., *Missile War under High Tech War* (Beijing: National Defense University Publishing House, 1993), pp. 66-67.

113. Wang, *Military Development,* pp. 80-82.
114. Wang, *Military Development,* pp. 80-82; "Overview of China's Nuclear Missile Situation," 2/95 (http://infomanage.com/nonproliferation/primer/chinabrief.html). China by the mid-1990s was said to possess between 14 and 17 ICBMs and between 70 and 90 Intermediate Range Ballistic Missiles (IRBM). The ICBMs have ranges of 9,300 miles (15,000 km) and 4,350 miles (7,000 km). The IRBMs have ranges of 1,700 miles (2,700 km) and 1,120 miles (1,800 km). Military Balance, quoted in Prager, "China: Waking Up to the Next Superpower." Mobile ICBMs apparently being developed by China include the 7,500-mile range DF-41 and the 5,000-mile range DF-31. Prepared Testimony of Richard D. Fisher.
115. Prepared Testimony of Richard D. Fisher.
116. James Risen and Jeff Gerth, "China is Installing a Warhead Said to be Based on U.S. Secrets," *New York Times* newswire, May 14, 1999.
117. "U.S. Probing Supercomputer Diversions," *IT Daily* (Asia-Tech Publications), June 13, 1997.
118. Wang, *Military Development,* pp. 91-92.
119. Liu et. al., *Missile War under High Tech War,* pp. 4-8.
120. *Ibid.*
121. *Ibid.,* pp. 8-15.
122. The discussion focuses on the versatility of missiles and the cutting-edge technologies that they rely upon. First, missiles are helpful in any type of battle, employing conventional, nuclear, chemical, or biological weapons. Second, missiles can employ a wide variety of guidance systems and technology, which means that their development is tied to the development of a host of modern technologies, from radars and infra-red light to electronic mapping. Third, missiles permit fighting over vast distances. Fourth, they are highly varied in their defense and attack capabilities and purposes. Fifth, they increasingly rely upon micro-electronic and automation technologies. Sixth, the same systems could be employed in multiple applications (e.g., surface-to-air or air-to-air). *Ibid.,* pp. 32-46.
123. "Overview of China's Nuclear Missile Situation."
124. This is weakened by the fact that China might consider a first use on Chinese soil against an invading force, and also by the possibility that China would use nuclear weapons against a nation that had not signed the nonproliferation treaty. For more information on China's nuclear policy, see "Overview of China's Nuclear Missile Situation." For more information on fears that China has aroused through apparent efforts to hedge the no first-use policy, see Brahma Chellaney, "China's Power Arouses Indian Disquiet," *The Jakarta Post,* December 20, 1996.
125. Jiang Baoqi et. al., eds., *A Study of China's Defense Economic Development*

Strategy (zhongguo guofang jingji fazhan zhanlue yanjiu), Beijing: National Defense University Publishing House, 1990, p. 49.

126. Li Huaixin, "Studying Military Economics with Chinese Characteristics" *(zhongguo tese de junshi jingji xue)*, in Li Lin and Zhao Qinxuan, eds., *Theory and Research on Military Economics in the New Era (xinshiqi junshi jingji lilun yanjiu)*, (Beijing: Military Sciences Publishing House, 1995), pp. 19-30.

127. For example, an "internal circulation only" (neibu) source published in 1990 by China's National Defense University argued that the primary problem with the organization of the military budget was that too much money was still siphoned off by salaries. Troop reductions were therefore considered essential. Jiang Baoqi et. al., China's Defense Economic Development Strategy.

128. See, for example, Wan Xiaoyuan and Wan Zilong, "Development Trends of Military Economics under Socialist Market Conditions" *(lun shehuizhuyi shichang jingji tiaojianxia junshi jingji fazhan qushi)*, *Military Sciences Economic Review (junshi jingji yanjiu)*, 1996 (12), pp. 10-13 (13).

129. China also marked the 70th anniversary of the founding of the PLA (on August 1, 1997) with calls for turning the army into a smaller force. "Streamlining the army with Chinese characteristics is the right choice for China in military modernization," said Jiang Zemin during the ceremonies. A People's Daily editorial added: "To walk the road of crack troops with Chinese characteristics requires the strengthening of quality and modernizing construction. . . . We must certainly . . . as quickly as possible make the shift from quantity to quality and from manpower to science and technology." *East Asian Strategic Review, 1997-1998* (Tokyo: National Institute of Defense Studies), 1998, p. 116; Mure Dickie, "China Says Army Should be Smaller, Tougher," Reuters, August 1, 1997.

130. China: Military Commission Meets on Demobilization, Morale, Ming Pao (HK), July 4, 1998, p. B10, in FBIS-CHI-98-185.

131. "More on Enhancing Defense Modernization" *(zai lun jiaqiang guofang xiandai huajianshe)*, *Military Sciences Economic Review (junshi jingji yanjiu)*, 1996 (4), p. 31.

132. The International Institute for Strategic Studies, *The Military Balance, 1997/1998* p. 179.

133. Liu Hsiao-hua, "Armed Police Force: China's One Million Special Armed Troops," *Wide Angle (kuang chiao ching)* (HK), 307 (April 16, 1998), pp. 42-47, in FBIS-CHI-98-134.

134. A journalistic article on the new equipment of the armed police for tackling Mafiosos, terrorists, and rioters can be found in Chou Kuan-wu, "New Equipment of Chinese Armed Police," *Wide Angle (kuang chiao ching)* (HK), 307 (April 16, 1998), pp. 72-79, in FBIS-CHI-98-141.

135. "China: Military Commission Meets on Demobilization, Morale."

136. Yan Xiaomeng, "Broadly on the Establishment and Perfection of a Social Security System for Servicemen" *(jianli he wanshan junren shehui baozhang tixi de longguan sikao), Military Sciences Economic Review (junshi jingji yanjiu),* 1995 (11), p. 83.

137. Wang Xiaoshu, "Briefly on Finding Places for Officers Transferred to Civilian Work: Contradictions and Countermeasures" *(qiantan dangqian junzhuan anzhi gongzuo de maodun ji duice), Transferring Chinese Army Officers to Civilian Work (zhongguo zhuanye junguan),* 1996 (2), p. 8.

138. *Ibid.*

139. *Ibid.*

140. "On the Work Distribution of Cadres Transferred to Civilian Posts" *(guanyu zhuanye ganbu de gongzuo fenpei), Transferring Chinese Army Officers to Civilian Work (zhongguo zhuanye junguan),* 1997 (2), p. 11.

141. *Ibid.*

142. Zhang Chuansheng, "Pondering the Current Effort to Find Work for Experts and Technical Cadres" *(cong zhuanye jishu ganbu anzhi xiankuang zhong yinchu de sisuo), Transferring Chinese Army Officers to Civilian Work (zhongguo zhuanye junguan),* 1996 (7), p. 17.

143. Liu Yichang and Li Lin, "On Construction of Defense Economics under Market Conditions" *(lun shichang jingji tiaojian xia de guofang jingji jianshe), Military Sciences Economic Review (junshi jingji yanjiu),* 1996 (3), p. 10.

144. "Nanjing Military Region Commander Chen Bingde on Military Theory, Reform," *China Military Science (beijing zhongguo junshi kexue),* 3 (August 1997), pp. 49-56, in FBIS-CHI-98-065.

145. Fang Jizuo et. al., "On the Legalization of Defense Expenditure Management," *Military Sciences Economic Review (junshi jingji yanjiu),* 1995 (8), p. 36.

146. Huang Ruixin et. al., "Problems of Financial Management in Military Expenditure Optimization," *Military Sciences Economic Review (junshi jingji yanjiu),* 1995 (10), p. 46.

147. Fang et. al., "On the Legalization of Defense Expenditure Management," p. 36.

148. "Taiwan Military Authorities Say Chinese Forces' Landing Drill 'Routine,'" Central News Agency, Taipei, November 27, 1995.

149. U.S. Department of Defense Report to Congress, "Security Situation in the Taiwan Strait," updated February 26, 1999. See http://www.defenselink.mil/

Chapter Three

1. Deng Liqun et. al., eds., *The Chinese People's Liberation Army, Vol. I* (Beijing: Contemporary China Publishing House, 1994), pp. 703-5.

2. These included a Central Committee Military Industrial Commission headed by Zhou Enlai, an Aviation Management Commission, a Ministry of Defense Industries, Ministries of Industrial Machinery focused on conventional and nuclear weapons production, a Defense Science and Technology Commission, and a Defense Industrial Commission.

3. John Gittings, *The Role of the Chinese Army* (London: Oxford University Press, 1967), pp. 176-201.

4. Sun Zhenhuan, ed., *The Construction of China's National Defense Economics (zhongguo guofang jingji jianshe)*, Beijing: Military Sciences Publishing House *(junshi kexue chubanshe)*, 1991, pp. 22-23.

5. *Ibid*, pp. 45-49.

6. Gittings, *The Role of the Chinese Army*, pp. 176-201.

7. *Ibid.*

8. Liu Yichang and Wu Xizhi, eds., *The Basics of National Defense Economic Studies*, Beijing: Military Sciences Publishing House *(junshi kexue chubanshe)*, 1991.

9. Gittings, The Role of the Chinese Army, pp. 176-201.

10. *Ibid*, p. 183.

11. *Contemporary China's Ordnance Industry (dangdai zhongguo de bingqi gongye)*, Beijing: Contemporary China Publishing House *(dangdai zhongguo chubanshe)*, 1993, p. 463.

12. Gittings, *The Role of the Chinese Army*, p. 226.

13. *Ibid*, p. 195.

14. *Ibid.*

15. Paul Humes Folta, *From Swords to Plowshares? Defense Industry Reform in the PRC* (Boulder, CO: Westview, 1992), pp. 48-49.

16. Deng et. al., *The Chinese People's Liberation Army, Vol. I,* pp. 705-6.

17. *Ibid*, pp. 702-703.

18. *Ibid*, pp. 705-6.

19. *Ibid*, pp. 706-707.

20. *Ibid*, p. 706.

21. *Ibid*, pp. 706-707. Another source states that in 1986, "the total value" of military-controlled production was 6.078 billion yuan; of this, 2.4 billion yuan (39 percent of the total) was civilian-use products. Liu and Wu, *The Basics of National Defense Economic Studies,* p. 185.

22. Deng et. al., *The Chinese People's Liberation Army, Vol. I,* pp. 706-707.

23. See, for example, Liu and Wu, *The Basics of National Defense Economic Studies,* pp. 100-102.

24. Sun Zhenhuan, ed., *The Construction of China's National Defense Economics,* p. 31.

25. Deng et. al., *The Chinese People's Liberation Army, Vol. I,* pp. 707-708.

26. *Ibid*, pp. 708-709.

27. *Ibid*, p. 708.

28. Shu-Shin Wang, *Military Development of the People's Republic of China after the 1989 Tiananmen Massacre* (Taipei: Chinese Council of Advanced Policy Studies, CAPS Papers, No. 5: 1994), pp. 91-92.

29. John Pomfret, "Jiang Orders Military to Go Out of Business," *International Herald Tribune,* July 23, 1998, p. 1.

30. "China's Defense-Industrial Trading Organizations" (Washington, D.C.: Defense Intelligence Agency, Reference Document PC-1921-57-95, 1995).

31. Interview with an officer at COSTIND, August, 1997.

32. *East Asian Strategic Review, 1997-1998* (Tokyo: National Institute of Defense Studies), 1998, pp. 113-114.

33. Wang, *Military Development,* p. 77; Cui Ning, "China: Hi-Tech Project Highlights 5 Areas," *China Daily,* April 3, 1996.

34. Huai Guomo (Vice Chairman of COSTIND), "Diligently Push On with the Sustained Development of Defense Conversion at Military Industrial Scientific Research Centers" *(nuli tuijin jungong keyan yuansuo junzhuanmin chixu fazhan), China Defense Science and Technology Information (zhongguo guofang keji xinxi),* 1996, 5-6, p. 9.

35. *Ibid,* pp. 11-12.

36. Parts of this list are provided in Liu and Wu, *The Basics of National Defense Economic Studies,* pp. 116-123.

37. He Liming et. al., "Military Production and Defense Development Strategies," *Military Sciences Economic Review (junshi jingji yanjiu),* 1996 (12), pp. 17-18.

38. *Ibid,* p. 18.

39. "Text of Defense White Paper," Xinhua, July 27, 1998.

40. Deng et. al., *The Chinese People's Liberation Army, Vol. I,* p. 322.

41. Bruce Swanson, "Naval Forces," in Gerald Segal and William T. Tow, eds., *Chinese Defense Policy* (London: Macmillan Press, 1984), pp. 85-86.

42. From G. Jacobs, "China's Amphibious Capabilities," *Asian Defense Journal,* January 1990, p. 64, cited in (Japan's) Office of Technology Assessment, "Other Approaches to Civil-Military Integration: The Chinese and Japanese Arms Industries," March 27, 1995 (http://www.gwjapan.org/ftp/pub/policy/miscpol/ota-cmi.txt).

43. Deng et. al., *The Chinese People's Liberation Army, Vol. I,* p. 323.

44. "Text of Defense White Paper," Xinhua, July 27, 1998.; "Deng Said Jiang Qualified Party Secretary," Beijing Xinhua News Service, August 8, 1997, in FBIS-CHI-97-220.

45. This includes over 70 airports, 25 wharves, and 300 rail lines, all open to civilian products. He Liming et. al., "Military Production and Defense Development Strategies," p. 18.

46. Wang, *Military Development,* p. 97.

47. "Text of Defense White Paper," Xinhua, July 27, 1998.

48. From 1984 to 1988, the navy opened 20 ports and wharves that were previously closed for commercial projects and profit-seeking businesses. The air force opened more than 40 airports, previously used only by the military, to civilian and commercial aviation. The army as a whole opened over 300 military railway lines, over 250 electric power lines, telegraph lines, oil extraction and processing facilities, and other resources for commercial ventures and civilian use. Deng Liqun et. al., *The Chinese People's Liberation Army, Vol. I*, p. 325.

49. *Ibid.*

50. 1.5 million soldiers are said to have participated in or carried out technical construction projects of every kind in poor areas from 1978 to 1987, with military science research and technology bureaus carrying out 1,300 projects in those areas. *Ibid.*, p. 322.

51. *Ibid.*

52. Liu and Wu, *The Basics of National Defense Economic Studies*, pp. 100-102.

53. "Text of Defense White Paper."

54. Deng et. al., eds., *The Chinese People's Liberation Army, Vol. I*, p. 324.

55. Li Zhonghu et. al., eds., *The Mobility Mechanism of National Defense High-Tech Production (guofang gaojishu chanyehua yunxing jizhi)*, Beijing: National Defense Industries Publishing House, 1995, pp. 182.

56. "Text of Defense White Paper," Xinhua, July 27, 1998.

57. Deng et. al., *The Chinese People's Liberation Army, Vol. I*, p. 328-329.

58. *Big Events of the Army's Production and Businesses (jundui shengchan jingying da shiji)*. Beijing: No date or publisher known for this source, borrowed from a Mainland analyst.

59. *Ibid.* Ellis Joffe states that the 999 Enterprise Group "combines over 30 companies operating under the General Logistics Department in the Shenzhen Special Economic Zone." Perhaps Triple Nine was counted as 30 companies at that time. See Ellis Joffe, "The PLA and the Economy: The Effects of Involvement," in Gerald Segal and Richard H. Yang, eds., *Chinese Economic Reform: The Impact on Security* (London: Routledge, 1996), p. 21.

60. Joffe, "The PLA and the Economy," p. 21.

61. Pomfret, "Jiang Orders Military to Go Out of Business," p. 1.

62. Five other firms include the Bureau of Military Equipment and Technology Cooperation (BOMETEC), the Huitong Corporation, China Electronic Systems Engineering Company (working on communications and electronics technology and equipment), Pinghe Electronics Company (producing military technology), and the China Zhihua Corporation (producing communications equipment, computers, image processing equipment, and navigation equipment). "China's Defense-Industrial Trading Organizations." (Washington, D.C.: Defense Intelligence Agency, Reference Document PC-1921-57-95, 1995).

63. These are the Kaili Corporation (also called (Carrie Enterprises), which works on communications equipment and publications; and Tiancheng Corporation. "China's Defense-Industrial Trading Organizations."

64. *Ibid.*

65. *Big Events of the Army's Production and Businesses.*

66. *Ibid.*

67. Liu Yichang and Li Lin, "On Construction of Defense Economics under Market Conditions" *(lun shichang jingji tiaojian xia de guofang jingji jianshe), Military Sciences Economic Review (junshi jingji yanjiu),* 1996 (3), pp. 8-15.

68. *Ibid.*

69. Sun, *The Construction of China's National Defense Economics,* p. 50.

70. *Big Events of the Army's Production and Businesses.*

71. *Ibid.*

72. Presumably, these are among the 670,000 full-time employees. Deng et. al., *The Chinese People's Liberation Army, Vol. I,* p. 709.

73. *Big Events of the Army's Production and Businesses.*

74. "Jiang Orders PLA-Owned Firms To Close," Xinhua, July 22, 1998, in FBIS-CHI-98-204.

75. "SETC Takes Over Military Enterprises," Ming Pao (HK), September 23, 1998, p A15, in FBIS-CHI-98-266; Lung Hua, "PLA Severs Ties with Enterprises," in *Hong Kong Economic Journal (Hong Kong Hsin Pao),* November 11, 1998, p. 24, in FBIS-CHI-98-320.

76. "China: PLA, Armed Police Told to Support Reform," Xinhua, April 21, 1998, in FBIS-CHI-98-111.

77. Pomfret, "Jiang Orders Military to Go Out of Business," pp. 1, 4.

78. Pai Chuan, "Command System of the Chinese Army," Hong Kong Ching Pao, 257 (December 1, 1998), pp. 40-42, in FBIS-CHI-98-346.

79. Benjamin C. Ostrov, *Conquering Resources: The Growth and Decline of the PLA's Science and Technology Commission for National Defense* (Armonk, NJ: M.E. Sharpe, 1991).

80. *Ibid,* p. 63.

81. Kenneth R. Timmerman, "The Peking Pentagon," *The American Spectator,* April, 1996 (http://www.security-policy.org/papers/96-D29at.html).

82. Folta, *From Swords to Plowshares?,* p. 7. For more on COSTIND, see also (Japan's) Office of Technology Assessment, "Other Approaches to Civil-Military Integration."

83. The U.S. Defense Intelligence Agency lists, as corporations under the control of COSTIND:
    - The Xiaofeng Technology and Equipment Corporation, which works closely with the PLA on computers, test equipment, robotics, and advanced technology.
    - The Xinshidai (New Era) Development Corporation, which

works on scientific cooperation and exchanges, exhibitions, and advanced technology.
- The Yuanwang (Group) Corporation.
- The Galaxy New Technology Corporation.
- The China Defense Science and Technology Information Center (CDSTIC).
- The China Association of Peaceful Use of Military Industrial Technology (CAPUMIT).

84. (Japan's) Office of Technology Assessment, "Other Approaches to Civil-Military Integration."
85. Huai Guomo, "Diligently Push On with the Sustained Development," pp. 11-12.
86. Twenty-four institutes employed U.S. $500,000 or less (presumably figures are on an annual basis), nine employed from $500,000 to $1 million; 12 from $1 million to $3 million; only 5 over $3 million. Huai Guomo, "Diligently Push On with the Sustained Development," pp. 9-10.
87. Sun, *The Construction of China's National Defense Economics,* p. 31.
88. (Japan's) Office of Technology Assessment, "Other Approaches to Civil-Military Integration."
89. Folta, *From Swords to Plowshares?,* pp. 50-51.
90. (Japan's) Office of Technology Assessment, "Other Approaches to Civil-Military Integration."
91. Sun, *The Construction of China's National Defense Economics,* p. 27.
92. *Ibid,* p. 32.
93. *Ibid,* p. 33.
94. These statistics are compiled mostly from two open sources: Information Office of the State Council of the PRC, "White Paper on Arms Control and Disarmament," Xinhua, November 16, 1995; and Liu Yichang et. al., The Study of Defense Economics (Beijing: Military Sciences Publishing House, 1993), pp. 65, 122. A slightly older source provides the following statistics, which differ slightly but represent a similar trend:

Military-Managed Production of Civilian-Use Products

1979	8.1 percent
1987	around 50 percent
1989	63.5 percent

See Sun, *The Construction of China's National Defense Economics,* p. 27.
95. Folta, *From Swords to Plowshares?,* p. 5.
96. *Ibid,* pp. 49-50.
97. Li Yintao, "A Research on the Stages of Defense Conversion in Science and Technology Industries" *(guofang keji gongye junzhuanmin fazhan jieduan yanjiu), Military Sciences Economic Review (junshi jingji yanjiu),* 1996 (2), p. 22.

98. Sun, *The Construction of China's National Defense Economics,* p. 177.

99. *Ibid.*

100. "China Investment: Defense Sector to Open," Economist Intelligence Unit, July 23, 1997.

101. "Construct a Modernized National Defense, Develop High-Tech Military Industries," *(jianshe xiandaihua guofang, fazhan gaojishu jungong),* from the Ninth Five-Year Plan of the National Defense Science and Technology Industries, in China Defense Science and Technology Information *(zhongguo guofang keji xinxi),* 1996, 5-6, pp. 18-21.

102. Li Yintao, "A Research on the Stages of Defense Conversion," p. 22. Somewhat different statistics are suggested by a Western source: Folta, *From Swords to Plowshares?;* see especially pp. 130-133.

103. *Ibid,* pp. 18-21.

104. The article states: "The MII provides enforced occupational management in military electronics, to initiate a development strategy, policy direction and planning in military electronics research, to set up and consolidate the enforcement of planning in Armed Forces and Defense Science and Technical Industry Commission." "China: Information Industry Ministry Outlined," *China Electronics (zhongguo dianzi bao),* July 10, 1998, p. 1, in FBIS-CHI-98-236.

105. For more details on MII, see Warren H. Rothman and Jonathan P. Barker, "Ministry Profile: Information Overlord," *China Economic Review,* October 23, 1998. http://www.rothmanbarker.com.

106. "Internet Use Growing in PRC," Hong Kong Wen Wei Po, September 22, 1998, p. A5, in FBIS-CHI-98-270.

107. "Implement Defense Conversion as our United, Guiding Principle: Follow the Track of Sci-Tech and Economic Unity" *(guanche junmin jiehe de fangzhen: zoushang keji yu jingji jiehe de guidao),* in China Defense Science and Technology Information *(zhongguo guofang keji xinxi),* 1996, 5-6, p. 24.

108. *Ibid.*

109. *Ibid.*

110. "Crisis Offers Challenge for Shipbuilding," Xinhua, December 24, 1998, in FBIS-CHI-98-358.

111. *Ibid.*

112. "Look Toward National Economic Construction: Speed Up Shipbuilding Defense Conversion in Military Industrial Research Institutes and Offices," in China Defense Science and Technology Information *(zhongguo guofang keji xinxi),* 1996, 5-6, p. 26.

113. *Ibid,* p. 26.

114. *Ibid.*

115. Sun, *The Construction of China's National Defense Economics,* p. 31.

116. "Look Toward National Economic Construction," p. 26.

117. Liu and Wu, *The Basics of National Defense Economic Studies,* p. 99.

118. See also Sun, *The Construction of China's National Defense Economics,* p. 30.
119. Sun, *The Construction of China's National Defense Economics,* p. 32.
120. "China's Defense-Industrial Trading Organizations."
121. (Japan's) Office of Technology Assessment, "Other Approaches to Civil-Military Integration."
122. *Contemporary China's Ordnance Industry,* p. 468.
123. *Contemporary China's Ordnance Industry,* p. 551. Exact statistics on the number of employees located in defense industrial bureaus have not been found by this author. The book cited above suggests one million employees in the Ministry of Ordnance Industry alone. But other sources suggest all of the Defense Industrial Ministries together may not employ much more than that. According to a recent Xinhua article, around one million workers are employed in the "national defense science, technology and industrial" bureaus. The article suggests, but does not clearly state, that this "one million" figure represents the number of civilians working in all of the former defense industrial ministries. Perhaps this figure does not include the workers in the businesses run by these ministries? Some statistics are also rendered more opaque by the fact that the largest defense industrial bureaus, MII and Shipbuilding, are not always counted as defense industrial bureaus. See Xi Qixin and Tian Zhaoyun: "On the Avenue Bathed in Sunshine—A Factual Account of Deng Xiaoping and Jiang Zemin Showing Concern for the National Defense Industry's Shift to Civilian Undertakings," Xinhua, February 22, 1998, in FBIS-CHI-98-060.
124. "Construct a Modernized National Defense," p. 20.
125. *Ibid.*
126. "TV Series on Military Airplanes Completed," Xinhua, August 14, 1997.
127. "Construct a Modernized National Defense," p. 20.
128. Sun, *The Construction of China's National Defense Economics,* p. 25.
129. Liu and Wu, *The Basics of National Defense Economic Studies,* p. 99.
130. Deng Liqun et. al., *The Chinese People's Liberation Army, Vol. I,* p. 515.
131. Lt. Col. Wang Chunyuan, China's Space Industry and Its Strategy of International Cooperation (http://www-leland.stanford.edu/group/CISAC/test/pub/recent.html#anchor214994)
132. "China's Defense-Industrial Trading Organizations."
133. The 20 organizations are as follows:
     - China Academy of Launch Vehicle Technology (CALT), also called the First Academy or the Beijing Wanyuan Industry Corporation. This is in charge of space launch vehicles, mission analysis, and interface coordination.
     - The China Chang Feng Mechanics and Electronics Technology Academy or the Second Academy, with responsibilities to produce spacecraft and components.

- The technology academy of China or Third Academy.
- The Hexi Chemical Corporation or Fourth Academy.
- The Chinese Academy of Space Studies or the Fifth Academy, which assists in the production of satellites and recoverable payloads.
- The China Space Civil and Building Engineering Design and Research Institute (CSCBI) or the Seventh Academy.
- The China Space Civil and Building Engineering Design and Research Institute or the Seventh Academy.
- The Shanghai Academy of Space Flight Technology, also labeled the Shanghai Bureau of Astronautics or Eighth Academy, which assists in first and second stages of space launch vehicles and altitude control, guidance, and stabilization systems.
- The China Academy of Basic Technology for Space Electronics or the Ninth Academy.
- The China Great Wall Industry Group.
- The China Great Wall Industry Corporation, which assists in space launch services, space technology and equipment, and is a "prime contractor" for space services; the China National Precision Machinery Import and Export Corporation, which produces all types of missiles, rocket engines, radars, precision machinery, optical instruments, medical equipment, household electrical appliances, tools, and fixtures.
- The China Jiangnan Space Industry Company Group.
- The Sichuan Aerospace Industry Corporation.
- The China Sanjiang Space Group.
- The Shaanxi Lingnan Machinery Company.
- The China Astronautics Industrial Supply and Marketing Corporation.
- The Harbin Institute of Technology.
- The Feihuan Corporation.
- The Beijing Tongha Measuring Instruments Corporation.

From "China's Defense-Industrial Trading Organizations."

134. Liu and Wu, *The Basics of National Defense Economic Studies,* p. 99.
135. "Construct a Modernized National Defense," pp. 18-21.
136. *Ibid.*
137. Information Office of the State Council of the PRC, "White Paper on Arms Control and Disarmament."
138. $5 billion is a profit estimate provided in 1995 by the Research Institute for Peace and Security. See Research Institute for Peace and Security, Asian Security, 1995-1996 (London: Brasssey's, 1995), p. 99. Interviews in 1996 suggested a somewhat higher figure.

139. Information Office of the State Council of the PRC, "White Paper on Arms Control and Disarmament."

140. Sun, *The Construction of China's National Defense Economics,* p. 21.

141. One list of goods in an open source is provided by Liu et. al., *The Study of Defense Economics,* p. 152.

142. Information Office of the State Council of the PRC, "White Paper on Arms Control and Disarmament."

143. There are no statistics available on the nationalities of the foreign partners. See Information Office of the State Council of the PRC, "White Paper on Arms Control and Disarmament."

144. According to one isolated source, the entire army apparently had established some 200 joint ventures, or jointly-funded enterprises, in 1992, and the number of jointly-funded enterprises was growing fastest in the air force, which managed 46 of these projects. Yet it is not clear if these were international or domestic joint ventures. *Big Events of the Army's Production and Businesses.*

145. Karl W. Eikenberry, "Explaining and Influencing Chinese Arms Transfers" (Wash., D.C.: Institute for National Strategic Studies [National Defense University] McNair Paper 36, February, 1995), p. 7. See also John W. Lewis, Hua Di, and Xue Litai, "Beijing's Defense Establishment: Solving the Arms Export Enigma," *International Security* (Spring, 1991), pp. 89-93.

146. See also Shigeo Hiramatsu, "China's Nuclear Arms Development and Arms Transfers to the Third World," *Asia-Pacific Review,* 2:1 (Spring, 1995), pp. 188-189.

147. Tim Weiner, "U.S. and Chinese Aid was Essential as Pakistan Built Bomb," *International Herald Tribune,* June 2, 1998, p. 4.

148. The GLD also controls China Xinxing Corp., which lists among its products food, clothing, and construction materials. (Japan's) Office of Technology Assessment, "Other Approaches to Civil-Military Integration."

149. "Overview of China's Nuclear Missile Situation."

150. (Japan's) Office of Technology Assessment, "Other Approaches to Civil-Military Integration."

151. *Ibid.*

152. Liu et. al., *The Study of Defense Economics,* pp. 118-120.

153. "PRC Law on National Defense, Fifth Opinion of the Eighth National People's Congress, Promoted March 14, 1997 and Endorsed by PRC 'Chairman' Jiang Zemin" (released by Xinhua, March 14, 1997)

154. "More on Enhancing Defense Modernization" (*zai lun jiaqiang guofang xiandai huajianshe*), *Military Sciences Economic Review* (*junshi jingji yanjiu*), 1996 (4), p. 31.

155. Joffe, "The PLA and the Economy: The Effects of Involvement," p. 15.

Chapter Four

1. Figures taken or computed from *China Statistical Yearbook, 1996* (Beijing: China Statistical Publishing House, 1996), pp. 222, 231, and 255; and *China Statistical Yearbook, 1986* (Beijing: China Statistical Publishing House, 1986), pp. 516, 520, and 535.

2. Deng Liqun et. al., eds., *The Chinese People's Liberation Army, Vol. I* (Beijing: Contemporary China Publishing House, 1994), p. 669.

3. *Ibid,* p. 579.

4. *Ibid,* p. 320.

5. *Ibid,* p. 669.

6. Jin Zhude and An Weimin, "[Employing] Twice the Development and Key Deployment of National Defense Resources: A New Exploration on the Concept of Defense Conversion" (*guofang ziyuan de arci kaifa he zhongxin peizhi: dui junzhuanmin gainian de xin tansuo*), *Chinese Military Industry News* (*zhongguo jungong bao*), September 6, 1996, p. 3.

7. Luo Yuwen, "PLA General Defends 1999 Military Budget," Xinhua, March 8, 1999, in FBIS-CHI-1999-0310.

8. *Ibid.*

9. Information Office of the State Council of the PRC, "White Paper on Arms Control and Disarmament," Xinhua, November 16, 1995.

10. "Text of Defense White Paper," Xinhua, July 27, 1998.

11. The 1998 White Paper claims militia and reserve requirements are indeed part of China's expenditure on national defense—but it is perhaps intentionally unclear if this means that these requirements are included in the defense budget. "Text of Defense White Paper," Xinhua, July 27, 1998.

12. This does not count 3.7 billion yuan in welfare (pensions for retired personnel, schools, and hospitals for families of officers) listed elsewhere in the budget and discussed in the White Paper; nor does it count expenses to build and maintain living quarters. Information Office of the State Council of the PRC, "White Paper on Arms Control and Disarmament," Xinhua, November 16, 1995.

13. Starting with a U.S. dollar figure, one Mainland article claims that China spends around U.S. $2,000 per soldier per year, just under three times the figure provided in the White Paper. Since the statistic is in dollars and designed as a comparison with U.S. spending on soldiers (said to be around $150,000 per soldier), it is not clear if it came from an internal or external source, or what it is based on. No year for the statistic is provided either. At an exchange rate of 8.2 yuan to the dollar, this would leave around 1,370 yuan per month budgeted for each soldier. He Liming et. al., "Military Production and Defense Development Strategies," *Military Sciences Economic Review* (*junshi jingji yanjiu*), 1996 (12), pp. 14-19 (12).

14. "PRC Law on National Defense, Fifth Opinion of the Eighth National

People's Congress, Promoted March 14, 1997 and Endorsed by PRC 'Chairman' Jiang Zemin" (released by Xinhua).

15. Liu Rongpu, "Some Considerations on the Inputs of Military Expenditure" *(dui junfei touruu de jidian sikao), Military Sciences Economic Review (junshi jingji yanjiu),* 1996 (5), pp. 39-40.

16. Liu Yichang and Wu Xizhi, eds., *The Basics of National Defense Economic Studies,* Beijing: Military Sciences Publishing House *(junshi kexue chubanshe),* 1991, p. 217.

17. "On Deng Xiaoping's Thinking on Military Expenditures" *(deng xiaoping xin shiqi junfei sixiang chutan), Military Sciences Economic Review (junshi jingji yanjiu),* 1995 (8), p. 24.

18. He Liming et. al., "Military Production and Defense Development Strategies," *Military Sciences Economic Review (junshi jingji yanjiu),* 1996 (12), p. 16.

19. "Today, almost all of the world's armies are heading in the direction of 'less money for living allowances, lowering maintenance costs, raising development.' Without cutting into living standards of soldiers, the only way to cut living allowances is to cut soldiers from the rolls.

   Although our nation has implemented a massive decommissioning of one million soldiers, it still has the largest army in the world, and soldiers' living allowances account for more than 30 percent of all military expenditures. . . . Our nation [still] has a need to cut the number of soldiers." He et. al., "Military Production and Defense Development Strategies," p. 17.

20. Shaoguang Wang, "Estimating China's Defense Expenditure: Some Evidence from Chinese Sources," *The China Quarterly,* 147 (September, 1996), p. 891.

21. *Ibid,* p. 893.

22. Interview with a PLA contact, May 22, 1997.

23. Total values of defense expenditures estimated by Shaoguang Wang are listed in the conclusion and compared, adjusting for inflation, to values at the beginning of the reform period:

Item	Amount (billions of yuan)	Compared to 1978 (in real terms)
official defense budget	43.2	about the same
military R&D	6.4	about the same
militia	0.7	much lower
PAP	5.0	new
subsidies for the production of weapons	3.0	much lower
earnings from the PLA's economic activities	8.0	much higher
earnings from the PLA's arms sales	0.2	new
TOTAL	66.5	slightly higher

For more details, see Wang, "Estimating China's Defense Expenditure," p. 910.

24. This statement is based upon a 1980 report and a 1992 report by the CIA. See Paul H. B. Godwin, " 'PLA, Incorporated': Estimating China's Military Expenditure," in Gerald Segal and Richard H. Yang, eds., *Chinese Economic Reform: The Impact on Security,* London: Routledge, 1996, p. 62.

25. "Taiwan 'White Paper' Lists PRC Capabilities, Invasion Exercises," Taipei Lien-Ho Pao, March 25, 1998, p. 4, in FBIS-CHI-98-086.

26. For the ACDA estimate and others, see Godwin, " 'PLA, Incorporated,' " pp. 62-67.

27. See for example Richard D. Fisher (Senior Policy Analyst, the Heritage Foundation), "China's Purchase of Russian Fighters: A Challenge to the U.S.," Heritage Foundation press and internet release, July 31, 1996.

28. Fang Jizuo et. al., "On the Legalization of Defense Expenditure Management," *Military Sciences Economic Review (junshi jingji yanjiu),* 1995 (8), p. 40.

29. *Ibid,* p. 37.

30. Deng et. al., *The Chinese People's Liberation Army, Vol. I,* p. 515.

31. For limited information on the relationship between these industries and national defense, see also Wang Pufeng et. al., *On Modern National Defense (guan xindai guofang gai)* (Chongqing: Chongqing Publishing House, 1993).

32. Wang, "Estimating China's Defense Expenditure," p. 892, 896-7.

33. "Russia Expects to Increase Cooperation with China in Military Technology," Interfax News Agency, July 27, 1997.

34. *Ibid.*

35. Lei Qingshan et. al., eds., *Introduction to the National Defense Reserves (guofang houbeijun gailun),* Beijing: National Defense University Publishing House, 1989(?), pp. 324, 327, 328.

36. For details on the history, organization, and purpose of the PAP, see Liu Hsiao-hua, "Armed Police Force: China's One Million Special Armed Troops," Hong Kong Kuang Chiao Ching, 307 (April 16, 1998), pp. 42-47, in FBIS-CHI-98-134.

37. The International Institute for Strategic Studies, *The Military Balance, 1997/1998* (Oxford: Oxford University Press, 1998), p. 265.

38. *Ibid.*

39. Godwin, " 'PLA, Incorporated' " p. 71. Poly Group is owned by the General Staff Dept., Kaili Company by the General Political Dept., and Xinxin by the General Logistics Department. Wang, "Estimating China's Defense Expenditure," p. 907.

40. François Godement, "China's Arms Sales," in Gerald Segal and Richard H. Yang, eds., *Chinese Economic Reform: The Impact on Security* (London: Routledge, 1996), p. 100. Godement throws water on the idea that China's arms sales could be highly significant strategically or financially:

A remarkable aspect of . . . large conventional arms sales by China in the 1980s is that they have never been appraised as likely to upset any regional balance. With few exceptions—concerning mostly weapons sold at a later date—Chinese arms sales, like their predecessor from the 1950s, were assessed more for their political nuisance value than for their actual potential. The available literature is often full of deprecative comments regarding the 'poor quality' of these weapons, suggesting that the motivations of the buyers are second rate: they are either Third World customers filling up their armies with cheap, low-tech arms which more likely than not they will not use in actual international conflicts (Egypt, Pakistan, Iraq and to a lesser extent Iran, Thailand), or 'Fourth World' states attempting to set up regular armies (Somalia, Sudan, Bangladesh, Zimbabwe) or 'pariah states' which have nowhere else to go: Libya, North Korea, Burma today, as well as the Khmer Rouge.

From *Ibid*, p. 98.

41. Godwin, " 'PLA, Incorporated,' " p. 71.
42. Wang, "Estimating China's Defense Expenditure," pp. 909-910.
43. Liu Yichang and Li Lin, "On Construction of Defense Economics under Market Conditions" *(lun shichang jingji tiaojian xia de guofang jingji jianshe), Military Sciences Economic Review (junshi jingji yanjiu)*, 1996 (3), p. 10.
44. "Deng Said Jiang Qualified Party Secretary," Beijing Xinhua News Service, August 8, 1997, in FBIS-CHI-97-220.
45. Wang, "Estimating China's Defense Expenditure," p. 906.
46. Wu Yubang, "The Centralized Nature of Financial Management and Centralized and Unified Leadership of the Army" *(caiwu guanli de jizhongxing yu jundui jizhong tongyi lingdao)*, in Li Lin and Zhao Qinxuan, eds., *Theory and Research on Military Economics in the New Era (xinshiqi junshi jingji lilun yanjiu)*, (Beijing: Military Sciences Publishing House, 1995), p. 55.
47. See for example, Liu Yechu and Chen Daixing, "Deng Xiaoping's Thought on Military Economics: The Basic Points and Impressive Views" *(lun deng xiaoping junshi jingji sixiang de jibendian jiqi weida yiyi)*, in Li Lin and Zhao Qinxuan, eds., *Theory and Research on Military Economics in the New Era (xinshiqi junshi jingji lilun yanjiu)*, (Beijing: Military Sciences Publishing House, 1995), p. 17; see also Huang Min and Teng Yong, "Basic Discussion of Deng Xiaoping's Thought on the Benefits of Military Economics in the New Period" *(qiantan deng xiaoping xinshiqi junshi jingji xiaoyi sixiang)*, in Li Lin and Zhao Qinxuan, eds., *Theory and Research on Military Economics in the New Era (xinshiqi junshi jingji lilun yanjiu)*, (Beijing: Military Sciences Publishing House, 1995), p. 72.
48. Li Huaixin, "Studying Military Economics with Chinese Characteristics" *(zhongguo tese de junshi jingji xue)*, in Li and Zhao, *Theory and Research on Military Economics in the New Era*, p. 22.
49. See also *Ibid*, pp. 19-30.
50. Huang Ruixin et. al., "Problems of Financial Management in Military

Expenditure Optimalization," *Military Sciences Economic Review (junshi jingji yanjiu),* 1995 (10), p. 46.

51. Liu and Li, "On Construction of Defense Economics under Market Conditions," pp. 10, 12.

52. On the other hand, it may be that the primary expense for the military housing construction is labor costs, which are not factored in accurately. Chen Zaibing and Sun Bolin, "On Securing Housing for Soldiers" *(lun junren zhufang baozhang),* in Li and Zhao, *Theory and Research on Military Economics in the New Era,* pp. 352-358 (354).

53. At current rates, this might be a salary bill for nearly a million civilian employees. It is unlikely that this includes employees of enterprises, or any bills paid by the State Council to its subordinate defense bureaus and committees. Zhang Geng, "Explore Road of Developing Socialized Logistic Support with PLA Characteristics", *The PLA Daily (jiefangjun bao),* November 10, 1998, in FBIS-CHI-98-331.

54. Jiang Baoqi et. al., eds., *A Study of China's Defense Economic Development Strategy (zhongguo guofang jingji fazhan zhanlue yanjiu),* Beijing: National Defense University Publishing House, 1990, p. 49.

55. "China Orders Military Draft Registration," Reuters, October 20, 1993.

56. Fang et. al., "On the Legalization of Defense Expenditure Management," p. 36.

57. *Ibid.*

58. In July 1998, upon the approval of the State Council and the Central Military Commission, the four major army departments (General Staff, General Politics, the General Logistics, and General Armaments) jointly issued a circular on distributing the "Plan For Implementation of the Servicemen Insurance System" throughout the armed forces. China's servicemen insurance system thus became operational. "Items of servicemen insurance mainly include injury and death insurance, ex-service pension insurance, and ex-service medical insurance." This reform was implemented to ensure that servicemen will enjoy social security treatment according to state stipulations after retiring from military service. "Servicemen insurance funds are to be borne jointly by the state and the individuals. The insurance premium standards are to be set in the light of those governing state public servants and staff members and workers at the same posts and grades while embodying the military professional characteristics." China's Servicemen Insurance System Becomes Operational, Xinhua, July 9, 1998, in FBIS-CHI-98-190.

59. Huang et. al., "Problems of Financial Management."

60. Fang et. al., "On the Legalization of Defense Expenditure Management," p. 36.

61. Deng et. al., *The Chinese People's Liberation Army, Vol. I,* p. 669-670.

62. Jiang et. al., *A Study of China's Defense Economic Development Strategy,* p. 50.

63. Fang et. al., "On the Legalization of Defense Expenditure Management," p. 36.

64. For one Chinese source seeking to disprove a "zero-sum" formulation of military spending vs. economic growth, and emphasizing the ways that military spending and economic growth could be complementary: "A Study on the Relations Between Military Expenditure and Economic Growth" *(guofang kaiji yu jingji zengzhang de guanxi yanjiu), Military Sciences Economic Review (junshi jingji yanjiu),* 1996 (5), pp. 34-38.

65. *"xinshinian, jiushinian, xiuxiupupu you shinian. . . ."* Jiang et. al., *A Study of China's Defense Economic Development Strategy,* p. 50.

66. Richard A. Bitzinger and Bates Gill, *Gearing Up for High-Tech Warfare? Chinese and Taiwanese Defense Modernization and Implications for Military Confrontation Across the Taiwan Strait* (Taipei: Chinese Council of Advanced Policy Studies, CAPS Papers No. 11: September, 1996), pp. 17, 19. No examples of "stagnated" disciplines are provided here.

67. "More on Enhancing Defense Modernization" *(zai lun jiaqiang guofang xiandai huajianshe), Military Sciences Economic Review (junshi jingji yanjiu),* 1996 (4), pp. 30-33.

68. Fang et. al., "On the Legalization of Defense Expenditure Management," pp. 35-36.

69. Liu Shuxin, "A Few Thoughts on the Military's Economic Development Strategy in Coastal Areas Facing High-Tech Regional War Under Modern Conditions" *(dui gaojishu jubu zhanzheng tiaojianxia yanhai diqu junshi jingji fazhan zhanlue de jidian sikao),* in Li Lin and Zhao Qinxuan, eds., *Theory and Research on Military Economics in the New Era (xinshiqi junshi jingji lilun yanjiu),* Beijing: Military Sciences Publishing House, 1995, pp. 100-106.

70. Fang et. al., "On the Legalization of Defense Expenditure Management," pp. 35-36.

71. "On Deng Xiaoping's Thinking on Military Expenditures," p. 26.

72. Jiang et. al., *A Study of China's Defense Economic Development Strategy,* p. 51.

73. "On Deng Xiaoping's Thinking on Military Expenditures," p. 26.

74. Jiang et. al., *A Study of China's Defense Economic Development Strategy,* p. 51.

75. Fang et. al., "On the Legalization of Defense Expenditure Management," p. 35.

76. *Ibid.*

77. *Ibid;* Li Minggeng (from the Institute of Military Sciences), "The Influence of High-Tech, Regional War on Military Economic Resources Distribution" *(gaojishu jubu zhanzheng dui junshi jingji ziyuan peizhi de yingxiang), Military Sciences Economic Review (junshi jingji yanjiu),* 1995 (8), pp. 67-69.

78. Li, "The Influence of High-Tech, Regional War," pp. 67-69.

79. *Ibid.*
80. *Ibid.*
81. *Ibid.*
82. Fang et. al., "On the Legalization of Defense Expenditure Management," p. 35.
83. Liu and Wu, *The Basics of National Defense Economic Studies,* p. 177.
84. Huang and Teng, "Basic Discussion of Deng Xiaoping's Thought on the Benefits of Military Economics in the New Period," p. 75.
85. Liu and Wu, *The Basics of National Defense Economic Studies,* p. 177.
86. *Ibid.*
87. Fang et. al., "On the Legalization of Defense Expenditure Management," p. 35.
88. Li Jinggong, "Briefly on Improving Military Expenditure Supply" *(xiantan gaijin xianxing junfei gongying fangfa), Military Sciences Economic Review (junshi jingji yanjiu),* 1995 (11), pp. 42-45.
89. Wu Yubang, "The Centralized Nature of Financial Management and Centralized and Unified Leadership of the Army" *(caiwu guanli de jizhongxing yu jundui jizhong tongyi lingdao),* in Li and Zhao, *Theory and Research on Military Economics in the New Era,* pp. 52-58. The author is from the General Logistics Dept. of the Chengdu Military Region.
90. Wu, "The Centralized Nature of Financial Management and Centralized and Unified Leadership of the Army." See especially p. 54.
91. Fang et. al., "On the Legalization of Defense Expenditure Management," p. 39.
92. *Ibid.*
93. *Ibid,* p. 40.
94. No details are provided on why this might be the case. Ibid.
95. Jin Zhude and An Weimin, "[Employing] Twice the Development and Key Deployment of National Defense Resources: A New Exploration on the Concept of Defense Conversion" *(guofang ziyuan de arci kaifa he zhongxin peizhi: dui junzhuanmin gainian de xin tansuo), Chinese Military Industry News (zhongguo jungong bao),* September 6, 1996, p. 3.
96. Liu, "Some Considerations on the Inputs of Military Expenditure," pp. 39-40.
97. Fang et. al., "On the Legalization of Defense Expenditure Management," p. 40.
98. A list of relevant laws is provided in Wan Xiaoyuan and Wan Zilong, "Development Trends of Military Economics under Socialist Market Conditions" *(lun shehuizhuyi shichang jingji tiaojianxia junshi jingji fazhan qushi), Military Sciences Economic Review (junshi jingji yanjiu),* 1996 (12), p. 13.
99. Jiang Baoqi et. al., *A Study of China's Defense Economic Development Strategy,* pp. 51-53.
100. Godwin, " 'PLA, Incorporated,' " p. 74.

Conclusion

1. Panitan Wattanayagorn and Desmond Ball, "A Regional Arms Race?" *The Journal of Strategic Studies,* 18:3 (September, 1995), pp. 149-150.
2. The International Institute for Strategic Studies, *The Military Balance, 1997/1998* (Oxford: Oxford University Press, 1998), p. 168.
3. Wattanayagorn and Ball, "A Regional Arms Race?" pp. 150-151.
4. *Ibid,* pp. 151-152.
5. *Ibid,* p. 153.
6. Renato Cruz de Castro, "Interactive Naval Development of Three Northeast Asian States," *Contemporary Southeast Asia,* 17:3 (December, 1995), p. 319.
7. Wattanayagorn and Ball, "A Regional Arms Race?"
8. The International Institute for Strategic Studies, *The Military Balance, 1997/1998,* p. 162-164.
9. *Ibid,* p. 101.
10. *Ibid,* p. 102.
11. *Ibid,* p. 101.
12. Research Institute for Peace and Security, Asian Security, 1997-98 (London: Brassey's, 1997), p. 71.
13. *Ibid,* p. 68.
14. *Ibid,* p. 68.
15. *Defense Guide of Japan,* (Tokyo: Japanese Self Defense Forces Publication, 1995), pp. 38-39.
16. The International Institute for Strategic Studies, *The Military Balance, 1997/1998,* p. 101.
17. *Ibid,* p. 103.
18. *Ibid,* pp. 101-102.
19. *Ibid.*
20. *Ibid,* pp. 181-183.
21. *Ibid,* p. 166.
22. *Defense Guide of Japan,* pp. 38-39.
23. "The latest activities conducted by the GSDF [Ground Self Defense Force] include the JAL plane crash incident, the Fugen volcanic disaster, wind and flood disaster caused by Typhoon 19, and the earthquake on the southwest coast of Hokkaido." *Defense Guide of Japan,* pp. 18-23.
24. Cruz de Castro, "Interactive Naval Development of Three Northeast Asian States," p. 331.
25. See also Wattanayagorn and Ball, "A Regional Arms Race?" p. 163.
26. Cruz de Castro, "Interactive Naval Development of Three Northeast Asian States," pp. 329-330.
27. Stockholm International Peace Research Institute, *SIPRI Yearbook, 1997: Armaments, Disarmament and International Security* (Oxford: Oxford University Press, 1997), p. 226.

28. *Defense Guide of Japan,* p. 34.
29. *Ibid,* p. 32.
30. Stockholm International Peace Research Institute, *SIPRI Yearbook, 1997,* p. 226.
31. *Defense Guide of Japan,* p. 26.
32. *Ibid,* pp. 12-13.
33. A chronology of these tensions is provided in Research Institute for Peace and Security, *Asian Security, 1997-98,* pp. 20-25:

> 14 July, 1996: Seven members of the Japan Youth Federation land on one of the northern Senkaku islets and construct a makeshift lighthouse.
>
> 28 August, 1996: Protest in front of a Hong Kong government building against Japan during a visit of Foreign Minister Ikeda.
>
> 4 September, 1996: Japanese Maritime Safety Agency prevents Hong Kong journalists from landing on the island.
>
> 9 September, 1996: Members of the Japan Youth Federation land on the island to build a new lighthouse.
>
> 12 September, Taipei County Council passes a resolution barring Japanese companies from participating in county enterprises. Four days later, Taiwan Provincial Assembly passes a resolution to exclude Japanese companies from bidding on public works contracts.
>
> 15 September: Protest in HK attracts 10,000.
>
> To the Japanese, the significance of the controversy was that it demonstrated how deep anti-Japanese sentiment runs in the Chinese-speaking world, and how this is one of the unifying forces in "greater China." Still, Taiwan is unwilling to work with the Mainland on the issue, although their interests and views are parallel.

34. The International Institute for Strategic Studies, *The Military Balance, 1997/1998,* pp. 183, 185.
35. *Korea Annual, 1997* (Seoul: Yonhap News Agency, 1997), p. 95.
36. *Ibid,* p. 94.
37. *The Defense of Japan, 1995* (White Paper of the Japanese Defense Agency) (Tokyo: Japanese Defense Agency, 1995).
38. Stockholm International Peace Research Institute, *SIPRI Yearbook, 1997,* p. 232.
39. *Ibid,* p. 231.
40. Michael Richardson, "East Asians Fear Rivalry for Nuclear Arms Might Drift their Way," *International Herald Tribune,* June 3, 1998, p. 5.
41. See also Jonathan D. Pollack and Young Koo Cha, *A New Alliance for the Next Century: The Future of U.S.-Korean Security Cooperation* (Santa Monica, CA: RAND, 1995), p. xiv.
42. Research Institute for Peace and Security, *Asian Security, 1997-98,* p. 143.
43. "India Shrugs Off Sanctions and Boosts Military Budget," *International Herald Tribune,* June 2, 1998, p. 4.

44. James Heltzman and Robert L. Worden, eds, *India: A Country Study, Fifth Edition* (Washington, D.C.: Federal Research Division, Library of Congress, 1996), pp. 583-594.

45. *Ibid,* p. 598.

46. *Ibid,* pp. 600-601.

47. *Ibid,* p. 564.

48. John Kifner, "Kashmir at the Heart of Crisis," *International Herald Tribune,* June 3, 1998, p. 5; Molly Moore and Kamran Khan, "In Kashmir, the Shooting Never Stops," *International Herald Tribune,* June 3, 1998, p. 1.

49. Heltzman and Worden, *India: A Country Study,* p. 564.

50. *Ibid.*

51. John F. Burns, "India's New Defense Chief Sees Chinese Military Threat," New York Times e-news release (www.nytimes.com), May 5, 1998.

52. Heltzman and Worden, *India: A Country Study,* p. 563.

53. "Text of Defense White Paper," Xinhua, July 27, 1998.

54. Heltzman and Worden, *India: A Country Study,* p. 588.

55. Alan Bullion, "India and UN Peacekeeping Operations," *International Peacekeeping,* 4:1 (Spring 1997), pp. 98-114.

56. See also Introduction, note 26.

57. Donald Hugh McMillen, "Chinese Perspectives on International Security," in *Asian Perspectives on International Security* (NY: St. Martin's Press, 1984), p. 179.

58. Lieutenant Michael Studeman, "Calculating China's Advances in the South China Sea: Identifying the Triggers of 'Expansionism,'" *Naval War College Review,* 51:2 (Spring, 1998), pp. 68-90.

59. *Ibid.,* p. 85.

60. Many details on the Spratly Island disputes between China and Vietnam are contained in Harish Mehta, "Vietnam Ending the Shooting Between Vietnam, China," *Business Times* (Singapore), February 26, 1993.

61. Chang Pao-Min, "Vietnam and China: New Opportunities and New Challenges," *Contemporary Southeast Asia,* 19:2 (September, 1997), p. 137.

62. Mehta, "Vietnam Ending the Shooting Between Vietnam, China."

63. Ji Guoxing, "Maritime Jurisdiction in the Three China Seas," Institute on Global Conflict and Cooperation, the University of California, 1995, p. 24.

64. The International Institute for Strategic Studies, *The Military Balance, 1997/1998,* pp. 194-195.

65. Stockholm International Peace Research Institute, *SIPRI Yearbook, 1997,* p. 235.

66. The second exercise probably had implications for China's military planning vis-à-vis Taiwan, but in this case specific references were made in China's account of the exercise to China's hopes to defend the Senkakus against Japanese incursion. Evan A. Feigenbaum, *Change in Taiwan and Potential Adversity in the Strait* (Santa Monica: RAND, 1995).

67. "China Conducts Military Exercise, Seizes Island," Reuters, September 22, 1996.

68. "Taiwan 'White Paper' Lists PRC Capabilities, Invasion Exercises," Lien-Ho Pao (Taiwan), March 25, 1998, p. 4, in FBIS-CHI-98-086.

69. U.S. Department of Defense Report to Congress, "Security Situation in the Taiwan Strait," updated February 26, 1999. See http://www.defenselink.mil/

70. "Taiwan 'White Paper' Lists PRC Capabilities."

71. Felix K. Chang, "Conventional War Across the Taiwan Strait," Orbis, 40:4 (Fall, 1996), pp. 577-607.

72. "Taiwan 'White Paper' Lists PRC Capabilities."

73. U.S. Department of Defense Report to Congress, "Security Situation in the Taiwan Strait."

74. "Taiwan to Lift Martial Law on Quemoy, Matsu," Reuters, July 16, 1992.

75. East Asian Strategic Review, 1997-1998 (Tokyo: National Institute of Defense Studies), 1998, p. 127.

76. The International Institute for Strategic Studies, The Military Balance, 1997/1998, pp. 180-181.

77. Ibid., pp. 187-188.

78. Ibid., p. 191.

79. Ibid., pp. 191-192.

80. "Philippines Sends Fighters, Ship to Spratlys," Reuters, February 16, 1995; "Manila Says China has Cut Back Force in Spratlys," Reuters, February 12, 1995.

81. Donald M. Seekins, "Burma-China Relations: Playing with Fire," Asian Survey, 37:6 (June, 1997), pp. 525-539.

82. Leszek Buszynski, "Southeast Asia in the Post-Cold War Era: Regionalism and Security," Asian Survey, 32:9 (September, 1992), p. 834.

83. Ibid., p. 838.

84. See also [Navy Senior Colonel] Yan Youqiang and [Navy Senior Colonel] Chen Rongxing, "On Maritime Strategy and the Marine Environment," China Military Science (Beijing Zhongguo Junshi Kexue), 97:2 (May, 1997), pp. 81-92, in FBIS-CHI-97-197.

85. This assumes the population grows to 1.5 billion people. Colonel Xu Xiaojun, "China's Grand Strategy for the 21st Century," in Michael D. Bellows, Asia in the 21st Century: Evolving Strategic Priorities (Washington, D.C.: National Defense University, 1994), pp. 21-41 (see especially pp. 21-22, 27).

86. "Chi Haotian Speaks on PRC Defense Policy," Xinhua, February 17, 1998, in FBIS-CHI-98-048.

87. U.S. Department of Defense Report to Congress, "Security Situation in the Taiwan Strait."

88. Hans Binnendijk and Patrick Clawson, eds., 1997 Strategic Assessment:

Flashpoints and Force Structure (Washington, D.C.: National Defense University Press [Institute for National Strategic Studies], 1997.

89. "Text of Defense White Paper," Xinhua, July 27, 1998.

90. Li Qinggong Wei Wei, "The World Needs a New Security Concept," *The PLA Daily (jiefangjun bao),* December 24, 1997, p. 5, in FBIS-CHI-98-015.

Index